MAELSTROM

Maelstrom: Christian Dominionism and Far-Right Insurgence illuminates the latest outbreak of right-wing extremism in America. This book reviews the cyclical nature of right-wing resurgences in American history, dismisses the appropriateness of the word "fascism" to explain them, and then describes in depth the goal of "reconstructing" American institutions on the basis of biblical principles. It critiques the popular view that far-right politics is carried by stupid, socially isolated, nuts. To this end, it discusses the logicality of the "big lie" and examines in detail how people are recruited into the far-right, by entertaining the theories of authoritarianism and resource mobilization. Finally, it characterizes how the ends-oriented rationality of far-right activists differs from the mini-max criterion of rationality utilized by the ordinary person. This can motivate them to be violent and can frustrate efforts by the government to control them.

James Aho is Professor Emeritus at Idaho State University where he has taught for over forty years. Recognized as a Distinguished Researcher and Teacher, he is the author of many books, including *Far-Right Fantasy: A Sociology of American Religion and Politics*, *Body Matters: A Phenomenology of Sickness, Disease and Illness* (co-written with his son, Kevin), and *Sociological Trespasses: Interrogating Sin and Flesh*. Aho is also the author of two award-winning studies of religiously motivated political violence, *The Politics of Righteousness: Idaho Christian Patriotism* and *This Thing of Darkness: A Sociology of the Enemy*.

Routledge Studies in Fascism and the Far Right
Series Editors:

Nigel Copsey
Teesside University, UK

Graham Macklin
Center for Research on Extremism (C-REX), University of Oslo, Norway

This book series focuses upon national, transnational, and global manifestations of fascist, far-right and right-wing politics primarily within a historical context but also drawing on insights and approaches from other disciplinary perspectives. Its scope also includes anti-fascism, radical-right populism, extreme-right violence and terrorism, cultural manifestations of the far right, and points of convergence and exchange with the mainstream and traditional right.

Love, Hate and the Leader
A Fascist Childhood
Trevor Grundy

Memory in Hungarian Fascism
A Cultural History
Zoltán Kékesi

The Right in the Americas
Distinct Trajectories and Hemispheric Convergences, from the Origins to the Present
Edited by Julián Castro-Rea and Esther Solano

Far-Right Ecologism
Environmental Politics and the Far Right in Hungary and Poland
Balša Lubarda

The Right and the Nation
Transnational Perspectives
Edited by Toni Morant, Julián Sanz and Ismael Saz

Metapolitics, Algorithms and Violence
New right activism and terrorism in the attention economy
Ico Maly

Plínio Salgado
A Brazilian Fascist (1895–1975)
João Fábio Bertonha

For more information about this series, please visit: www.routledge.com/Routledge-Studies-in-Fascism-and-the-Far-Right/book-series/FFR

MAELSTROM
CHRISTIAN DOMINIONISM AND FAR-RIGHT INSURGENCE

James Aho

NEW YORK AND LONDON

Cover image: © Shutterstock

First published 2024
by Routledge
605 Third Avenue, New York, NY 10158

and by Routledge
4 Park Square, Milton Park, Abingdon, Oxon, OX14 4RN

Routledge is an imprint of the Taylor & Francis Group, an informa business

© 2024 James Aho

The right of James Aho to be identified as author of this work has been asserted in accordance with sections 77 and 78 of the Copyright, Designs and Patents Act 1988.

All rights reserved. No part of this book may be reprinted or reproduced or utilised in any form or by any electronic, mechanical, or other means, now known or hereafter invented, including photocopying and recording, or in any information storage or retrieval system, without permission in writing from the publishers.

Trademark notice: Product or corporate names may be trademarks or registered trademarks, and are used only for identification and explanation without intent to infringe.

ISBN: 978-1-032-48887-5 (hbk)
ISBN: 978-1-032-48883-7 (pbk)
ISBN: 978-1-003-39126-5 (ebk)

DOI: 10.4324/9781003391265

Typeset in Times New Roman
by KnowledgeWorks Global Ltd.

Contents

Epigram	*vi*
Acknowledgments	*vii*
Introduction	1
1 The Collection: A Study of Right-Wing Extremism	7
2 The American Far-Right: Historically and Sociologically	12
3 Christian Dominionism and Its Critics	22
Interlude 1: Fetus Fetish	33
4 Christian Dominionism and Violence	36
5 The Big Lie: Its Model, Making, and Motive	47
6 The Danse Macabre: Deadly Miscommunications	58
Interlude 2: God and Guns	69
7 The Case of the Minor Family	71
8 Revisiting Authoritarianism	77
9 "Fascism" Reconsidered	88
References	*97*
Index	*104*

Epigram

Sodomites are reptilians. . . It's not God's fault, he told nations how to deal with that. He told the nations that he ruled, put them to death. Put all the queers to death.
(Pastor Joe Jones, Shield of Faith Baptist Church, Boise, Idaho (Bringhurst 2022))

Acknowledgments

It is my honor and pleasure to acknowledge the encouragement, guidance, and financial support that my colleagues at Idaho State University have given me over the years, including the decade since my retirement from the classroom. Without them, this project would never have been completed. With apologies to those whom limited space requires that I omit mentioning by name, without being exhaustive, there is Gesine Hearn, who served as my last Department Chair, and gave me valuable insights into primary and secondary documents relating to modern German culture (see Chapter 8); social phenomenologist, Deirdre Caputo, who has never hesitated to help me overcome my technological disabilities; my beloved friend, Mark McBeth, one of my first undergraduate students and now Chair of the Political Science Department at ISU; environmental sociologist, Trina Running; and present Sociology Department Chair and sociologist of religion, Jeremy Thomas.

In addition to these are my three sons, all of whom, as professors themselves, never cease to amaze and inspire me: Ken, an alpine botanist (at Idaho State University); Kevin, a phenomenologist of the lived body (and Chair of the Department of Philosophy and Communications at Florida Gulf Coast University), and my favorite jazz pianist, Kyle (at Missouri State University).

Finally, is my wife, Margaret, my loving companion, personal editor (who recommended the title of this book), award-winning poet, teacher, and fellow adventurer, since the time we first met in 1966 at Washington State University. Margaret, this book is dedicated to you.

I thank the following organization, and magazine, book, and journals listed below that published parts of the following chapters:

Chapter 1, "The Collection," first appeared as "The James Aho Collection" in "Political Extremism and Radicalism in the Twentieth Century: Right-Wing Extremism" by Cengage Learning (EMEA) Ltd.
Chapter 2, "The American Far-Right Historically and Sociologically," first appeared as "What is the American Far Right?" in *Tablet Magazine*, 2019. Available at: https://www.tabletmag.com/jewiish-news-and-politics/250728
Chapter 5, "The Big Lie," first appeared in 2022, under that same title in *Religious Othering: Global Dimensions*, ed. by Mark Juergensmeyer, Kathleen Moore, and Dominic Sachsenmaier, London & New York: Routledge Press.
Chapter 6, "The Danse Macabre," first appeared in *Sociological Spectrum*, 2006, vol. 26 (4), pp. 1–17. For reprints and permissions: https://www.tandfonline.com/
Chapter 8, "Authoritarianism Revisited," first appeared in *Critical Sociology*, 2020, vol. 46, pp. 329–41. For reprints and permissions: https://uk.sagepub.com/en-gb/eur/journals-permissions

Introduction

Different terms have been used to en-frame the emergence of a global-wide social system. Some of the more popular are "Westernization," "Europeanization," "Occidentalism," "modernization," "civilization," and "Americanization." Whichever word we use to title it, academic consensus credits it to a combination of instantaneous electronic communications; mass tourism and migration; transnational corporate trade relations whose commodities are marketed through globally appreciated advertising tokens; international banking and finance; multinational industries in entertainment, music, sport, and military hardware; and finally, experimental laboratory science and bio-medicine.

Anthropologist Mattias Gardell (2003) agrees that the planet is rapidly becoming a "single place," a unitary "global village." But he also acknowledges that there has been an "explosion" of "tens of thousands" of new "fundamentalist" religious groupings, both within and without the boundaries of the major world confessions, each of which seeks to "relativize" (i.e., critique and undermine) the sacred truths of competing religious associations. Jeffrey Kaplan (1997, xiv) puts it this way: The unifying effects of globalization have brought in their wake an upsurge of "apocalyptic millenarian" movements, each of whose gods is jealous of their rivals, and whose devotees mount defensive stances toward non-believers, and against whom they can be deadly aggressive. By "apocalyptic millenarianism," Kaplan assures us that he is not referring to the notion of "progress," as espoused by enthusiasts of globalization, but the announcement of something very different, specifically, the "denouement [or end] of history" altogether, as a prelude to something entirely new and better.

Mark Juergensmeyer (2000) uses the fact of globalization's unifying and destructive forces to account for "the global rise of religious violence." For example, he cites the case of the Brooklyn-educated physician and Zionist terrorist, Dr. Baruch Goldstein, who murdered more than 30 Palestinian worshippers at the Tomb of the Patriarchs in Hebron, Israel, February 25, 1994; the al-Qaeda-linked bombing of the World Trade Center in New York City in 1993, a decade prior to the immeasurably more deadly attack on that same facility on 9/11 in 2001; and the strike on the Tokyo subway by the Buddhist sectarian group known as Aum Shinriko, March 20, 1995, during which 12 commuters were killed and hundreds of others injured by sarin gas.

What we are witnessing in globalization, in other words, is a "paradoxical tension" (Gardell 2003, 3) or, as Hegel might have put it, a "contradiction" between "centripetal" and "centrifugal" pressures. The centripetal pressures of globalization draw people away from the margins toward a putative world center (which, for Hegel, was the axis he saw running from Berlin and Paris to London). On the other hand, globalization's centrifugal pressures drive people away from this center outward toward the periphery. Nor is this the end of the story, for in a very real sense the centripetal (centralizing) thrust of globalization is in part the very thing that occasions the centrifugal (decentralizing) reaction against it. And the reaction *against* centralization—particularly, when

DOI: 10.4324/9781003391265-1

it is violent—can in turn be a major "cause" of efforts to promote further centralization. But even this is too simplistic to encompass what is happening on the ground. Let us look at it more closely.

Even when the centripetal (unifying) pressure of globalization comes in the form of a smiling invitation by an attractive online "influencer" to adopt a globally favored dance step, music taste, dress style, sport, or food preference, the apocalyptic millenarian may well experience this as an "existential threat" to "traditional values."[1] And the deadlier the millenarian response is, the more urgent will be calls to adopt more benign, homogeneous "modern values."

The same is true of globalization's liberating spirit and democratic impulse, wherein everyone is expected to assess the worth of others on the basis of their individual accomplishments instead of their skin color, religious confession, gender, or social class. This can occasion a negative reaction which, if and when it becomes deadly, can spur even more heated efforts to promote equality and democracy.

Or once more, consider the subtle pressure that globalization places on commercial enterprises to adopt the same globally recognized principles of instrumental rationality (such as double-entry bookkeeping) if they wish to see their businesses succeed; or the same mini-max (cost-reducing, income maximizing) standards of health-care management, education administration, and production, implemented by college-certified specialists, instead by one's own kin, court favorites, or dependents. This can drive a reaction against that pressure on the part of those who have vested interests in traditional forms of accountability and in customary ways of organizing work relations. But if that reaction goes so far as to occasion violence, this can compel victims and witnesses to the destruction to double down and modernize even more rapidly and thoroughly.

Finally, there is the inducement that globalization places on people everywhere to adopt the same globally endorsed "ultimate concerns" (Paul Tillich), which invariably "diminish the field of competence of God" (Gardell 2003, 13). Particularly, when it comes to dealing with matters like drug trafficking, climate change, famine, pandemics, mass migration, or military invasions. So overwhelming can the wheels of globalization's centripetal "juggernaut" seem to the apocalyptic millenarian, that words like "extermination," say, of White man, or of manhood generally, or "death" of God, seem like fitting metaphors to describe what is happening. ("Juggernaut" comes from the Sanskrit name of an incarnation of Vishnu—Hinduism's God of the world—whose devotees are so enthralled by His visage that they allow themselves to be crushed to death by the car that conveys Him from village to village.)

Gardell, for one, disputes the empirical accuracy of this rather foreboding vision of globalization's future. In the first place, he says, there is no *single* globalization process. Rather, there are multiple "non-isomorphic paths of globalization," each of which is capable of creating ruptures and conflicts "at every level." In part, this is because globalization cannot possibly proceed at the same pace in all of society's sectors. Instead, there are inevitable institutional "lags," wherein material factors like new hand tools or new modes of travel are adopted more readily than objects in the realm of ideas (such as faith credos, ethical principles, and the like). Given this, the *actual* process of globalization moves less like a well-oiled machine than it does an "organized diversity" or "a complex, overlapping, disjunctive order" (Arjun Appadurn, in Gardell 2003, 7), which is another way of saying that, in reality, there is no demonic conspiracy behind globalization, as apocalyptic millenarians suppose; no secret plot. On the contrary, due to "functional differentiation," every sector of society, from health care, education, commerce, science, and politics, to the military, and more, is able to "evade centralized control," and in so doing, follow its own internal logic.

Nonetheless, Gardell does grant that globalization in *any* sector has little respect for race-based job assignments and hierarchies; for long-standing customs, for non-rational moral convictions, and for clan-based forms of solidarity, all of which globalist elites view as "obstacles to progress," or as practices that need to be abandoned by "forward-looking" peoples. This is a major reason why apocalyptic millenarians express outrage at those same globalist elites; some going so far as to proclaim, "we don't want to be citizens of the [globalizing] world, but citizens of the United States" (or of Russia, or India, or Japan, etc.) (Pat Buchanan, in Gardell 2003, 10). It is this negative reaction against the centripetal thrust of globalization, says Gardell, that lies behind the "great millennial struggles" of our age. And it is the impetus too behind the explosion of American patriot militias that first began showing up in the late 1970s, as well as the rise of so-called Aryan revolutionaries; not just in America, but throughout continental Europe, England, India, and Australia, as well. The irony is that these so-called Aryan revolutionaries and their allies have been drawn together *electronically*, through one of the primary vectors of globalization, the Internet: through "flows" of news commentary, conspiracy tales, discussions of military tactics, dating services, and legend-making. Of these legends, one of the most dangerous "tell[s] of a once glorious [e.g. White] race sinking into a corrupting morass of decay and filth" (Gardell 2003, 11).

Maelstrom[2] examines a major centrifugal force that has taken root in the very heart of one of the leading outposts of the globalization project, the United States of America. The name given to it by its proponents is "Christian Dominionism" (CD). CD is neither a church nor a denomination. Instead, it is a rapidly growing, para-religious movement that has penetrated, among countless other Christian groups, Baptist, Presbyterian, Pentecostal, Catholic, and Mormon congregations throughout the country. Like other instances of apocalyptic millenarianism—such as the Hindu nationalist *Bharatiya* Janata Party or orthodox Jewish nationalism—CD views the centralizing moment of globalization with alarm, as an "existential threat" to its existence.

The definitional extension of "CD" overlaps that of the softer-sounding, more popular label, "Christian Nationalism" (CN) (cf. Miller 2021).[3] Adherents of CD, however, are different from CNs in being more certain about their moral convictions, and thus more willing than CNs to resort to high-powered weaponry to achieve their goals. This is evident in CD's preference for the noun "Dominionism" to describe themselves—which harbors suggestions of combat, conquest, and domination.

Although I was unaware of the phrase "CD" when I began researching it in 1985, it is a movement that has fascinated me since 1984 when I first heard of a religious group located in northern Idaho, and dedicated to, among other things, the imposition by force, if necessary, of White Christian rule over the earth and earthlings. Its title was the Church of Jesus Christ-Christian, or, as it was more widely known at the time, the Aryan Nations Church. When rumors began circulating about the Church's ties to the terrorist group I discuss in Chapter 1, I realized that I was perfectly, if rather perversely, situated geographically to satisfy my curiosity.

Chapter 1, "The Collection," discusses how I initially went about conducting my investigation, and it relates some of the unsettling things I discovered, including about myself. The heart of this chapter originally served as the Introduction to a repository of material now housed in the Eli Oboler Library on the Idaho State University campus in Pocatello. Readers can use it to access the large, and until 1980, largely underground, body of written and oral documents about, and especially by, the contemporary American ultra-right. There are newsletters, broadsides, pamphlets, periodicals, books, recorded sermons, and even correspondence I engaged in with a number of convicted right-wing terrorists.

Chapter 2, "The American Far-Right Historically and Sociologically," is an expanded version of a much shorter article that first appeared in *Tablet Magazine* in 2019. It is included here to provide readers with some background into the succession of right-wing insurgencies that have plagued America since the time of its founding (ca. 1800). This, to disabuse ourselves of the impression that what is going on today is somehow extraordinarily unique. However, the chapter *does* pay particular attention to the decade after 2010, when alarums were rung by self-proclaimed American "conservatives" about what (to them) was the horrifying specter of "matter out place" or of "filth," to use Mary Douglas' (1966) characterization: the presence in the White House of a Black man. Not just one of a number of ordinary servants who supposedly know their place in the so-called natural order of things, but an "alleged" (this word is theirs) *Black* American President. One, furthermore, with the off-putting middle name of "Hussein." The panicked reaction to Barack Obama's imagined menace has continued long after his eight-year term in office ended in 2016, well into the years of the Trump and Biden presidential administrations.

One of the most historically significant and, to me, interesting outcomes of the years after 2010 has been the unapologetic embracement of elements of CD doctrine and policies by leading figures in the Republican Party (or GOP = Grand Old Party). Chapters 3–8 examine several implications of this fact.

Chapter 3, "Christian Dominionism and Its Critics," begins by surveying the roots of the CD movement in the ferment that began building within the fundamentalist Christian community in the early years of the *20th* century. It then goes on to consider the ironic posture that CDs assume toward scientific inquiry. During the course of this discussion, we will consider CD's own, surprisingly (at least to me) impressive, scientific enterprise in fields like biblically inspired medicine, anthropology and race, geology, history, and political economics. The thrust of my argument is that while CD is definitely not anti-intellectual, its approach to these and related subjects is in fact explicitly opposed to what passes in secular universities and research institutes as bona fide scientific methodology.

Chapter 4, "Christian Dominionism and Violence," is broken into two parts: From the Inside and From the Outside. Part One, From the Inside, discusses CD immigration policy, and its program to reintroduce slavery to America. From the Outside, Part Two, argues that whether it is clothed in the uniforms of law enforcement officials or in the camouflage and balaclavas of private militias, CD has been deeply implicated in political violence since at least the middle 1980s. Yet the thesis of the chapter is that the cause(s) of Dominionist-related violence are not found in the theology of CD alone. In addition, other factors, some of which at first glance appear to have little to do with religion, play an equally important role. Here, I introduce a "value-added" causal model of domestic terrorism, which takes into consideration not only the matter of religious belief, but also considerations like easy access to military hardware, a disinterest in or an ignorance of religious extremism on the part of state authorities, and perhaps most important, the espousal by Dominionist preachers of norms that encourage their congregants to resort to combat arms to solve social (and personal) problems. (For an example of this, see the Epigram to this book.)

For all my talk about norms, restraints, and opportunities, the fact remains that what people believe to be true remains essential to understanding why they act toward the world as they do. In regard to collective violence, one of the most dangerous convictions is, "Thank God We're Not Like Them." This was the title given to an international, interdisciplinary workshop conducted out of the University of California-Santa Barbara in conjunction with Goettingen University, Germany in 2018 and 2019. Several of the papers presented at this workshop have since appeared in book form in *Religious Othering: Global Dimensions* (Juergensmeyer et al. 2023). My contribution to that book, "The Big Lie," is also the title of Chapter 5.

The phrase "Big Lie" gained currency around November 2019 when, after failing to re-secure the presidency for himself, Donald Trump and his followers insisted that Joe Biden's victory had been fraudulently "rigged" and thus Trump's rightful claim to the office had been "stolen." While this is indeed an example of craven dishonesty, as I use the phrase, "Big Lie" has a more expansive and inflammatory meaning. It refers to a centuries-old mythos that alleges the existence of a secret Jewish (or in more recent renderings, Masonic, Jacobin, Jeffersonian, Jesuit, Communist, Democratic Party, or liberal Deep State) Plot to establish a reign of evil on earth. The goals of the chapter are, first, to describe the archetypal features of the Big Lie and the attributes of its major character: that is, the Mason, the Jew, the Communist, or the Deep State operative. The second goal is to survey the tools used by big liars in concocting their fables. And the third goal is to reflect on their motives in doing so. It closes by entertaining one possible reason for the Big Lie, namely, the allure of an even *bigger* lie, that by means of it believers can deny or pretend that they have escaped their existential precariousness and contingency; or to say it more frankly, their own death and decrepitude.

Chapter 6, "The Danse Macabre," is a refined version of a piece first published by *Sociological Spectrum* in 2006. It deals with one of the enduring paradoxes of politics, namely, that *all* sides to a violent dispute will demonize their opponents by deploying variations of Big Lies. That is, they will first tag each other with disparaging labels and then go about devising legends to validate those labels. Next, they will indelibly imprint the labels and legends in the hearts and souls of impressionable youngsters. Then, finally, they will ritually offer each other up as sacrificial victims to their respective delusions. As they do so, each party will experience themselves as innocent of the tragedy that ensues and will exhibit the same aggrieved surprise when the violence they have inflicted on others returns to haunt themselves. It traces recent examples of this process of (mis)communication by reconstructing three intertwined incidents involving Christian Dominionist insurgents and federal law enforcement officials: the bloody shootout near Ruby Ridge, Idaho (1992); the fiery destruction of the Branch Davidian sect compound in Waco, Texas a year later; and the culmination of this series of *dansee macabre* in what was at the time the deadliest domestic terrorist attack in American history: the bombing of the Oklahoma City federal building in 1995.

At this point, a fair question to ask, is "why?" What is it that lies behind our avidity to join with allies to abet and applaud the killing of others? When I initially stepped into the field in 1985, I was pretty certain I knew the answer: In one way or another, I supposed, the perpetrators of collective violence—in this case, right-wing extremist violence—are "SIC." That is, they are either Stupid, socially Isolated, and/or Crazy. But in testing the veracity of this conceit against reality, I came to learn that people can become racists, anti-Semites, Islamophobes, and misogynists, in the same way that I and my friends had become vegetarians, environmentalists, peace activists, and in some cases, *left*-wing extremists: through the attachments we forge with those already in the movement at issue. Among other things, this suggests that for the most part people don't join (what pass in common jargon as) "hate groups" because they necessarily have a pre-existing animosity (although sometimes they do). Rather, they first *join-with* people in hate groups and then begin altering their worldviews (including their hostilities) so as to nourish and strengthen those bonds. Second, I learned that another idea I held—that "once a hater, always a hater"—is demonstrably false. On the contrary, just as vegetarians can convert to meat-eating and pacifists into pro-war advocates, haters can occasionally come to respect, admire, and even love those whom they earlier disdained (cf. Aho 1994, 122–51). Chapters 7 and 8 are attempts to understand these facts.

Chapter 7, "The Case of the Minor Family," examines how people can join (and, when they do, leave) hate groups from the standpoint of Sociology. In other words, it illustrates how social pulls and pushes can radically affect the lives of otherwise ordinary people. By focusing on "Lisa Minor" (an alias), the chapter relates how she got involved with, and later fled from, the Aryan Nations Church. My account of Lisa's conversion to and apostasy from the Aryan Nations Church is indebted to her sister, "Alice" (also an alias). Alice graduated with a BA degree in Sociology from Idaho State University and was herself a cultist of sorts. However, in her case, an amateur New Age practitioner. While reflecting on the stories of Lisa and Alice, as well as that of Lisa's husband, Ed, and a handful of others, we will have occasion to wonder if, perhaps, a purely a sociological account of conversions and defections overlooks some essential facts about religious conversions and apostasies. That is to say, if a sociological accounting of one's biography is not exactly incorrect, it does seem to overlook some fundamental aspects of human being. These relate to one's private psychodynamics—that is, the very things that professional sociologists are trained *not* to see, or at least to ignore. But human beings are rarely just passive objects, pulled and pushed like stones in a river, by external forces over which they have no control (Wallis 1982). Rather, they are active agents who can mold those forces to suit their own personal whims.

Chapter 8, "Authoritarianism Revisited," published by *Critical Sociology* in 2020, examines what one of these "internal psychodynamics" might be: In the case of right-wing extremism, it is authoritarianism. Here, I sketch the emergence of the concept of the "Authoritarian Personality" (AP) in post–World War I Germany and trace its use by professional social psychologists today. I then discuss the rather startling explanation for the AP offered by (the mostly Jewish, Marxist) affiliates of the Frankfurt University Institute for Social Research in the early 1930s. This, as they witnessed in horror the rise of Nazism in Germany and Austria (and after they left Germany, in America as well). The heart of the chapter is a phenomenological description of the sado-masochistic impulses that undergird the AP: growling aggression toward the weak, coupled with dog-like submission to their reputed masters.

One popular (liberal) disparagement directed at CD, and at American right-wing extremism generally, is that it is merely fascism with a different name. Chapter 9, "Fascism Reconsidered," addresses the validity of this assertion by considering a recently published book on the subject, *Against the Fascist Creep* (Ross 2017). Here, I take the opportunity to re-examine one of the key assumptions that informs my approach to the American far-right. To paraphrase Blaise Pascal, who flourished in 17th-century France, it is that people never inflict terror on others "so completely and cheerfully" as when they are driven to do so by religious convictions. My argument, first mentioned in Chapter 2, is that viewed historically, American right-wing insurgencies are not accurately understood as "fascistic" phenomena at all, but as expressions of sincerely held religious—in this case, evangelical Protestant—beliefs, sensibilities, and impulses.

Notes

1 The following characterization of the threats sensed by apocalyptic millenarians is based on Talcott Parsons' (1971) layout of what he calls "modernization," which Gardell (without acknowledging him by name) appears to use. For an accessible introduction to the modernization process and its resulting discontents see Edward Banfield (1967).
2 According to *Webster's New World Dictionary of the American Language*, "Maelstrom" = a violently confused, turbulent or dangerously agitated state of mind, conditions, or affairs.
3 Kelefa Sanneh (2023) has critiqued, "Christian Nationalism" by pointing to its vagueness and to the evident differences among its various adherents, which range from unapologetic right-wing racism to left-leaning progressivism. It should become clear, as we go on, that Christian Dominionism leans far to the right.

1 The Collection

A Study of Right-Wing Extremism

On December 8, 1984, there was a shootout on Whidbey Island, Washington, between US federal marshals and a gang of White Christian Dominionists (CDs). It ended with the gang's safe-house burning to the ground, and the roasted body of its leader, dead, in a bathtub. The gang called itself the Secret Brotherhood (Ger. *Brüders Schweigen*) or as I title it here, the Order; its intent was to ignite a race war by shutting-down shipping lanes in Puget Sound, just offshore, west of Seattle. Within a year, nearly two dozen of its members had been prosecuted for 67 different crimes, including arson, robbery, counterfeiting, the largest armored car heist in American history up to that time, and murder. One-quarter of the FBI's manpower resources were devoted to the investigation of the Order, and millions of dollars.

The Order was alleged to have ties to a religious group headquartered in northern Idaho known as the Church of Jesus Christ Christian-Aryan Nations (hereafter, "AN"). Being a Professor at Idaho State University in Pocatello, Idaho, I was geographically situated to study the Order more closely; what began as a simple inquiry turned into a multiyear investigation. One of its products was this chapter (hereafter, "the Collection"). The Collection is housed in the Eli Oboler Library on the campus of Idaho State University (ISU). Parts of the Collection are also available online, at Cengage Learning (Aho 2020). Another product was two books (Aho 1991, 1994), and then a third (Aho 2015) written during the presidency of Barack Obama, when many of the ideological themes first promulgated by the Order were resurrected by the American TEA (Taxed Enough Already) Party and various ancillary groups.

Initially, my inquiry had two goals. The first was to causally explain why and how people become committed to right-wing extremism, "from the outside," so to say, from the standpoint of an objective scientist. This entailed scores of face-to-face and phone interviews with self-identified CDs, as well as snail-mail correspondence with several convicts who were imprisoned at the time for their involvement in terrorist activities. One of them has since been executed by the State of Ohio for a series of racially motivated murders. My correspondence with him is also housed in the Collection.

Another document in the Collection is the Nehemiah Township Charter. This is a notarized plan for a White CD utopia, signed by nearly 20 separate activists, several of whom would become infamous for their involvement with the Order, and some of whom I interviewed.

The point of gathering this data was to assess (or "test") the validity of the prevailing social psychologies of the contemporary American far-right. At the time these boiled down to a variation of what, in the Introduction, I call "SIC" theory: that right-wing extremists are either stupid (or to say it more politely, have fewer years of formal education than their more conventional peers), socially isolated, and/or crazy. The Collection contains academic literature that elaborates on this theory and offers critiques of it. The Collection also houses newspaper accounts from the mainstream press that routinely take SIC theory for granted as true.

DOI: 10.4324/9781003391265-2

My second goal was to sympathetically understand (Ger. *Verstehen*) the CD movement "from the inside," from the perspective of its adherents. This required what anthropologists call "participant observation" of their lectures, sermons, workshops, demonstrations, and conventions. It also required that I immerse myself in their "library of infamy" (Aho 1994, 68–83): their short-wave radio broadcasts, magazine articles, taped sermons, newsletters, books, and pamphlets. Today, much of this material is relatively easy to obtain online. During the first stages of my research, however, it existed largely underground, and it took networking, sleuthing, and investments of time and money to access it.

To this end, I secured a modest faculty grant from ISU to underwrite my research, after the grant Committee dismissed concerns that I was putting myself in danger. Happily, my representative on the Committee defended the project by arguing that I was an adult and supposedly knew what I was getting into. Naturally, I appreciated his sentiment, but in truth all I really knew about CD was from newspaper articles and a handful of TV exposés. I would soon find myself exposed to a level of cravenness and cynicism that I was scarcely equipped to handle, intellectually or emotionally. More unsettling was my discovery that CDs are not in fact SIC but have levels of formal education comparable to those of their nonradical peers, if not a bit more than the average American; that they are deeply integrated into their local churches, workplaces, and neighborhoods; and by all appearances, they are rational—if not in a means-oriented, benefit-maximizing way, then in an ends-oriented determination to establish a racially pure Christian republic, regardless of what this might cost themselves or others.

After winding several hundred miles through the northern Rocky Mountains on my first field trip into the belly of the right-wing beast, I arrived at a pristine, glacier-carved lake and to Coeur d'Alene, a pleasant resort town situated on its forested shore. The first thing to strike me was the paradoxical coupling of natural beauty to hate. How, I asked myself, could such a verdant place give rise to such reported mendacity?[1]

Sociologists don't normally answer questions like this by sitting at a desk. Instead, they go into the field to personally meet their subjects. I still vividly recall fretfully pacing the floor of my motel room, building-up courage to interview my first "neo-Nazi." Earlier that morning, I had thumbed through the yellow pages of the phonebook and found the number for the AN under the "Church" listings, just above that for the Church of Jesus of Christ of Latter-day Saints (Mormon). A cheerful female voice answered, "Good morning, Church of Jesus Christ Christian-Aryan Nations. May I help you?" What followed was an appointment to meet its pastor, Richard Butler, at a local restaurant.

Butler arrived in a suit, carrying a passel of pamphlets and taped sermons, and accompanied by a burly bodyguard: a pastel-blue-shirted and twill-panted older man, born and raised in the Idaho county in which he still lived. Contrary to my expectations, neither man was wild-eyed nor stupid, although both were paranoid. And, as I found out the next day, for good reason. This is when the bodyguard was arrested for paying an undercover FBI agent for having supposedly "assassinated" the person who was believed to have betrayed the Order to authorities. Evidently, the bodyguard had offered to pay a sizable amount to anyone who could offer photographic evidence of the informant having been killed. After learning of the offer, the FBI is said to have doctored a photo of the informant, giving him the appearance of being beheaded; when the bodyguard was shown the photo, he wrote out a check and the bodyguard was immediately taken into custody.

As for myself, however, the important thing was the pastor's passel, filled with reading material for my edification. And indeed, it did open the door to a bizarre world, if not quite in the way the pastor intended. These documents are all now part of the Collection. In them are tales of Jewish conspiracy and Federal Reserve Bank intrigue, allegations of IRS tax scams, and reports of Soviet weather-war operations. There are scientific-sounding Holocaust denials, jeremiads against the granting of civil rights to "unqualified" minorities (read: "Black people"), anti-vaccination screeds, indictments of Communist "brainwashing" in public schools, and alternative histories of Israel and modern America.

Of the latter, most intriguing were "proofs." These draw on everything from pyramidology—alleging a direct tie between those who erected the Egyptian pyramids and the architects of Stonehenge—to biblical prophecy. And from these to medieval heraldry, legends, numerology, and hack linguistics (Aho 1991, 105–13). For example, according to the AN, "British" is a conjunction of the Hebraic terms *b'rith* (covenant) + *ish* (people). Thus *they*, not the Jews, are the supposed inheritors of the Covenant; and Abraham was not the forefather of the Jews, but the first "Britisher." Even the title of the British language, "English," is supposedly a corrupted version of the Hebrew words: *an* (one) + *gael* (stammering) + *ish* (man).[2] As is the name of Britain's first king, "Brutus." AN linguists claim that Brutus got his name from "*barat*," the ancient Phoenician word for "fortune." This ostensibly explains why, historically, the British have enjoyed such immense prosperity. That the Phoenicians were well known for their seamanship accounts for how these so-called people of the covenant arrived on the tiny island of Britain in the first place.

Again, according to the documents now in the Collection, the 13 stripes on the American flag stand for the original 13 tribes of ancient Israel—not: the 13 colonies—and that America was the terminus of their centuries-long wanderings. Presumably, this is "verified" by the fact that "July the Fourth" has 13 letters, and so on. That these and related claims and proofs are ridiculed by professional linguists and historians has little bearing on the fervency with which they have been embraced by the AN community.

Another item that the pastor brought to the restaurant was a copy of the AN newsletter, *Aryan Nations Calling*, together with its book catalogue. From this I ordered additional materials which are now also in the Collection, as well as the titles and postal addresses of groups ideologically allied with the AN. One of these was Barrister's Inn (then headquartered in Boise, Idaho), which marketed itself as a clearing house for information on the rights of juries (to refuse a judges' orders), and on "pro se" (for oneself) litigation. A second group was the National Alliance, a bona-fide neo-Nazi outfit which had its own monthly slick, *National Vanguard*, and book catalogue. A third group advertised in *Aryan Nations Calling* was the LaPorte, Colorado Church of Christ, located just west Fort Collins, several of whose members were caught-up in the prosecution of the Order. From the LaPorte church, I secured a subscription to its periodical, *Scriptures for America*, several years of which are housed in the Collection. In short, this is how I navigated the world of CD: step by step over many months. And like any long-distance traveler, I went through a series of feelings, from anticipation, dread, frustration, and excitement, to exhaustion.

For instance, there was the moment when I realized I had finally "arrived." It was a July morning after I had negotiated a pine-shaded gravel road to the AN compound on my way to be a participant observer at its annual Aryan World Congress. I came to a guard house and a gate manned by two masked sentries armed with assault rifles. Beside them was a sign, emblazoned with the warning: "Whites Only." The guards strode to the car and demanded identification. I showed them my blue ID card, which had been certified by Rev. Butler. They glanced at my name, back to my face, then smiled. "Jim Aho. We've been waiting for you." The gate rose; I meandered further up the road, the woods swallowing my way back to the highway.

When conference attendees were invited to participate in its opening ceremonies, I imagined a routine American flag-raising and the singing of the National Anthem. Instead, the loudspeakers blurted, "Aryan warriors, attention!" Immediately, scores of men who previously had been aimlessly milling about formed into military ranks. "Aryan warriors, salute," came the next command, and a hundred straight arms shot into the air. And then, before I could shamefacedly withdrawal from the stage, the notes of the "Horst Wessel Song" began to play. This is named after a German Nazi Storm Trooper from the 1930s who is said to have been martyred for the cause.

Embarrassed at having become, perhaps, *too much* a participant, and not enough a detached observer, I fell into conversation with the person standing next to me. Claiming to be a fifth-generation Mormon, he proudly handed me a copy of the book he had just self-published, *Amendment to the Constitution* (Pace 1985). It calls for the rescission of those constitutional amendments that outlaw slavery in America and that grant ex-slaves birth-right citizenship. *Amendment* is now part of the Collection; it is discussed in depth later in Chapter 4.

An equally jarring experience occurred during the *closing* ceremonies of the conference, the ritual igniting of a 30-foot tall, rag-enshrouded cross. I'll never forget the scene (Aho 1993):

> Out of the recesses of a thick fir forest, a single file of white-robed men, women, and children eerily emerge, led by two torch bearers. Two hundred in number, all deathly still. Some wear high conical hats masking their faces and cut with round black eyeholes. But most are bareheaded ... their visages grim and focused. There is an explosion of fire. Night turns into midday. Although I am standing some distance from the spectacle at the wood's edge, my face warms with the heat. I search to give my feelings words. The first that comes to mind is "power!" In terror mixed with shame at my naivete, I realize I have for too long dismissed these people as frequenters of a harmless diversionary lark. This rite I am witnessing goes back centuries, connecting the participants not only with each other in the present, but with their faceless ancestors in the past. For a moment I understand for the first time how races are truly rejuvenated; not by books and posters, but by drama. This is not, the high priest (formally, titled a "Kludd") explains, a symbol of racial violence; nor is it a desecration of a Christian icon. It is instead a sign of mutuality and defense. Its source is the Celtic practice of lighting seacoast pyres as guide signals. It has since, he says, become "a light to guide the white in the darkness of these times."

As for the Collection, the most pivotal step in its construction began about 10:00 AM on a Wednesday, March 1986, as I was preparing to give a class lecture. The phone rang; the voice on the other end told me that her mother had just died, and that she had left behind boxes of far-right material. She went on to say that her mother had once taught German at the AN academy: a one-room school dedicated to instilling in children "the 4 Rs": reading, 'riting, 'rthmetic, and race. Now that her mother was gone, the daughter said, she didn't know what to do with the boxes, the contents of which, she assured me, she disagreed with. If I can't find someone to take the items, she said, I'm just going to burn the whole lot. Please don't, I replied. Mail the boxes to us; we'll pay the postage. Within a week the boxes began to arrive, a different one every day for about a week. Unwrapping them was like being the recipient of gifts at a perverse potlatch, each box bearing new surprises. A large portion of the Collection comes from this donation.

The world of CD is vaster, more complex, and more nuanced than anything that can be portrayed in a few paragraphs; the Collection contains materials from all its regions. First, are documents that deal with specific issues like gun-rights, school prayer, modern medicine, abortion, bussing, and Ten Commandments monuments. This style of CD is episodic, and it rises and falls as public concerns come and go. Second is ideologically driven CD, an orientation that transcends momentary fluctuations of public opinion, and is characterized by an all-encompassing Manicheism: a division of the world into absolute good (us) and evil (them). This style of CD is in turn divisible into two major types, depending on whom or what the cosmic evil is alleged to be. The first type is preoccupied with the so-called Aryan race, and it posits the "Jew" as the archetypal villain, although there is debate over what, exactly, "Jew" stands for: Is it a religion or is it a race? The second type of ideologically driven CD is obsessed with the "organic" Constitution: the original articles of confederation plus the Bill of Rights. Here, the definitive enemy is not the Jew, but an imaginary non-ethnic entity such as the "Illuminati," the "Insiders," "Shadow Government," or "Dark Command." This type of CD is less concerned with matters like "race-mixing" and immigration than it is with "free-market capitalism," banking and tax-policy, and government regulations.

Having said this, it is essential to bear in mind that these ideological trajectories are not mutually exclusive. One thing that makes CD so difficult for outsiders to comprehend is how the word "Jew" (or those with Jewish surnames) can be conflated with menacing specters like the "Hidden Hand" or the "Deep State," and how facilely these categories can be implicated in everything from the quest for LGBTQ rights, drug abuse, and foreign wars, to domestic gun massacres, climate change, and infectious diseases.

What is important is not to be overwhelmed or discouraged by the sheer mass of the Collection. As noted above, I spent well over a decade exploring the world of CD, yet it still remains largely an unfathomable mystery. One of the objects of this book is to aid readers to get a handle on what CD is, where it comes from, and what its future might be.

Notes

1 For a comparable experience of the paradoxical coupling of natural beauty to hate in northern Idaho, see Mathias (2022b). For an account of a similar situation by the same author—this, involving LifeGate Church, in Pennsylvania—see Mathias (2022a).
2 Professional linguists claim that the word "English" actually comes from "Angle," the name of the German tribe who overran what is now modern Britain.

2 The American Far-Right

Historically and Sociologically

The American far-right of the second decade of the 21st century is a congeries of self-identified "Sovereign Citizens" (who, like Walt Whitman, take pride in being "entire unto themselves"); "3%ers" (an allusion to the mythical number of Americans who fought the British during the Revolutionary War); "Oath-Keepers" (so named for having taken an oath, often as police officers or as members of the military, to defend the US Constitution from foreign and domestic enemies), and armed Hawaiian-shirted "Boogaloo" warriors, who are either patiently awaiting the "Big Luau" ("CivilWar.2") or trying to "accelerate" its arrival. There are also Proud Boys (who boast of their White Euro-American racial heritage), Qanon conspiracy-mongers, and elderly White TEA Party retirees on Medicare and Social Security, who resent having to support brown and black-skinned "free-loaders"; play-acting Odinists, who prefer the ethical "purity" of ancient Norwegian paganism over the moral ambivalence of mainline Christianity; "f**k yeah" gun-nuts; and Silicon Valley "hipster fascists," enchanted by the same Ayn Rand who once served as the guiding light of their grandparents. This is to say nothing of buttoned-down Mormon "freemen," anti-vaxxers, anti-taxers, and Doomsday Preppers; black-clad, self-identified neo-Nazi storm-troopers; and their Confederate flag-waving Klan cousins. And these are only some of those who, as Max Weber might have said, live *for* right-wing politics, for whom it is a calling. But there are also those who live *off* the extremist right by marketing over-the-counter male enhancement pills, rare coins, and silver ingots; Czech gas masks, military-style firearms, and cheap Belize real estate; "White Pride World Wide!" coffee mugs, t-shirts, and bumper stickers, and red "MAGA" ball-caps. And we must never forget the venders of unregulated nutraceuticals, survival go-packs, and home security systems; and, especially, the robotic algorithms that oversee largely unregulated online social media platforms—for example, Instagram, Telegram, Gab, Facebook, Parlor, Twitter, and so on—that profit off traffic in outrage, and whose near cousins broadcast the most titillating of their messages on 24 hours a day hate radio. These and countless other trajectories are overseen by handfuls of millionaire and billionaire funders of non-taxable "educational foundations" and "charities" that are staffed with the "great minds" of the conservative movement, which, as we shall soon see, is not conservative at all. Without being exhaustive, here we find Groundswell, Project Veritas, Making America Great, Moms for America, First Liberty, and the Conservative Action Project, and so on.

All of this poses a problem for sociologists, namely, how to count their number? Given, one, their overlapping and sometimes contradictory affinities; two, the fact that group names and individual affiliations are transitory; and three, that far-right operatives have seized control of GOP (Republican Party) apparatuses throughout the Deep South, the Midwest, and the Rocky Mountain region, lending them a patina of conventional legitimacy, the short answer is: No one can be certain. But this, we do know:

To begin with, the American appetite for right-wing extremism has always been relatively small. Citing survey data gathered in 2013 by the highly respected Pew Research Center, Devin

Burghart (2014) reports that only 0.14% of Americans (i.e., 14 for every 1000 citizens) admit to being dues-paying members of the TEA (Taxed Enough Already) Party, which is among the most newsworthy radical right-wing groupings of the present era. And he estimates the number of "sympathizers" varies anywhere from 20% to 40% of the public, depending on the crisis of the moment. Active supporters (as indicated by Facebook "likes") comprise just 2% of the adult American population.

Second, continuing a pattern that goes back at least six decades, the large majority of TEA Partiers are White males from the sparsely populated states of Alaska (which is no. 1 in terms of per capita membership), Montana (no. 2), Wyoming (no. 3), and Idaho (no. 4). This comports with data gathered in the 1980s on the per capita number of right-wing extremist headquarters by state (Aho 1994, 153).

Third, whatever its reputed size, right-wing extremism in America is a cyclical phenomenon. In other words, while there has never been a time without government-bashing bigots and racists, there have also been moments when these sentiments capture larger fractions of the popular imagination. But just as quickly, these moments dissipate like morning fog. Furthermore, without suggesting that the process is automatic, these upsurges seem to occur about once every 30 years or so. Arthur Schlesinger's, Sr. (1965) and Jr. (1986), who use a 30-year marker to account for American political dynamics, argue that economic booms and busts may affect the amplitude of these insurgencies, but by themselves, they have little connection to *when* they occur. Instead, they attribute extremist outbreaks to successive younger generations for whom rightest ideas are still novel, fresh, and exciting. These eventually supersede their tired, cynical elders until they themselves become bored, and the movements they lead fade away.

Right-Wing Movements in American History

The first outbreak occurred around 1800, and it involved revelations of an Illuminati conspiracy. These concerns found expression in a pamphlet which has since served as a template and guidebook for conspiracy-mongering down to the present day: John Robison's *Conspiracy against All the Religions and Governments of Europe* (1967 [1798]). In response to the pamphlet the Federalist Party, led by New England "Presbygationist" (Presbyterian and Congregational) ministers and academics, enacted legislation to fend off what they feared was a seditionist plot by Jeffersonian and Jacobin revolutionaries to overthrow the republic. Rumor had it that the alleged plot was being roused to action by itinerant Methodist and Baptist ministers who were preaching to the ill-educated rural French and Irish populations of Virginia, Kentucky, and Tennessee. As a solution, the Federalists passed a series of four Alien-Sedition Acts. These so angered the alleged conspirators, that Thomas Jefferson used them to fuel his successful campaign for President and to repeal all the Acts, but one: that allowing for the deportation of alien enemies (i.e., those same rural French and Irish immigrants).

In 1830 a new menace appeared on the political scene: Freemasonry. This is a quasi-religious organization, originally designed for Protestant males, possibly envious of the robes, incense, and magical rites enjoyed by their Catholic neighbors. (It was out of Freemasonry that the Illuminati, just mentioned, was said to have emerged a generation earlier.) One version of the story claimed that Freemasonry had ties to a newly founded Christian sect known as the Church of Jesus Christ of Latter-day Saints (Mormon), whose leader once had been a Mason, and whose sacramental ceremonies bore an uncanny similarity to Masonic rites. Indeed, legend went so far as to claim that the word "Mormon" itself had been concocted from the last names of two men who were supposedly murdered by the Freemasons after they disclosed its wickedness to the public: William *Mor*gan and Timothy *Mon*roe. When salacious tales were related about the LDS religion and polygamy, anti-Masonic/anti-Mormon hysteria swept across the nation into the states of the Old Northwest. And an Anti-Masonic Party was founded, briefly rose to prominence, and then disappeared. In the meantime, the leader of the LDS Church had been assassinated and the Governor of Missouri had issued an extermination order on his followers, who fled from there to Illinois, and ultimately to safety in the high desert of the inter-mountain West, where many of their descendants still reside.

By 1860 the long-simmering Southern distrust of Yankee businessmen, who were manning their factories with free immigrant—Irish and German—labor, was being reframed as an insidious plot to destroy the slave economy of the South. As proof, rumors were floated of an impending "war of Northern aggression" to be expedited by a horde of radical Abolitionists, led by a silver-tongued "tyrant," misnamed "Honest Abe." Both Abolitionists and slaveholders cherry-picked passages from the King James Bible and the Constitution to bolster their positions, but gentlemanly debate soon led to fisticuffs and this to the brandishing of pistols—even in the halls of Congress. Threats of state nullification of "unconstitutional" laws followed, and this by intimations of secession from the Union. Tensions finally came to a head in the form of a preemptive attack on federal troops manning Ft. Sumter in South Carolina. The American Civil War commenced, and in less than a decade hundreds of thousands on both sides were killed. Even after the Confederate States surrendered, and the (male) slaves emancipated and formally granted citizenship rights, the price in human blood paid for victory was considered so unforgivable that descendants on both sides of the Civil War, at least thus far, have been reluctant to seriously entertain the possibility of a second.

The White Christian nativist American Protection Association (APA) was cobbled together in the 1890s, and it eventually grew into the largest political action group seen in America up to that time (with an estimated 3 million members). Sympathizers of the APA targeted different types of so-called unAmericans depending on the region in question, and with varying results. In the once Confederate South, for example, a terrorist group known as the Ku Klux Klan (KKK) was devised, and took up arms against Black freedmen in an effort to "redeem" the so-called lost cause (slavery). The Klan enforced Jim Crow segregation laws through public lynchings. (Of the 4742 lynchings staged in America from 1882 to 1968, over one-third alone occurred in the single decade between 1891 and 1901 [UMKC n.d.].) In the mining districts of California, Colorado, Montana, and Idaho, on the other hand, nativist hostility focused primarily on immigrant Asian laborers, whose camps were looted and whose residents were murdered. In the upper Midwest and Northeast states, it was Roman Catholics who felt the brunt of hate. Catholicism, of course, had long been an object of disdain for WASPs. Witness the Know Nothing Party of the 1840s and 1850s, an anti-Irish, anti-German crusade that ultimately turned against itself and collapsed over the question of slavery. But in the 1890s a visibly different type of Catholic began arriving on American shores: swarthy, short, and black-haired. Like their Irish and Germans forbears, they were accused of carrying with them Jesuitical plans to impose Papist rule on the country. But rather than fending off the threat directly with guns, for the most part APA sympathizers went after the intoxicants that popular legend associated with them: beer, wine, and whiskey. America's first "war on drugs" was declared and an Anti-Saloon Party established to fight it. Victory was declared in 1919 with the passage of an anti-alcohol Prohibition Amendment to the Constitution (which was repealed in 1933 [Gusfield 1986]).

Immediately after the First World War (1918) and the Bolshevik revolution that followed it, American authorities announced the presence of a new domestic peril; one supposedly more dangerous than the Illuminati, the Masons, the Mormons, the Catholics, and the Blacks of earlier eras: Communism. Stories were told about a secretive international conspiracy (COMINTERN), a monstrous cabal what was linked to already extant legends of union thuggery, Jewish "pinheads," and once more, to slavish papists. One result of the "red scare" was the passage of a series of increasingly onerous anti-Asian immigration restrictions in the far West. Another was a revived KKK to replace the original organization of the same name, but which had since been brought to its knees by rumors of embezzlement and revelations of sexual scandal. An award-winning movie, "Birth of A Nation," celebrating the Klan's rebirth, was shown to the public by presidential invitation at the (Woodrow Wilson) White House. As this was happening, the Klan seized control of state governments from Indiana to Oregon and points south. But the new KKK eventually lost its luster too, during the Great Depression of the 1930s, its members splintering into various proto-fascist grouplets like the Black Legion, the Silver Shirt Legion, and the German-American Bund, all of which are now mostly lost to memory.

Thirty years after the first red scare, an enterprising World War II veteran, "Tail Gunner Joe" McCarthy, helped revive memories of COMINTERN by claiming that now it had infiltrated the State Department and the movie studios of "Kosher Valley" (Hollywood) (an unsubtle reference to Jewish movie moguls). The conspiracy was also said to be implicated in the placement of fluoride in the water systems of local municipalities, so as to weaken the bones (and fighting prowess) of American youth; and of those same boys being "brainwashed" by "useful idiots," as liberal arts professors were then called. Loyalty oaths were ordered and investigations conducted into internal subversion. Some who objected to the proceedings were jailed for contempt of Congress; those who cooperated were blacklisted from further employment in sensitive industries. Yet, within a few years the second red scare too had passed—with the exception of a tiny, if noisy, John Birch Society—mostly without regret. Like a shingles virus, right-wing hysteria once again receded back into the spinal cord of the American body politic, awaiting an opportunity for its next stress-induced eruption.

Predictably, this came in 1980, 30 years after the dawn of McCarthy era, after a gigantic "Washington for Jesus" rally, staged by a consortium of White evangelical preachers who titled themselves the "Moral Majority, Inc." The election of an affable, if decidedly conservative, President—Ronald Reagan—followed, and with him a lapdog Congress eager to do his bidding. The underlying goal of the so-called Reagan Revolution was to systematically dismantle the various "socialist" programs and agencies that had been set up to address the Great Depression and to fight World War II. However, its publicly stated goal was to put an end to a "holocaust" of infant murders (abortions) and to defend "traditional family values" against the supposed carriers of "secular humanism," which included the same "pointy-headed 'perfessors'" whom McCarthy had earlier reviled. This, along with their alleged followers: Black civil-rights activists, white-skinned "long-hairs," and their bra-less female liberation companions. The most radical Reaganites went further, taking-up arms and banding together in Christian patriot militias with titles like the *Brüders Schweigen* or Order (mentioned in the last chapter); they conducted "military exercises" in anticipation of an impending race war. Reaganism ended abruptly in 1995 after a disgruntled Iraq war veteran, Timothy McVeigh, blew up the Murrah federal building in Oklahoma City, killing 168 mostly female clerks and minority preschoolers. That is, until 2008 when a "black man moved into the White House": Barack Obama.

The birth of today's far-right insurgency was announced in 2009, almost precisely 30 years after the onset of the Reagan era. One of the few minor things that distinguishes it from its predecessors are the names of its reputed antagonists. Now, instead of Masons, Abolitionists, Papists, "Commies," and the like, they are said to be uppity gay men and transgender kids, "environmeddlers," and Muslim "terrorists," Black Lives Matter advocates, abortion doctors, and Mexican "rapists and criminals" (a Donald Trump label). Apart from this, however, details aside, everything else has remained the same. There is the same bombast and buffoonery; the same litany of affronts to Christian righteousness; the same tales of a diabolic plot—this time, organized by "Deep State" operatives; the same prognostication that these are the End Times; the same promises that calamity can be avoided, but only if God-fearing patriots "prepare war"; and the same assurance that their prophesied victory will culminate in a world of justice and peace.

Owing to financial improprieties, acts of domestic terrorism, and sexual shenanigans (involving, most notably, if not exclusively, the movements' religious spokesmen), earlier right-wing insurgencies all imploded amidst public ridicule and internal finger-pointing. Later, we will discuss whether the latest iteration, "Trumpism," will follow suit. But at this writing, there have already been investigations into possible tax, insurance, and banking fraud committed by Trump administration officials; guilty pleas and convictions for perjury and campaign violations by several of his closest associates; accusations of sexual harassment and worse; and two impeachments (and acquittals) of Trump himself for obstruction of justice. But more important than all this is that like its historical predecessors of 1800, 1830, 1860, 1890, 1920, 1950, and 1980, Trumpism has failed to credibly address what has always lain behind American right-wing outbursts, namely, the displacement of rural, White Christian women and men by one or more rising status groups.[1]

Status Displacement

Hannah Arendt (1967) calls those who are undergoing the mortifications of status displacement "superfluous men," an expression she adopts from Maurice Barrès, who used it to characterize those who were flocking to his (European) proto-fascist gatherings in the 1890s. The phrase favored by today's victims of status displacement, borrowed from French social theorist, Renaud Camus, is *le grand remplacement* (the great replacement). Whichever way we choose to en-frame it, displaced peoples experience their superfluity as the end of the world, *their* world, the only world they have ever known. The problem is that, like earlier instances of right-wing upheaval, instead of going after the political-economic causes of their discontent, today's right-wing rebels are encouraged to direct their fury against various *fetishes* or fictitious emblems of peril. These fetishes go by names like, "child sex-traffickers," "pedophiles," and "baby murderers"; "drug cartels," people from "shit hole countries" (Trump's slander); "elitist vaccinators," "government gun-confiscators," and the like. But the reality is that no number of "big, beautiful" (anti-immigrant) walls, minority voter restrictions, or anti-sharia laws—which is to say, typical far-right measures—are likely to relieve superfluous man of their existential precarity. Likewise, the defunding of public schools and colleges from which their children might benefit, passage of "right to work" laws that undermine their economic power, or denials of government-subsidized medical insurance to the economically challenged (which includes themselves). The same goes for Second Amendment "gun-sanctuary laws," the waving of "Don't Tread on Me" Gadsden flags, the erection of Confederate soldier monuments, compulsory public schooling in Christian patriotism (as in Trump's 1776 Project), anti-transgender bathroom bills, closures of backcountry public roads to protect the property rights of the wealthy, or the sharing of cryptic "Qdrops" (posted by "Qanon," a popular source of defamatory Internet memes). Nor will extra-legal measures such as the murder of Hispanic grocery shoppers, Black and Jewish worshippers, gay bar-hoppers, or abortion providers.

Arendt relates how, throughout the 19th and 20th centuries, European and American right-wing ideologues encouraged superfluous men to see themselves, not as "little men" or as "forgotten Americans" (or as "suckers" and "losers," to borrow two Trumpian smears), but as *Herrenvolk* (superior folk), or as "supermen" (*Übermenschen*), upon whose shoulders the fate of western civilization rests.

Apart from its undeniable cathartic appeal, the label "fascism" is inadequate for understanding the American far-right. As is, by the way, the term "conservatism," which should already be obvious. Ignoring that the term was not even coined until the 1920s, and then in Italy, "the word 'fascism'," to quote George Orwell, "is ... almost entirely meaningless, except in so far as it signifies 'something not desirable'" (Orwell 1944). Nowadays, it is routinely invoked to slander everything from "Islamo-fascism" to compulsive gym-going (or "body fascism" [Pronger 2002]), and from "technofascism" (computerized music) and "femi-nazism," to "eco-fascism" and "homo-fascism." There are even oxymoronic phrases like "liberal fascism" (Jonah Goldberg 2007), "anti-fascism" (which, taken literally, means "anti-fascist fascism"), and "the worst tyranny in American history": "COVID fascism" (Deace & Horowtiz 2023). More than empty, however, the word is simply misleading. True, there have always been tiny contingents of American males who pleasure themselves by dressing up in brown, black, or white shirts, jodhpurs, riding boots, and occasionally by donning swastikas. But significant American far-right extremist movements, like those touched on in the previous section, have never been a foreign import. Rather, they are largely homegrown. Unlike the secularized, pseudo-scientific oratory reminiscent of European-style fascisms, in other words, from the beginning (i.e., ca. 1800) the rhetoric of the American far-right has been informed by two unique American cultural features: liberal-sounding jargon and Christian evangelicalism. Let us take a moment to briefly examine each.

First, to sell itself in an extremely competitive political market, the American far-right has always found it helpful to incorporate liberal-sounding verbiage into its communications. Alexander Reid Ross (2017), whom we will meet again in the last chapter, speaks of this as the rhetorical gambit of "syncretic absorption." For example, instead of frontally attacking labor unions, the American far-right campaigns for "right to work" laws that have the effect of defanging them; instead of deriding "consciousness raising" as psychobabble, it appropriates the concept as a viable way to recruit and mobilize its own supporters; and instead of ridiculing the notion of "racial in-justice," it organizes demonstrations around that very idea and then goes on to argue that its primary victims are straight, rural, White Christian men and women.

At this moment, the American far-right is promoting "multiculturalism" and "White ethnic studies programs," so that the victims—that is, White people—of discrimination by liberal elites, can learn about their illustrious forbears. It lauds the importance of "biodiversity," while grieving the imminent "extinction" of the Caucasian race. It demands the right to "free speech" (against the tyranny of "political correctness"), insists on "freedom of religion" (i.e., the right to harass LGBTQ citizens and abortion providers), and advertises that peculiar American conceit, mentioned at outset of this chapter, the "Sovereign Citizen": the ostensibly independent, self-made ego. The incorporation of liberal-sounding verbiage into far-right oratory sometimes goes so far that without careful parsing it becomes a challenge to ascertain whether one is consulting a bona fide liberal-progressive screed, or one authored by a racist, a misogynist, or a bigot.

A second, even more telling, rhetorical feature of American far-right discourse has always been Christian evangelicalism. As far back as 1800, many of the most notable spokespeople on the far-right have been drawn from the ranks of the Protestant (and occasionally, Catholic) ministry. Without being exhaustive, we can think of Rev. Carl McIntire, for example, of the Christian Anti-Communism Crusade of the 1950s and 1960s, or of Father Coughlin, founder of the Christian Front; Rev. G. L. K. Smith (of the Cross and Flag); and one-time Methodist minister, Rev. Wesley Swift (who co-founded the Aryan Nations Church). This is to say nothing of the Revs. William S. McBirnie and Gerald Winrod. In the present era, the comparable figures are Baptist ministers like Jerry Falwell, Jr. and Sr., Franklin Graham (son of Rev. Billy Graham), Rev. James Hagee, and Rev. Robert Jeffress, and so on.

It is the evangelical connection that helps us grasp the far-right's perennial obsession with "sodomy" (i.e., with acts said to hamper the presumed "natural end" of sexuality, such as contraception, masturbation, pedophilia, abortion, and homosexuality). Perhaps even more, it explains the far-right's "disgusted" beguilement with unrestrained female flesh and with activities associated with it, like rock 'n roll and jazz, two colloquial references to sex; with the "new addiction" (pornography), and with "hot drinks" and "drugs."

The evangelical fervor of the American far-right has rarely been more evident than in its most influential contemporary expression: Christian Dominionism (CD), the subject of this book. CD gets its title from the Book of Genesis which admonishes believers to assume "dominion" over the entirety of earth, including its human denizens. Estimates are that over 80% of those who voted for Donald Trump in the 2016 presidential election were CDs (Burton 2018).

Not surprisingly, there are different varieties or brands of CD, which should become clear in the next few chapters. But all of them share the same two convictions. The first is what I call the "Big Lie." Briefly, this is the insistence that there exists a demonic plot to "satanify" America; that every private concern and public issue—from insomnia, unemployment, and the opioid crisis, to wildfires, COVID-19, massacres, hurricanes, and so on—is attributable to it. And that if nothing is done to avert it, the End of the World is nigh. The second conviction concerns the "something to be done." This is the idea that American institutions must be remade or "reconstructed" after the directives of the "organic" Constitution (the original articles plus the two dozen or so amendments) and the Bible, read literally.

Trump and Trumpism

Donald Trump was legitimately beaten in the 2020 presidential election by an elderly, moderate liberal, Joe Biden, who garnered the largest plurality of ballots in American history, despite barely moving from his basement studio to campaign: 81+ million votes. As critics feared he might, Trump cried that the election was fraudulent, a sentiment that eventually came to be shared by over three-quarters of the GOP (or about 35% of the electorate). Although Trump's own Attorney General testified to a select House of Representatives hearing that Trump's claims were "nonsense" and "bull shit," and wondered aloud whether Trump had been "separated from reality," his supporters demanded that various state and federal courts formally rule on Trump's complaints. This included the Supreme Court, one-third of whose judges had been "pre-selected" (according to his liberal critics) by Trump himself, precisely for this purpose. After more than 60 of the courts refused to hear his complaints, Trump angrily responded, now even more vehemently, that in actuality it was *he* who had won, and in a "landslide" to boot. He went on to urge his supporters to "#Overturn" the election so as to "Stop the steal."

To avoid drowning in a dispute that would distract us from the focus of this book, I will ignore the Trump administration's attempt to subvert Biden's electoral victory by sending to Congress slates of fake Trump electors from several highly contested states—for example, Arizona, Pennsylvania, Georgia, Michigan, Wisconsin, and so on. Instead, I want to briefly say a few words about what has come to be known as the "insurrection," when thousands of angry Trump supporters "invaded" the capitol building during the electoral ballot count, in an effort to stop Biden's election from being certified.[2]

After what is reported to have been an "unhinged," "crazy" midnight meeting at the White House, December 18, 2020, during which Trump was repeatedly reminded that he had in fact lost, he is said to have proposed using the military to seize voting machines from the states just mentioned. However, calmer voices urged that instead he call for a "big protest in D.C. on January 6," the day on which Biden's election to the presidency was to be officially certified. Trump agreed with this, and the next day he tweeted, "Be there. Will be wild."

Given its marching orders, the far-right ecosystem sprang into action, broadcasting over the air and through cyberspace, invitations to its audience to attend the planned protest rally. A handful of online luminaries even went as far as to promise a "red wedding" on that day. Supposedly, this was an allusion to a cable TV Game of Thrones scenario during which guests are invited to a wedding feast, then trapped inside a room and killed. "Mother f *** er, you better look outside, you better look out January 6," warned one tweeter. "Kick that f ***ing door open and look down the street." "There's going to be a million-plus geeked-up, armed Americans. All Hell is going to break out."

Days prior to the planned protest rally, one of President Trump's closest legal advisors is said to have asked a young female staff person, "Are you excited?" about what was about to happen. "Things might get real, real bad on January 6." When the staffer heard this, she admitted to the select House committee investigating what *did* occur, to being "alarmed."

As it turned out, the protest rally, which Trump later called a "love feast," took place as scheduled. First, on the grounds of the US capitol and then, once its guarded doors were breached, inside the capitol building itself. This, by a bellowing crowd of flag-waving, MAGA-hatted protestors, who honored themselves with titles like "Proud Boys," "3%ers," and "Oath Keepers." Several of the protestors were recorded live on TV beforehand describing their intention to hunt down and kill "Nancy" (the derisive appellation they gave to Democrat Speaker of the House of Representatives, Nancy Pelosi) as well as Vice President, Mike Pence, who up to that point had been a reliable Trump sycophant. Evidently, Pence was targeted for being insufficiently enthusiastic about Trump's false election claims.

When he learned about plans that some of the demonstrators were going to hang Pence, Trump tweeted, "Mike deserves it." "They [the rioters] weren't doing anything wrong." They were, he continued, simply reacting to the (supposed) fact that Pence "didn't have the courage to protect the Constitution or the Country." One Trump staff member is reported to have gone so far as to propose that administration officials "blame" Pence's (anticipated) lynching "on anti-fa" or on "BLM" (the Black Lives Matter movement).

At this writing, there is still argument over what role, if any, Trump personally played in igniting the violence that occurred on the 6th. Those who claim that Trump and his staff planned and orchestrated the whole affair, point to a meeting held in the Willard Hotel, downtown in Washington, DC, on January 5th, the night before the protest took place. Trump's Chief of Staff (who participated by phone) and Rudy Giuliani are both said to have attended, along with leaders of two of the right-wing paramilitary groups just mentioned: The Proud Boys and the Oath Keepers. While Trump defenders dispute this, one thing is clear: At a speech he gave to a small crowd of protestors, on a plot of grass known as the "ellipse," located just off the capitol grounds, the morning of January 6, moments before the "storming" of the capital, Trump spoke about his intention "to be with you" (i.e., the protesters) and to "fight like Hell" for the movement. This, by "walking down" the street to the capitol building with the protesters, and then once there, confronting lawmakers.

After his speech, Trump's staff cautioned him against verbalizing what sounded to several of them as a threat, at the risk of being prosecuted for committing "every crime imaginable," including obstruction of justice and incitement to riot. In a huff, Trump pointed to the tiny audience that had just witnessed him speak, and asked what happened? He was told that the capitol police had refused to grant entry to scores of protesters, after they were magnetically screened (via megnatometers, devices that measure magnetic fields around objects) for carrying with them what amounted to a small arsenal of combat hardware, including brass knuckles, Glock pistols, combat-appropriate radio equipment, tear gas cannisters, face masks, helmets, steel spear tips affixed to flag poles, knives, bear spray, body armor, and at least one AR-15 semi-automatic rifle. To ease concerns that the police might have had about his own safety, Trump is said to have assured them that "they [the protesters] are not here to hurt me." He then went on to demand that they "let my people in."

Two heavily armored black SUVs arrived on the scene; Trump was seen climbing into the first and ordering the driver to proceed to the capitol building. The driver is reported to have politely replied, no sir, we're going straight to the White House. Trump then allegedly blurted, "I'm the f *** king President. I'm going." Although reports differ over what happened next, a "scuffle" is said to have ensued, during which Trump allegedly "lunged" at one of the security officers to get control of the SUV's steering wheel, while "grabbing" the driver by his "clavicles" [collarbones].

Eventually, the SUV did arrive back at the White House, where a lunch meeting was already in session. Once inside, Trump is reported to have had a temper tantrum, during which he threw his meal, together with its serving dishes against the wall. (A staff member who acknowledged that she helped clean up the mess claims that it was at that point that she and several of her colleagues, having witnessed similar scenes before, began contemplating invocation of the 25th Amendment to the Constitution to remove Trump from the office of the presidency. This, to save his "legacy.") Other attendees, however, proposed that Trump address the nation on TV, call for "healing," and condemn the rioters, whom Trump evidently wished to see pardoned. After some 187 minutes (or over three hours) passed, during which he is said to have reveled at videotaped images of the protest riot, Trump is reported to have consented to the TV address. He subsequently appeared on camera where he urged the rioters to "go home, in peace." He then added, "We love you." He neither mentioned, nor did he apologize for, the storming of the capitol.

As it turned out, the so-called love feast resulted in a number of deaths, including that of one foul-mouthed female rioter who was shot in the neck by police as she and others tried to storm the Senate chamber by shattering windows on the locked entry doors. The police too suffered hundreds of separate of injuries, and at least two are said to have had heart attacks as a result. (Two other policemen are reported to have later committed suicide, along with at least three protestors.) For their part, close to one thousand demonstrators were arrested and are, at this writing, being prosecuted for various misdemeanors and felonies, ranging from criminal trespass and vandalism, to assault and battery, and seditious conspiracy. Ironically, more than a few of them had proudly posted self-incriminating video clips of their misdeeds online, or they boasted about them on message boards that were easily accessed by authorities.

Millions of citizens witnessed the affair on TV and expressed shock at the level to which American political "discourse" could descend. Critics contend that had any of the 60 or so courts mentioned at the outset of this section ruled in Trump's favor, the American experiment as a democratic republic would have come to an end. That SCOTUS and the other courts all refused to act as Trump and his supporters thought they should, lent credence to an alternative suggestion, at least in liberal circles, that Trump had come to exemplify the very thing he had facilely accused his opponents—including Joe Biden—of being. Namely, "a loser."

Those who equate Trump the man with Trumpism the movement, see in these developments the finish of both. Observers closer to the movement, however, insist that even if one grants that Biden *did* win the election, his victory has merely amplified Trump's and his followers' grievances. And they go on to warn of more guns in the streets, of possible secession from the country, and even a second civil war—all to be undertaken in the name of Christ and Liberty. What we can be more confident of is this: If the 30-year generational cycle of right-wing insurgencies and recessions is any basis for prediction, Trumpism is likely to suffer the same fate.

One of the most telling signs of this likelihood is the flurry of smiley-faced commercial ads that followed each five-minute cable news segment of the insurrection on the afternoon and evening of January 6. There are even rumors that Trump officials sought to *trademark* the protest slogan, "Stop the steal!" and market it for sale. Add to this, were increasingly shrill GOP calls for more "officially-sanctioned fraudits" of balloting in GOP-run states.

The likely end of Trump the man, if not Trumpism the movement, of course, hardly means an end to right-wing fanaticism in America. On the contrary, a facsimile of Trumpism, likely under the guise of a catchier movement title, should reappear in 2040 or so, that is, about 30 years after 2009, when the TEA Party rose to prominence. Underlying this possibility is the assuredness of boredom, of a narcotizing ennui on the part of the American public, perpetually on the lookout for tantalizing distractions from its personal problems, and grown tired of endless conspiracy-mongering that elevates cortisol levels, but accomplishes little else. This will likely inspire *more* cryptic End Times prophecies, in this case issued by younger, more attractive strongmen (and women). And as always, there will be a coterie of fawning pulpiteers to mobilize their congregants to hate a new, yet to be identified, domestic enemy.

Conclusion

To say it again, then, American right-wing insurgencies seem to occur approximately every 30 years or so, yet only a relatively small portion of any given generation is drawn to them. The question of what differentiates this portion from the conventional majority has led to a virtual library of academic and journalistic commentary. And one thing we learn from it is that there is little empirical support for the ever-popular theory that right-wing extremists are, or ever have been, characterologically SIC: stupid, socially isolated, and/or crazy. The evidence available today indicates that the typical ultra-rightist has attained a level of formal education comparable to that of their more temperate peers, and occasionally a lot more. And even the most pugnacious among them, if not already dead or moldering in federal prison, have not been shown to be clinically insane. Finally, given that people tend to be galvanized to act via the social networks of which they are a part—through their family ties, workplace relationships, prayer groups, and friendships—true isolates are the last and least likely to become activists of *any* sort, let alone right-wing activists. In fact, the marriages of right-wing radicals appear to be about as stable as those of the average citizen, if not more so. And while many come from rural regions where they mine, log, ranch, and farm, there is little support for the hypothesis that they are any more geographically transient or more socially alienated than their temperate neighbors (for more on these comparisons, see Aho 1991, 135–63).

But there is one factor that *does* seem to distinguish right-wing extremists from those who are not. It is authoritarianism (Dean & Altemeyer 2020). By this, I mean a disposition to inflict gratuitous pain on the downtrodden, coupled with a yearning to debase oneself before their purported superiors—even when those superiors mock them and/or advance policies detrimental to their practical economic interests. To be sure, authoritarianism in this sense has never been restricted to extremists on the right. Proponents of equality and democracy can be just as cruel, and certainly as servile, as ultra-rightists. But left-wing extremism is the subject of another study. In what follows here, our concern is exclusively with the most outspoken and dangerous devotees of the American far-right, Christian Dominionists.

Notes

1 The most comprehensive application of this hypothesis to American political history can be found in Lipset and Raab (1970).
2 The following account of the January 6, 2021, insurrection is based on the findings of the select House of Representatives Committee public hearings, broadcast on mainstream TV channels, over a several week period during the Spring and Summer of 2022. These findings are exhaustively available in print (cf. Thompson [Chairman], 2022). For an excellent summary and critical assessment of this report, see Lepore (2023).

3 Christian Dominionism and Its Critics

The Roots of Christian Dominionism

Until the late 1960s, American Protestant evangelicalism was primarily a "pre-political movement" (Diamond 1996, 92), whose concerns had to do with personal salvation, individual achievement, and on the need of believers to comply with legitimate authorities. Where there was any talk of building a better society, it was generally limited to discussions about the appalling conditions on Native American reservations and on missionary work in the Far East and in Central and South America. Gerard Colby's and Charlotte Dennett's, *Thy Will Be Done* (1995) offers an exhaustive account of the challenges faced by the mostly young, male missionaries of this period, not the least of which were linguistic. (The Summer Institute of Linguistics and its associated Human Relations Area files, both of which were originally established to address the linguistic problem, eventually played pivotal roles in the development of the profession of Anthropology in America. Both were initially funded by the Rockefeller Foundation and, ultimately, by the Rockefeller-owned Standard Oil Company.) And then, of course, there were the physical perils and health issues that the missionaries faced, and the occasional gruesome deaths they suffered as a result.

While the focus on foreign missionary work has never disappeared, by the 1970s, under the auspices of a different style of religiosity, partly associated with the Southern Baptist convention, and with dissident Presbyterians, American evangelical concern began to shift back to the United States. So much so, that by the middle 1980s Rev. George Grant (1987, 50–51) could confidently assert that "Christians have ... a holy responsibility to reclaim the land [meaning, the United States] for Jesus Christ – to have dominion in the civil structures [i.e., the government, economics, charity, and education, etc.], just as in every other aspect of life and godliness." In other words, "*it is dominion that we are after not just a voice ... Not just influence... Not just equal time. It is dominion we are after. World conquest*" (my emphasis).[1] Grant goes on to write that this is what Christ has commissioned believers to achieve. "We must win the world with the power of the Gospel. And we must never settle for anything less."

The opening section of this chapter addresses how the doctrine of Christian Dominionism, as promulgated by Rev. Grant, came into existence, its source(s). In the section after that, we deal with the surprisingly sophisticated, if rather ironic, logic that underlies CD thinking, particularly in regard to modern science. The story begins with a Baptist layman named Stewart Lyman.

Stewart Lyman

Conservative American Christians were already calling themselves "fundamentalists" when they formally declared "war on modernism" in 1919. This was barely a year and a half after the end of World War I and the frightening ferment that followed in the tracks of the Bolshevik Revolution in

Russia. Above all, there was the seemingly never-ending turmoil of race riots in American cities, and the Palmer raids conducted out of a newly formed FBI, to ferret out and deport supposedly disloyal immigrants to this country.

The declaration of war on modernism expressed views that had been developed at least a decade earlier in a 12-pamphlet series of essays authored by 64 different conservative biblical scholars: *The Fundamentals: A Testimony to the Truth*. The Fundamentals in turn was financed by a devoted lay-evangelist who, like John D. Rockefeller, was himself an oil magnate: Stewart Lyman (1840–1923). Lyman had earlier cofounded and headed the Union Oil Company (Unocal), which came to be known for its bright orange Union 76 gas station signs. He also founded Biola University (shorthand for the Bible Institute of Los Angeles), which gained local notoriety for the huge "Jesus Saves" neon signs that were affixed atop its downtown dormitory. (The campus has since been moved to La Mirada, California, just east of downtown LA).

The content of *The Fundamentals* was the culmination of a series of Bible conferences held after 1870 in response to concern at, one, mass immigration to America by Jews and Eastern European and Italian Catholics (who are rebuked in *The Fundamentals* as practitioners of "Romanism"); two, Mormonism (which at the time was still practicing polygamy). Then, a pamphlet each was devoted to discussing "cults," such as Spiritualism (an early precursor of contemporary New Age philosophy), the Jehovah's Witnesses, and Christian Science. A fourth concern was the growing popularity of the liberal-progressive Social Gospel movement, and with it, the concept of "higher criticism" (meaning, a "modern" way to read the Bible, allegorically instead of literally); and fifth, the association of both the Social Gospel and the higher criticism with Germany, with Prussian militarism, and with the atrocities of World War I.[2]

In the face of these and related challenges to Christian orthodoxy, *The Fundamentals* offered a return to what it insisted was the true source (*ad fontes*) of Christianity, namely, a faith "cleansed of all impurity," which would brook no compromise with the "spineless," "godless pseudo-Christians" whom the pamphlets accused of having brought America "floundering to the brink of death." A decade later, the condemning accusers would include Rev. Carl McIntire and a handful of his closest associates.

The McIntire Consortium

After graduating from Princeton University Theological Seminary, Carl McIntire (d. 2002) assumed his first pastorate in the Presbyterian Church, USA, in 1931. But before long, he and a number of his supporters left the Church after losing an ecclesiastical court dispute regarding the proper way to understand End Times (eschatological) prophecy. The issue at stake was whether the Book of Revelation should be read as prophesying that Christ will return to earth *after* the Millennium (and thus, after associated events like the Rapture, the Tribulations, the war of Armageddon, etc.), the position upheld by *post*-millennialists, like John D. Rockefeller, Sr. Or should the Book of Revelation be interpreted as saying that the Second Coming will occur *prior* to the Millennium (the position maintained by *pre*-millennialists). McIntire and his allies aligned themselves with the pre-millennialists.

After years of failed attempts to secure preaching positions in recognized denominations, McIntire (along with the Revs. Fred Schwarz and Billy James Hargis) established their own schismatic *Bible* Presbyterian Church (in 1962). The adjective in its title reflected their conviction that they were among the few carriers of an authentic Christ-centered Bible message.

While readers may wonder why these events have any salience for CD today, they turn out to be important in at least two ways. First of all, a preoccupation of pre-millennialists has always been the study of contemporary world events so as to detect signs of the Second Coming: for example, the Soviet revolution of 1917 in Russia, or the establishment of the state of Israel three decades later in 1948, and the re-gathering of the Jews after centuries of exile. Both events were interpreted by pre-millennialists as unmistakable signs of Christ's imminent return, and by implication a warning to prepare oneself for the catastrophes that were about to befall non-believers (cf. Lindsey 1970). This explains McIntire's and Hargis's fiery diatribes against gambling, drink, and drugs; against homosexuality and public-school sex education; against fluoridated public water systems; Darwinism, labor unions, and racial integration, and above all, against Communism.

Second, and more prosaically, McIntire, Schwarz, and Hargis were never content merely to sit back and passively observe history unfold. Schwarz, for example, as a leading figure in the Christian Anti-Communism Crusade became known for his anti-Communism training schools, set up after World War II, and staffed with prominent conservative academics. But his most well-known venture was a nationally televised "Hollywood's Answer to Communism" rally staged in the Hollywood Bowl," October 1961. It featured the famed cowboy and cowgirl actors, Roy Rogers and Dale Evans, as well as the Oscar-winning movie celebrity, Jimmy Stewart, along with the Christian movie pseudo-hero, John Wayne. McIntire and Hargis, meanwhile, were drawn to the possibility of disseminating the Good News in what they believed was a more cost-effective—that is, cheaper and more "productive" manner—namely, over the air. At the height of his fame, Hargis was preaching daily 15-minute sermonettes on over 225 radio stations across the country; McIntire's "Reformation Hour" was broadcast on no less than 600+ stations nationwide.

More important, perhaps, than his radio shows, was McIntire's success at lobbying the Federal Communications Commission to liberalize its restrictions on religious broadcasting. Although he eventually lost his own private battle with the FCC for violating its Fairness Doctrine (by refusing to air his religious competitors' views), McIntire did succeed in encouraging it to begin selling airtime to the highest bidders in 1957. This eventually led to the unseating of a number of overly timid and comparatively staid local radio and (and later, TV) preachers, by media savvy, occasionally flamboyant, and politically adept preachers, who were willing to share the stage with captivating celebrity guests. The political talk show format, for example, pioneered by Rev. Pat Robertson's CBN (Christian Broadcasting Network) in the early 1960s, mixed "the latest national and international news" with gospel music performed by professional musicians, together with animated cartoons for the kids. Two beneficiaries of these developments were Rev. Jimmy Bakker and his wife, Tammy (d. 2007), whose marriage (and media empire) were shattered by exposés of their sexual infidelities.

"As the content of shows like these became more worldly," says Sara Diamond (1996, 98), and their audience sizes exploded into the millions, "religious broadcasting" became "the single most important resource in the mobilization of the Christian Right." The prime example of this, again, was Pat Robertson, who deftly deployed his own TV talk show, the 700 Club (broadcast on CBN), as a weapon in his ultimately failed attempt to secure the GOP presidential nomination in 1979.

Jerry Falwell Sr. (d. 2007) who, until the time of his first TV broadcast, was a rather obscure, if amiable, Southern Baptist minister with a megachurch in Lynchburg, Virginia, went on to found the Moral Majority, Inc. In its first year alone, it boasted a subscription list of 32,000 evangelical preachers and a treasury of donations totaling more than $1.5 million. With the support of a number of other right-wing Christian lobbies, the Moral Majority, Inc. staged a "Washington for Jesus" rally in 1980, which is estimated to have drawn over 200,000 believers. There, they hoisted American flags and Bibles, waved placards proclaiming "a world aflame in sin" (i.e., in "sodomy" and "fetal murder") and warned that "America must repent or perish." Five months later, they (hyperbolically and inaccurately) took credit for sweeping into office the most far-right President in half a century, Ronald Reagan, and a Congress eager to advance his so-called Reagan revolution (Lipset & Raab 1981).

The content of McIntire's, Hargis's, and Schwarz's speeches, lectures, sermons, and magazine and book publications prefigured the content of CD messaging still heard and read today. But what made the trio truly essential for the growing political influence of CD was their willingness to experiment with new technologies to deliver those messages. We've already mentioned Schwarz's anti-Communism training schools, and the adoption of radio and commercial TV to convey their lessons. But there was also Hargis's use of direct mail advertising to solicit money from the general public, and his hiring of Richard Viguerie (who was already a well-known big-data expert), to help organize mass-mail solicitations from specific target audiences.

Hargis helped co-found the "T-Party" (not: the later TEA Party of 2009) which preached anti-Tax, anti-Treason, and anti-Tyranny messages. And he devised a traveling circus-like road-show, devoted to Christ and Liberty, called "Operation Midnight Ride." OMR enlisted John Birch Society luminaries, like Gen. (ret.) Edwin Walker (whom the FBI once suspected of being involved in President John Kennedy's assassination) (Chapman 2012, 8). Nor was this Hargis's most ambitious project. His most "flamboyant plan" is said to have taken place in 1953, when he typed Bible verses on note cards, tied them to tens of thousands of gas-filled balloons, then launched the balloons from Chaims, West Germany, with hopes that they would land across the Iron Curtain (Chapman 2012, 3). Although the efficacy of the experiment is still unclear, it did attract the attention and financial support of the International Council of Christian Churches.

A seemingly more serious, certainly more straightforward, early source of CD was a fourth Presbyterian dissenter and McIntire disciple, Rev. Francis Schaeffer. Schaeffer would later break with McIntire and become a post-millennialist and be reabsorbed back into the mother denomination. From this, he went on to join the Coalition on Revival, which was founded by still another post-millennialist, Jay Grimstead. Together, they worked tirelessly to establish God's kingdom on earth, *now!* instead of waiting around for Christ's second coming. They did this by advocating the reformation of American institutions on the basis of "theonomic" principles (i.e., God's written law) (Baron 1992; Frame 1989; Rausch & Chismar 1983).

When Schaeffer and his wife left America to establish a retreat center called L'Abri ('the shelter') in Switzerland, he turned into a prolific author (until his death in 1984). His *A Christian Manifesto* (1982) is estimated to have sold over 200,000 copies in the first year alone; it has since been translated into multiple languages and boasts sales in the millions.

Following the lessons of Rousas Rushdoony's (1973) tome, *The Institutes of Biblical Law* (which is discussed in the next subsection), Schaeffer argued that while America originally was founded on biblical principles, it has since fallen away from the "Truth." This, he wrote, is primarily due to the influence of "secular humanism," which supposedly has replaced God with the concept of human "Progress." To avert further moral and spiritual decline, as had happened to the now-defunct civilizations of Greece and Rome, Schaeffer recommends the use of civil disobedience to end abominable practices like abortion—along the lines of Rev. Martin Luther King's non-violent campaigns against racial segregation. But in the event that civil disobedience is neither practical nor feasible, then Schaeffer reluctantly accedes to the necessity of using force. Leadership positions, assigned either by election or by appointment, in schools, businesses, hospitals, governments, and the like should, according to Schaeffer, be occupied by born-again Christian men. Once in office, they are mandated to begin "reconstructing" America according to biblical specifications.

Rousas John Rushdoony

Authorities such as Julie Ingersoll (2015) claim that the phrase "Christian Dominionism" is attributable to its considered "foundational" theologian, Rousas John Rushdoony. While the truth of her assertion can be disputed, it is undeniable that Rushdoony was one of its leading proponents.

He was among the first to write about a renewed faith, charged with responsibility "to subdue earth and exercise dominion over it": not only its plant life and animals but also its non-believing human creatures.

Raised by an Armenian emigrant family to America, who had first-hand knowledge of political persecution, Rushdoony became an inveterate skeptic of state authority, a stance later endorsed by Pat Robertson, Jerry Falwell Sr., and Francis Schaeffer. After being raised in a Congregationalist/Methodist household, he ended up as a Presbyterian and was ordained to the ministry in the Presbyterian Church, USA. He later transferred his loyalty and affiliation to a seemingly more orthodox Presbyterian congregation in Santa Cruz, California. From there, he went on to found the Chalcedon Foundation in 1955.

Rushdoony was deeply influenced by Westminster Theological Seminary faculty, particularly, by Professor Cornelius Van Til, a Dutch Calvinist theologian, who emphasized the fact of mankind's total depravity. Following Van Til's teachings, Rushdoony came to believe that, if not properly grounded in the inerrancy of the Bible, human-based knowledge by itself is inevitably "sinful, invalid nonsense." He cited this conclusion to justify his claim that there exists an irreconcilable gulf separating knowledge claims proffered by true believers (like himself), versus those advanced by "secular humanist" non-believers, including liberal, mainline scientists.

One of the Chalcedon Foundation's first associates was Gary North, who eventually married Rushdoony's daughter. North had earlier been involved with the Foundation for Economic Education, which espouses a variation of libertarianism, to which we will return later. And after North and his father-in-law separated, North went on to set up his own think tank in Tyler, Texas: The Institute for Christian Economics. In spite of their differences, however, North and Rushdoony continued to collaborate and to publish books concerning all aspects of human life.

Rushdoony's *Institutes of Biblical Law*, mentioned in the previous subsection, was explicitly modeled after John Calvin's own magnum opus of the same title. In it, Rushdoony articulates his hoped-for vision of an American future: It will be a "millennial kingdom," comprised largely self-sufficient, independent "Christian republics," each of which has few central administrative apparatuses, and with only small local governments set up to oversee the extended families they govern. Each family in turn is to be supervised by certifiably Christian men. Hence, there will be little, if any, need for property taxes, public education systems, or government welfare institutions. Additionally, there will be no pornography, embryonic stem-cell research, LGBTQ rights, sex education, or Darwinism.

Dominionist Bible Science and Sciences

While the phrase "Christian Dominionism" was not in wide use until Schaeffer, Rushdoony, and North popularized it, it has raised the fears and hackles of prominent liberal progressive thinkers. This, for its supposedly un-American and totalitarian ambitions, its alleged anti-intellectualism, and for its embracement of the methodology, if not the findings and theories, of modern mainstream science. In the following paragraphs, we address each of these concerns.

To begin with, regarding the claim that CD espouses totalitarianism, the reality is that American evangelical Protestantism has *always* shown an exuberant, expansive, we might even say, "dominionist" face to the world. Ingersoll (2015) has gone so far as to argue that virtually every major political development in American history—from the Revolution, the Civil War, and the Civil Rights movement; to Prohibition, Progressivism, and Female Suffrage—originated in and was nourished by evangelical enthusiasm. Thus, when the early liberal-progressive Social Gospel preacher Josiah Royce (1855–1916), to cite just one example of many, unabashedly proclaimed that the "divine solution" to *all* of humanity's problems would be the "Christianization of America and then the world" (Dorrien 2009, 7), he was doing little more than expressing a sentiment more or less taken for granted as indubitable at the time. Washington Gladden, a second Social Gospel preacher, says essentially the same thing, but even more pointedly. The goal of the Social Gospel, Gladden asserts, is to "socialize" or "humanize" Scripture, while "Christianizing" society; building God's kingdom on earth by insinuating "every great department [or institution] of society" with "Christian spirit and … Christian law" (quoted in Dorrien 2009, 70). The implication of this is that while contemporary CD may be off-putting to live-and-let-live readers unfamiliar with American (Protestant) history, there is little in it that is either particularly novel or un-American.

As to its totalistic aspirations in particular, which is to say, its yearning to remake or "reconstruct" the entirety of American society and the world, after biblical injunctions. Rev. George Grant's words, quoted in the second paragraph of this chapter, seem to support this contention. But before going too far down this path, let us turn once again to the comparable promise (or threat, depending on one's perspective) issued by Washington Gladden, a century earlier, that the goal of the Social Gospel program would be to infuse "every great department of society" with Christian life-force and to rule each according to the maxims of Christian law. True, Gladden's liberal progressive rendering of "Christian law" conflicts with that of the CD Grant, but the scope of his ambitions do not. For both Gladden and Grant, the guiding star in their heavenly firmament is the biblical maxim, "Thy will be done on earth as it is in Heaven" (Matt. 6: 10).

What *does* make CD different from other evangelical-inspired movements takes us to a third point. It is that unlike the Social Gospel, which Seymour Martin Lipset and Earl Raab (1970) characterize as "cultural baggage," loaded onto a political-cultural "locomotive" driven by upwardly mobile "winners" in the status competitions of a newly emerging American industrial empire, CD—at least according to Lipset and Raab—is carried by "losers." Or, to express it less vulgarly (using terms introduced in Chapter 2), the primary conveyors of CD are "superfluous men" who are undergoing the humiliations of marginalization and displacement by the relentless march (or "juggernaut") of globalization. And they are nostalgic for the time when they supposed *themselves* to be leading figures in world affairs. As their status prospects have dimmed, says Theodor Adorno, their religious reveries have provided them the thin gruel of symbolic compensation, becoming ever more "magnificent, demonic, and occasionally destructive" (Adorno 2020). One of the first documents of this was the vindication that many CD leaders enjoyed when, during the Reagan era, they heard news of an impending atomic-fueled apocalypse, seeing in it the judgment of (their own) angry God (Lindsey 1970; White 1983).

Fourth, and most importantly, let us assume as Richard Hofstadter (1963) does, that from its beginning American culture has been imbued with a populist skepticism of cloistered intellectuals and of intellectualism. If so, then once again there appears nothing new nor peculiarly un-American in CD's voiced antipathy toward mainline academic science, toward the "pencil-headed intellectuals" who practice it, and toward professional expertise generally (especially in bio-medicine and law). True, lay-Dominionist discourse can sometimes seem outlandish, if not entirely without humor. Take its Big Foot fantasizing, for example, its obsession with UFOs, its Qanon conspiratology, and its marketing of instruments like "spirit boxes," to communicate with deceased relatives. There are also its tales of alien abductions by Ebens who are said to inhabit the Zeta Reticula star system. (Are these not the "angels" spoken of in the Bible? Some CDs earnestly ask.) But as for the *theology* of CD, to quote Ingersoll (2015, 14–16), it exhibits an "elegant internal logic." From a handful of "presuppositions" or unassailable assumptions, skilled CD thinkers are able to derive countless empirical-like propositions and ethical pronouncements that touch on virtually every aspect of human life, from sexuality to early childhood education; and from banking and health care to foreign policy. All of which takes us to the subject of CD and modern science.

CD and Modern Science

There is a phrase that exhibits how intellectually sophisticated CD theology can seem. The phrase is "epistemological self-consciousness." While this does sound cryptic, and even a bit intimidating, on closer view it is perfectly straightforward. In fact, it has a rather *post-modernist* ring that can charm the naïve reader. Let us look at it more closely.

Whether what they assert about mainstream science is accurate or not, CDs claim that it labors under the illusion of "value neutrality." This is supposedly why mainstream scientists insist that only science is capable of depicting reality *as it is*. But the concept of value neutrality is a fraud, say CDs. It is a shield behind which mainstream scientists hide their actual atheistic, god-denying, biases.

At one time this may have been a radical critique (e.g., this is precisely the criticism directed against modern science in one of the 12 pamphlets in *The Fundamentals* series described earlier). But today it is an axiom familiar to most academic social psychologists (who are themselves mainstream scientists): It is that no human cognition, scientific or otherwise, can ever be fully value neutral. On the contrary, all perception, all thinking, and all memory—which is to say, all knowing—is unavoidably infused through and through with ultimately unprovable, value-laden assumptions, the veracity of which must be accepted, for want of a better word, on faith. This includes the most detailed laboratory findings, the most intricate probabilistic accounts of past occurrences, and the most accurate predictive forecasts. In other words, *human knowers can never be value neutral*.

As used by CDs, the phrase "epistemological self-consciousness" means two things. First, it means that a knower acknowledges the truth of the previous paragraph, and that, therefore, one can never know things-themselves. Second, it means that the knower is willing to disclose what their *own* particular value-biases are. To the degree that mainstream academic science denies having any such presuppositions—which, as we just said, is highly questionable—then it follows that it and its practitioners are epistemologically *un*conscious, and their work is therefore conducted in bad faith.

Among the many implications that follow from the idea of epistemological self-consciousness is that the adoption of any set of presuppositions over another is never a trivial event. Rather, it is a *vital existential decision*, a choice that necessarily "kills-off" alternative ways of being there in time and space, of existing in the world. What these alternatives are, at least from the standpoint of CD, takes us to a fifth clarification.

Of the myriad values and presuppositions on which a knower might conceivably draw, CDs say there are two basic types. Reduced to essentials, these represent the familiar metaphysical division between God and Satan, and its associated echoes: Goodness and Evil, Righteousness and Wickedness, Right-hand versus Left-hand, White skin versus Black, and the Male principle versus that of the Female.

According to CD, the *second* of the alternatives in this series of dualities rests on the presupposition that nature and mankind are the sole sources and measure of all things. This includes the entire textual product of mainstream academic science, as well as that of its near cousin, the "secular humanities." In CD theology, both the mainstream sciences and the secular humanities locate the causes and the end purposes of earthly affairs in dis-enchanted matter riven from, or separated from, God; or, in other words, the self-seeking, God-absent, God-denying ego.

In contrast to this, the first principle in the pairings understands God the Father to be the Alpha and Omega, the Prime Mover and ultimate End, from which all things come and toward which they are moving. God, as represented in that singular text whose very words are said by CDs to be dictated by Himself: The King James Bible. In CD thinking, the King James Bible offers a unitary, internally consistent, and verbatim account of reality as it truly is.

It follows, then, that if one seeks edification and moral guidance from the Evil/Wicked/Left-handed (= sinister)/Female/Black dimension of reality, then they are ipso facto allied with Satan, the Liar, and eternal bearer of "fake news." But if instead one seeks out and adheres to the Word of God, they are positioned to be His disciples, and therefore messengers (evangelists) of "good news." Among other supposedly good news, at least from a neo-Calvinist perspective, is that humankind is totally depraved (as St. Augustine long ago understood[3]) and is thus unable to redeem itself through individual good works and/or social reform. Nonetheless, some human beings have been "unconditionally elected" (i.e., through no credit of their own) by God for eternal life in Heaven.

A multitude of hypotheses and moral directives are logically derivable from the good news. This gives CD the appearance of being a publicly sharable, "objective," system of knowledge, analogous to, and supposedly as rigorous as, if not more so, than mainstream science. The result has been a proliferation of CD-inspired "biblical sciences" (or "Bible sciences"), each of which is comprised a mixture of what secular-humanist audiences might deem factual, together with "alternative facts" (held to be true only by CDs). That CD is eager to advertise itself as "scientific" underscores how deeply embedded it is in the Liberal-Enlightenment tradition, which it outwardly claims to repudiate.

The Bible Sciences

It is essential to bear in mind our earlier observation that neither the mainline sciences nor the Bible sciences commence their inquiries with bare facts alone from which they derive various theories. Instead, each sets out with *conjectures* about reality, from which they deduce hypotheses that alert them to what should be attended to, and what can be ignored. Mainstream science derives its hypotheses from the prevalent paradigms in its recognized sub-specialties. The hypotheses in the Bible sciences are derived from a literalist reading of the Bible.

This, however, does not mean that the two styles of inquiry are formally (or logically) identical. Far from it. Bible scientists amass facts to verify or to amplify hypotheses they already know to be true. Mainstream science does the opposite: It sets up experiments that put its hypotheses at risk of refutation. In the event that a hypothesis in a particular case is not refuted does not imply that it is, therefore, true, but only that it has earned a bit more corroborative plausibility. But even after being corroborated in this way countless times, "all [mainstream scientific] theories [are] without exception" hypothetical, "even if we feel unable to doubt them any longer," says philosopher of science, Karl Popper (1965, 51). In other words, *all* mainstream scientific theories, in principle, can be subjected to further testing and possible rejection. Which is a long way of saying that mainstream science is an enterprise in unending skepticism, while the Bible sciences are practices (or instances) of dogged dogmatism.

On the face of it, this may seem to be a minor difference, but it turns out to have major implications. For as Popper also tells us (1965, 35–37)—here, regarding the Bible scientist's goal of validating or confirming their hypotheses—"the world is full of verifications ..." "It is easy to obtain confirmations ... if we look for them": of the existence of God, for example, of Big Foot, of "chemtrails," of alien abductions, or of Deep State conspiracies. There is even "first-hand testimony" that one-time President Barack Obama was not actually born in the United States to a woman, but "hatched," like a reptile, at a secret military installation on Mars. (The testifier in this case claims to know this because he himself was supposedly hatched and raised at the same facility and came to know Barack, simply, as "Barry.")

For our purposes, however, the most important difference between mainstream sciences and Bible sciences is not so much methodological, as it is practical. For unlike mainstream inquiries, the various Bible sciences have few, if any, established customs or institutions of double-blind, prepublication peer-vetting (or screening) of book and article submissions, wherein neither the author nor the reviewer is able to identify the other. Although double-blind peer reviewing is by no means perfect, it does have an anti-corruptive, corrective effect. Where double-blind peer reviewing is absent, there is relatively little control over what ends up being published, read, or aired. True, many Bible scientists are college graduates; some are fine writers. But relatively few seem to be credentialed in the disciplines they presume to discuss professionally. Rather, they typically have degrees in marketing, corporate leadership, law, religious studies, or (as in the case of Rushdoony) childhood education. Furthermore, while some of the colleges at which Bible scientists have matriculated offer "doctoral" degrees, most of them have less than scintillating academic reputations. Ingersoll (2015, 132–34) reports on the resentment that Bible scientists have of mainline science critics, whose "persecution" they attribute to the mainline scientists having been "brain-washed" at liberal universities.

Let us briefly turn now to the different Bible sciences. That there even exist such phenomena, belies Theodor Adorno's (2020) oft-repeated assertion that contemporary right-wing discourse has no refined theories or ideology but is merely a bag of rhetorical "slogans" and "tricks" that appeal to "authority-bound" audiences.

As evidence against this, take Christian geology, a sub-specialty of creation science (Ingersoll 2015, 119–39). Creation science in turn is based on the presupposition that, details aside, the Book of Genesis is empirically accurate: earth really *was* created in "six days." (Naturally, there is debate over what constitutes a biblical "day.") Starting with this presupposition, Bible geologists may debate the merits of "gap theory" or of various "fossil-flood theories," but they will not question the veracity of Genesis itself. "Gap," by the way, refers to the centuries that are said to have passed between the "first" creation (that of planet earth) and the "second," which gave us Adam and Eve. Fossil-flood theories demonstrate how the flood of Noah's time, as loosely portrayed in Genesis (Chapters 6,7, and 8), explains the rock strata—visible, say, in the Grand Canyon or in the Rocky Mountains—and the fossils interred there.

There is also Christian climatology, Christian biology, and Christian demography (for the latter, see Elmer & Elmer 1984). Christian demography has informed CD policy recommendations regarding the immigration of non-Christians and non-White people to America, which takes us to biblically grounded race science. This presumes to offer genetic and anatomical accounts of why darker-skinned peoples supposedly have never produced advanced civilizations. Clue: it is supposedly because they are inferior intellectually to White Euro-Americans, as proven by the shapes of their skulls (George 1962). (When he wrote this widely disseminated pamphlet, Wesley George was a Professor of Biology at the University of Alabama.)

There is even a biblically inspired medical science. This is based in part on a rejection of, or at least a high degree of skepticism about, germ theory, that is, the conjecture that bacteria, viruses, fungi, prions, and the like, cause diseases. With the denial of germ theory, the technologies that mainstream bio-medicine recommends as cures for disease come into dispute: for example, the cauterization of infected flesh, its surgical removal, and/or vaccinations. CD-influenced medicos reverse the causal connection said to exist between germs and disease, maintaining that, just as garbage attracts hungry insects, putrefying (diseased) flesh draws its own "garbage eaters": those same pesky bacteria, viruses, and fungi (Aho & Aho 2008, 90–95). It follows, then, that to rid the body of germs, one must first cleanse it of the filth that attracts them. This, by deploying a tactical regimen of "nutraceuticals" (non-pharmaceutical, hence un-licensed, food supplements), high colonic enemas and water consumption, cellular oxygenation (through e.g., vigorous exercise), a diet of low pH-level (basic) foods, vaccine-avoidance, and directed prayer.

There is also biblical archaeology and Christian historiography. The first accepts as basically (if not precisely) true, the stories about Israel as recounted in the first fifteen books of the Old Testament: for example, Israel's enslavement in Egypt, its escape past receding sea waters under the guidance of Moses, Jacob's conquest of the Promised Land, the establishment by David of a unified kingdom, the erection of a magnificent palace in Jerusalem under Solomon, and so on. To confirm these stories—recall, the object of Bible science is not to challenge or to test its claims, but to validate them—Bible archaeologists conduct digs, some of which are well-financed by their government sponsors, to unearth the relevant potshards and tin relics (Margalit 2020).

For its part, Christian historiography pays special attention to American history, showing how and why it is the "exceptional" nation CDs suppose it to be. The idea here is that history should never be read merely as a succession of human acts, but as a *theophany*, an account of how God, through His image and likeness (i.e., humankind), has become manifest over time. Hence, the tales about the Mayflower Compact, the Declaration of Independence, the American Constitution, and so on are never complete if simply taken as depictions of negotiations and the like between individuals or interest groups. Rather, they are most fully and truly grasped as the unfolding of God's Will on earth (Ingersoll 2015, 189–215). This approach to history can also be used to explain (and occasionally, to justify) less reputable events in America's past, like the enslavement of Black Africans; or in the case of Europe, the Holocaust.

Because of its direct policy implications, perhaps the most important Bible science is political economics, as expounded by the erstwhile presidential candidates Ron Paul, his son, Rand, both of whom are beholden to the massively prolific (self-published) CD author mentioned earlier, Gary North, and his one-time father-in-law, Rousas Rushdoony. One of the fascinating ironies of CD political economics is the debt it owes to the Austrian free-market advocate, Ludwig von Mises, and to the (now deceased) staunch atheist, pro-abortionist, and allegedly Benzedrine-driven Russian-Jewish immigrant novelist, Ayn Rand (to whom Rand Paul is not related). Adding to the irony is that Ayn Rand is a proponent of the "virtue," as she honors it, of untrammeled egotism and selfishness (Rand 1961). On the face of it, this seems to contradict CD's otherwise vocal devotion to the idea of submission to God, about which we will have more to say, momentarily.

The core principle of Bible-based political economics is free-market absolutism and hostility to government meddling in commerce.[4] And with this, skepticism about the issuance of government-printed fiat-money, government-run central banking, and progressive income taxes. Bible-based political economists also oppose the idea of government-subsidized private health insurance (e.g., Medicare [for retirees], Medicaid [for the indigent], and Obamacare), government-run housing and/or housing-subsidies, government nutritional programs for the poor, and Social Security, all of which they consider to be "socialistic." CDs oppose as well government consumer protection regulations, environmental protection laws, and land "seizures" for use as public parks and wildernesses. But perhaps the most vilified CD targets are state "propaganda agencies" like the Public Broadcasting System and National Public Radio, liberal movie-making "lie factories," and public schools and colleges, all of which are said to "brainwash" their audiences. Assuming that any of these functions are necessary, which most CDs doubt, they should be farmed out to private profit-making corporations or to non-profit NGOs, preferably, to churches and extended families.

Conclusion

The stated goal of Christian Dominionism is to enhance the glory of God, regardless of the price that must be paid by democratic institutions to do this; by the principle of distributive social justice (which CD considers a Marxist-Leninist myth), by women, by children, and most notably (by what CDs view as) the ultimate concern of secular humanism: the individual ego and the notion of self-actualization. All of these ideas are judged, in one way or another, to be of Satan in the sense written about in the previous section.

CDs do occasionally grant, like utilitarian philosophers, that liberal policy measures like those just mentioned might well benefit humankind by advancing health, intelligence, lowering crime rates, and so on. But whether this is true or false, cost/benefit estimates are ancillary to the overall Dominionist project, not its final calculation.

This is not to say that CD is irrational or anti-rational, but that it is rational in a very different way than commonly understood. Max Weber (1964, 115–17) illuminates this in his discussion of the difference between the practical expediency (or *Zweckrationalität* [Ger.]) of the "average man" (who obsesses over the cheapest and/or fastest ways to achieve goals) versus the "ends-driven" *Wertrationalität* of the "principled man." Weber goes on to characterize ends-driven rationality as the motivation behind both the revolutionary "hero" and the pacifist. For the impulse of both the hero and the pacifist, he says, is to do what is right, *regardless of what this might cost themselves or, for that matter, others.*

Yet, while CD is far from being irrational, it can verge on being in-humane, anti-human, or, if one prefers, "sadistic." But its sadism (if that is the proper word) is never merely callous nor vindictive. For it is also *masochistic*. That is, its seeming harshness and cruelties—which should become clear in the following chapters—are not offered as ends in themselves, as in Nazi nihilism. Rather, they are advertised as holy obligations. From the standpoint of the CD activist, politician, official, or pundit, in other words, it is not *their* will that is being enacted, but His. By actively working to instill public policies that reflect God will, CDs experience themselves as promoters of true freedom. This is how the CD resolves what may appear to outsiders to be a contradiction between submission to God's law and untrammeled egotism, alluded to above.

With unvarnished frankness, then, CD illustrates how easily the craving for perfection can be confused with the will of the Almighty, the result being what many would consider evil. Samuel Taylor Coleridge says it this way: "And the devil did grin/for his darling sin/is pride that apes/humility" (Batchelor 2004, 156).

Notes

1 For Michelle Goldberg's rendering of this same quote, see Michelle Goldberg (2007, 41). See also Wilson (2019b).
2 The Social Gospel movement, in which Josiah Royce and Washington Gladden played pivotal roles, got its inspiration in part from the *Verein für Sozialpolitik* (Union for Social Politics), which was founded in Germany in 1873. The *Verein* is considered history's first effective lobby established to promote government-run programs like unemployment compensation, medical insurance, and retirement pensions. American preachers first became aware of the *Verein* through allusions to it in the writings of late 19th-century German immigrants to America, such as Friedrich List and Francis Lieber (Herbst 1965). Other Americans came into direct contact with the *Verein* while studying at German universities during what was known at the time as their *Wanderjahre* (wander-years). A few did both. One of these was Albion Small, who originally set out to be a Baptist minister like his father. But after coming across Lieber's writings as an undergraduate at Colby College, Maine, he was inspired enough to abandon his pulpit ambitions, sail across the Atlantic, and sit-in on the lectures of Gustav Schmoller, a self-titled "socialist of the chair" and a *Verein* leader at Berlin University. Small returned home with a Prussian wife and with a passion to establish what became the world's first Department of Sociology at the University of Chicago, a program originally dedicated to spreading the Social Gospel message (Small 1925). In its early years, virtually the entire Sociology faculty at Chicago comprised men partial to the Social Gospel; several of whom were ordained Baptist ministers. (The University's founding itself was underwritten by the Baptist multi-millionaire, John D. Rockefeller, Sr.)
3 Augustine maintains that even though their iniquity is not yet evident, from the moment of conception every human being is "soiled by sin and doomed to death and justly condemned" (Augustine 1960, book 13, chap. 14).
4 For more on CD political economics, see Aho (2016, 85–105).

Interlude 1 Fetus Fetish

In a momentous decision—*Dobbs v. Jackson Women's Health*—announced on Friday, June 24, 2022, the Supreme Court of the United States (SCOTUS), overturned *Roe v. Wade*, a ruling enacted in 1973 that legalized abortion throughout America. Now, each "sovereign" state will have the sole responsibility to deal with abortion, as it deems proper. News of the decision was greeted, on the one hand (by Christian Dominionists), with tears of gratitude, as a "crowning achievement," and as a victory for "state's rights" and God's own wishes; on the other (among advocates of *Roe v. Wade*), with grief-stricken weeping. This is analogous to what might obtain were the anti-slavery 13th Amendment to the Constitution to be declared null and void (for this possibility, see the subsection titled, "Slavery," in Chapter 4).

Put aside for the moment that President Donald Trump, who nominated three of the most outspoken concurring justices in Dobbs, was supported in the 2016 presidential election by less than half the voting public, and that even months after Dobbs was announced, fully two-thirds of Americans still endorsed *Roe v. Wade*. This raises numerous questions about its enforceability (more on which below). But here, let us spend a few words considering several other issues that Dobbs raises, which are directly pertinent to this book.

The most important of these, introduced in another context near the end of Chapter 3, is that although Christian Dominionism is by no means irrational, nor its proponents "crazy," it and they are nonetheless rational in a very different way than what passes as "rationality" in contemporary political discourse. To illustrate what I mean, turn once again to the distinction made by Max Weber, between *Zweckrationalität*, cost-minimizing practical expediency, versus *Wertrationalität*, the orientation of what Weber calls the conscientious, "principled man." *Wertrationalität*, says Weber, is the action orientation of a person driven by uncompromising religious convictions and/or by revolutionary principles and who therefore gives little thought to the harm that may accrue to others, or even to themselves, as a result. *Zweckrationalität*, by contrast, is the action orientation of the "average man" (also Weber's phrase). Because the *Wertrationalität* of the principled Christian Dominionist fails to take into consideration the human pain and suffering that might ensue from particular policy choices, it can border on being "inhuman," "anti-human," or even "sadistic." Nonetheless, as I point out in Chapter 3, the sadism of CD is far from the nihilistic cynicism we associate with Nazism. This is because, unlike Nazism, the CD project is explicitly undertaken, not to celebrate human powers, but to honor and glorify God and His will.

A revealing example of *Wertrationalität* is provided by a group of anti-abortion activists who call themselves "Abolitionists," members of a Christian Dominionist sect known as Apologia, located in Phoenix, Arizona. It seems they too were disappointed by the Dobbs decision (National Public Radio, August 23, 2022). Not because they felt it goes too far, but because it is not nearly radical enough. In the minds of Abolitionists, in other words, from the moment a sperm meets an egg, a full human person is brought into being. Thus, it follows that abortion is in effect homicide.

And furthermore, since the abortion-seeker herself is no mere victim, but an active participant in the procedure, then it also follows that she, not just her doctor, should be criminally punished, for manslaughter or murder. When the reporter conducting the interview wondered whether this would be ethically justified, the pastor of Apologia firmly and calmly replied, "We all deserve to die." He then went on to reassure the interviewer that "this is what the Bible teaches."

This leads us to a second point. It is that with notable exceptions, American social scientists and sociologists, even today, tend to overlook the degree to which deeply held religious beliefs and traditions can influence ostensibly secular affairs, particularly in regard to the making and enforcement of criminal laws. There are a number of reasons for this oversight. The simplest is that "spiritual matters"—for example, religious or mystical experiences, conversions, and faith convictions—are rarely, if ever, accessible to direct observation. Thus, they present immense challenges to anyone who claims to be a scientist. A second reason concerns a peculiar feature of American culture: the presumed separation of church from state, a popular dogma that is not mentioned in the Constitution. The problem here becomes evident in the matter of abortion, where six of the nine Supreme Court justices who ruled on Dobbs appear to be in sympathy with orthodox Christian social/moral philosophy, particularly in regard to sexuality and the female principle (i.e., Carl Jung's "anima").

The female principle occupies an inferior status in orthodox Christianity, as well as in other Abrahamic belief systems, like Judaism and Islam. The marginalization of female flesh is so deeply embedded in popular Christianity, Judaism, and Islam, that it is often taken for granted, and can remain invisible, even to well-educated believers. Along with this is the seemingly "audacious," prideful suggestion that females might conceivably have fundamental rights to control their own bodies.

All of which brings us to the heart of this Interlude: that much ballyhooed "core" American cultural ideal of "personal autonomy," "individual freedom," or, if one wishes, simply "individualism." One of the most striking things about the Dobbs decision is its apparent indifference to the consequences that a no-exceptions, nationwide abortion ban might have on this ideal. Not the least of these consequences would be an end to "privacy rights," most notably the right that Euro-American women have enjoyed for decades to seclude the most intimate details of their sexual lives from public scrutiny. And two, the right that women have had, until Dobbs, to protect the integrity of their bodies from compulsory intrusion. Jeanne Gerson explains what is at stake, this way: "Personal autonomy, the ultimate value that privacy enshrines, doesn't just buttress freedom; it *is* freedom" (Gerson 2022). And the contrary to freedom, she continues, is tyranny. In regard to the Dobbs decision, it is *religious* tyranny. This is to say nothing of the threat that Dobbs harbors to various "unenumerated rights," which are not mentioned by name in the Constitution, but which previous Court majorities have long recognized as reasonable extensions of the 14th Amendment (which requires states to provide equal protection under the law to all its citizens): for instance, the right of married couples to use artificial contraception, to marry persons of races different from their own; and/or to enjoy same-sex intimacy. Justice Clarence Thomas, an outspoken Dobbs-ruling supporter, argues all of these and more are now up for reconsideration as possible judicial "errors" (except for inter-racial marriage, of which Thomas himself is a beneficiary).

The ways by which Dobbs imperils personal autonomy (and freedom) become evident when thought turns, as it inevitably must, to when and how the new law can or should be enforced. For example, shall it now be a felony to avert an ectopic pregnancy, wherein a fertilized egg fails to properly implant itself in the uterus? This is a serious medical condition that can lead to infection and even to death for the mother. Or shall it be a felony to secure an abortion for a molar pregnancy, where there is an abnormal growth in cells that normally develop into a placenta (a potentially fatal condition for the mother)? Or shall it be a crime to avert a biologically normal pregnancy by crossing state lines to access abortion services provided in another state or in another country where abortion is legal? Or to access abortion services at clinics located on federal lands, such as Indian reservations, or at federal military facilities in anti-abortion states? And if so, what should be the punishment? On the basis of their understanding of biblical teachings, some Christian Dominionists propose that stoning, burning, or strangulation of the convicted woman be inflicted (Luscombe 2022).

But what if the expectant female, herself a likely victim of rape or incest, is a child of 13, 12, or even 10 years old? Shall she be barred from procuring mail-order abortion medicine from places where abortion is still legal? Or, on this same line, shall older menopausal women be prosecuted for purchasing Mifepristone (RU-486), the "morning after pill," for their pregnant daughters? Or for that matter, for themselves, as a first-line medication to treat their own severe psoriasis, endometriosis, or lupus? Women who reside in anti-abortion states already find it difficult to secure RU-486 because pharmacists and physicians fear being prosecuted for manslaughter.

All of these questions raise another: how should fertile females be monitored? By surveilling their ostensibly private electronic communications, perhaps? Some anti-abortion state legislators have gone so far as to propose licensing "bounty hunters"—analogous to men who kill predators like coyotes or bears for profit—to pursue suspected pregnant women, who cross state lines to obtain abortions, hold them on suspicion of homicide, and then return them against their wills to their home states for prosecution. Shall this be permitted? In America? All of this is to say nothing about abortion providers—doctors and nurses—or lay people, who aid and abet abortion-seekers by providing them housing and travel, and/or by underwriting their clinic fees, as some citizens and private companies in anti-abortion states promise (or threaten) to do?

Still another problem relates to the provision of fertility services. Take artificial insemination or IVF (in-vitro fertilization) which is available to women in a number of states. Once an egg has been fertilized, how should the resulting zygote be handled? Shall it be permissible to "store" it in a refrigerated unit for later use, at a set annual fee? But what happens if the mother cannot pay the storage fee? Or no longer wants the product? Can she or the clinic be held criminally liable for "child abandonment" or murder? To answer this in the affirmative suggests that a human zygote is indeed a bona fide human child, as the pastor of Apologia (see above) claims, with all the rights associated with this. But what if the zygote in question is not "viable?" This becomes important in states where it has been legislatively decreed, by little more than a simple majority vote (of primarily male legislators), that human life begins at the "moment of conception," and must thus be protected from that point on, at all costs. But for centuries, going back at least to St. Augustine, theologians have acknowledged that fetal viability is a problematic condition, until the moment of "quickening" or, to use the technical term, until the fetus has "fully formed." This, once again, raises the question of how to handle fetuses that can *never* fully form, as in ectopic or molar pregnancies, that put the woman at grave risk of infection or death. Should a medically induced life-saving abortion put her at risk of criminal investigation for homicide?

Related to the ultimately unanswerable question of fetal personhood, is the even more pressing issue of what constitutes an abortion? Need it necessarily involve a surgical procedure? Or, as is usually the case today, is it a matter of simply taking a pill (like RU-486) to induce a miscarriage? But if so, does the mere fact of miscarriage open the mother and/or her doctor to suspicion of homicide?

We cannot hope to answer concerns like these reasonably in a few short passages. But what they add up to is that far from putting an end to the debate about abortion, Dobbs merely reopens the door to a whole new world of hurt.

4 Christian Dominionism and Violence[1]

> There is a trite cruelty in the logic of the perfectly certain.
>
> (Bowler 2019, 119)

Despite their differences, all Christian Dominionists share the conviction that Christian men are to assume dominion over "all that moveth upon the earth" (Gen. 1: 26–28, 9: 2). Says CD activist, James Vincent Foxx, "we must have a deep desire to dominate without mercy. And if you refuse to dominate, then [we] will dominate you" (Foxx, in Mathias 2022b, 15).[2]

The phrase "all that moveth" encompasses birds, beasts, and fish, but also non-Christians and so-called non-human hominids. Regarding the latter, Rev. Richard Butler, the now deceased onetime head of the Aryan Nations Church, proclaims that "not everything that moves on two legs is human." In his case, he was referring to "negro beasts of the field ... whose' cannibalistic fervor ... cause[s] them to eat the dead and the living" (CSA n.d.).

In this chapter, the word "violence" encompasses the savageries of murder (lynching and assassination), bombing, rape, and mutilation, which is to say, acts which, because they are relatively rare, are newsworthy and drive most inquiries into the subject. But as developments in the first decades of the 21st-century show, a full understanding of the connection between CD and violence calls for a more expansive definition of the term. In Austria, France, Australia, England, Russia, Poland, Hungary, Brazil, the United States, and elsewhere, in other words, CD activists are using state apparatuses to implement agendas that violate human rights, or in other words, commit violence. But since these actions are garbed in the uniforms of officialdom and framed in legal jargon, they can go undetected, unreported, and are under-researched. To handle this challenge, the following discussion is divided into two parts. In Part 1, "CD and Violence on the Inside," we deal with violence in the second, broader, sense of the word. Part 2, "CD and Violence on the Outside," investigates CD's relationship to violence in the narrow sense, criminal violence.

CD and Violence on the Inside

As indicated earlier, there are different brands or styles of CD. One type is post-millennial (or Reconstructionist) CD. Another is pre-millennial CD. And then there is Identity Christianity (Clarkson 2016; Ingersoll 2015).

Post-millennial CD maintains that only *after* a Bible-based paradise has been in existence for 1000 years (a millennium), ruled by "kings for dominion," shall Christ reappear on earth. This style of CD is often found in the congregations of orthodox Presbyterian churches, which explains its penchant for remodeling or "reconstructing" American society on the basis of Calvinist rulings.

Pre-millennial CD, on the other hand, posits that Christ will come *prior* to the millennium of peace and justice; it expresses the goal of dominion as one of "reclaiming" America from the liberal-progressive "demons" whom they accuse of having "stolen" it. Among others, this style of CD is represented by Rev. Dr. James Kennedy, his protégé Janet Porter of Faith2Action.org, and by C. Peter Wagner, whose mega-church campuses are scattered in suburbs throughout the Deep South and Midwest.

The most well-known, if least popular, form of CD is Identity Christianity, which, to borrow Theodor Adorno et al.'s (1950) pejorative label, is carried by "cranks." Identity Christians maintain that *they*, not the Jews, are the direct descendants of Isaac, or "Sac," as they like to call him, hence, their supposed ethnicity as "Sons of Sac," "Sac-sons," Saxons, or more precisely, *Anglo-Saxons*. This means that "Judah's scepter" (i.e., the right to rule earth) has passed directly through them to their German, British, and American descendants (Allen 1930 [1902]).

Each brand of CD has its own prophetic founder(s) and unique history.[3] As for their legislative and judicial goals, however, they are in virtual unanimity: Unless a particular Old Testament ruling has been explicitly annulled by a saying of Jesus and/or the Apostles, it shall be legally binding in a reconstructed America, that is, in an America reclaimed for Christ.

Take the matter of male circumcision. Although it is considered a visible marker of male adherence to Judaism, the Apostle Paul says that it "means nothing" (I Cor. 7: 18–19; Rom. 2: 29). And he goes on to hope that "the knife slips" and the *mohel* cuts themselves (Gal. 15: 12). It therefore follows that circumcision shall not be mandatory for male citizenship in an America reclaimed for Christ. The same goes for the central ritual in Jewish life, the kosher meal (Aho 2002). For as Paul also teaches: "No food is unclean in itself" (Rom. 14: 14). "Do not wreck God's work over a question of food" (Rom. 14: 20).

On the other hand, insofar as neither Jesus nor the Apostles say anything against it, in a reconstructed America, all of the following may be subject to death by execution: disobedient teenagers, abortionists, witches, blasphemers, and heretics; astrologers, those who bear false witness in court, women who lie about their virginity; and adulterers, rapists, practitioners of bestiality and incest, and homosexuals (BCSE 2007). Yet, insofar as Jesus himself admonishes believers to be merciful—"Let he who is without sin cast the first stone" (John 8: 7)—then all but the most rabid CDs express a willingness to limit punishments for these acts to excommunication, fines, and jail terms. Or in the case of homosexuality, to "reparative therapy." One rare exception to this is Rev. Pete Peters (1992; see also the epigram to this book).

Predictably, achieving the proper balance between mercy and justice has ignited spirited debate among CDs, reflecting various degrees of misogyny, prudery, inanity, and financial and political self-interest. This is witnessed in controversies over gay marriage, transgender surgery, "drugs," and abortion. To avoid becoming mired in a tarpit of moral casuistry, I will ignore these debates here, except to say that American evangelicalism traditionally has limited itself to these sorts of questions. What is new and discomfiting (at least to non-Dominionists) is the expansion of focus by CDs to matters of political economics. To use its own jargon, the goal of CD is to "infiltrate" the "Seven Mountains" of modern society, engage the "principalities" (evil-doers) who presently control them, and defeat them in "spiritual warfare" (Wilder 2011). The phrase "Seven Mountains" is a biblical allusion to ancient Rome's seven hills. In CD, however, it is taken to mean the seven major institutions that comprise modern American society: the family, religion, arts and entertainment, the news media, education, business, and government.

To illustrate what the defeat of the "principalities" might entail, consider two CD policy recommendations: the first, regarding immigration to America and alien residency; the second, concerning the reintroduction of slavery.

Foreigners and Guest Peoples

In the Old Testament foreigners and guest peoples are permitted to reside in ancient Israel. Nevertheless, if they are not Israelites—or what we might call "Jews"—they are denied access to the Temple and to any rights associated with this (Deut. 23: 4–5). Among other things, this means they may be charged interest on loans, which is otherwise denied to Jewish creditors (Deut. 23: 20; Lev. 25: 35–8). As we will see in the next section, they also may be subject to enslavement. Jesus and the Apostles say little about these laws; but Jesus does urge his followers (who at that time were mostly Jews) to treat guests and foreigners with compassion. "For you were once strangers [in Egypt] too" (Matt. 25. Here, Jesus is drawing on the ancient nomadic custom of hospitality, as formulated in Ex. 22: 21; Lev. 19–34; and Deut. 10: 19).

Now let us assume, as CDs do, that analogous to the relationship between ancient Israel and Judaism, that America is a Christian nation, supposedly founded by Puritans with a "divinely preordained mission" to preserve and protect "the liberty and purity of the Gospel of our Lord Jesus."[4] Insofar as this is the case, then it follows that non-Christians may be permitted to visit and even work in America, but they shall not be granted citizenship, nor equal civil, political, or social rights under the Constitution. At their own discretion, however, local authorities may extend these benefits to them as a "courtesy" (Throckmorton 2011). But this shall only be on a temporary basis and may be revoked at the pleasure of those same authorities. In any case, once their permit to be in America has expired, they must leave.

This ruling applies to Muslims, Hindus, and Buddhists but also by implication, to atheists, Satanists, and practitioners of wicca. CDs acknowledge that the First Amendment to the Constitution protects religious expression, but they maintain that this pertains "only within the bounds of Christianity" (Rushdoony 1973, 294). The problem, of course, is that the extension of the word "Christianity" is contestable. This has the effect of putting Roman Catholics and Mormons, as well as non-evangelical Protestants at risk of expulsion. Prominent CDs such as the Revs. John Hagee and Cindy Jacobs view Catholicism as a "godless theology of hate" whose saints "honor the spirits of darkness" (Aho 2016, 90). Handfuls of CDs mouth similar complaints about Mormonism, which they consider a form of "oriental despotism," in part because of its (long-ago ecclesiastically banned, but allegedly still endorsed) practice of polygamy. What neo-Calvinist CDs find particularly objectionable is Mormonism's widely preached—but neither officially endorsed nor formally renounced—doctrine of human divinization: "As man is now God once was; as God now is, man may be" (first announced ca. 1840 by eventual Church President, Lorenzo Snow [Decker & Hunt 1984]).

It is worth noting that Dominionist-like bigotry was the impetus behind the immigration restrictions imposed on both Irish and German Catholics to America and on Mormons during the 19th century. It may also partially explain the enthusiasm among CDs today for imposing gratuitously cruel border control measures on (mostly Catholic-Mexican) refugees on America's southern border, which is not to deny that there is a racist component in these policies as well. Whatever the case, continued CD suspicions concerning Catholicism and Mormonism may presage the eventual collapse of the present-day cross-denominational Dominionist alliance.

Preferably, the expulsion of non-Christians from America can be accomplished voluntarily, by denying them access to affordable health care, welfare benefits, public schools, college grant monies, and driver's licenses. This is a position espoused by one-time GOP presidential nominee, Mitt Romney. But in the event that self-deportation is unfeasible, then CDs favor forcible deportation. As a guest on CD Glenn Beck's highly popular talk show, The Blaze, blurted: "Round 'em up and remove 'em. We don't care where you go, but you can't stay here." Both Romney and Beck are Mormons.

James Pace (1985) who claims to be a fifth-generation Mormon himself is an outspoken proponent of forced deportation. Yet even he expresses hope that it can be done with a minimum of pain and in a non-burdensome way, by financially reimbursing deportees who suffer property losses as a result (109–20). Pace writes that money presently "wasted" on public welfare programs can be re-budgeted to underwrite deportees' moving expenses, as well for the leasing of buses, boxcars, and airplanes to transport them to the Mexican border. He fails to address how ICE, the Immigration and Customs Enforcement agency, will deal with the millions of potential deportees who would likely undertake evasive action to stay in the country; or, for that matter, the even larger number of Americans who would come to their aid.

Those who *do* abet "criminal invaders," as CDs call unwanted immigrants, should, according to the Glenn Beck guest just mentioned, have their cars and houses confiscated and auctioned off. As for the farms, ranches, hospitality services, and food-processing plants that employ them: They should be subject to stiff fines and their owners imprisoned. But given that many of these businesses are located in the heart of Dominionist country, in the Midwest, and already consider themselves "over-taxed," CDs tend to favor lenience in their behalf. As for American metropolises that have declared themselves "sanctuary cities," however, and who refuse to help ICE expel unwanted immigrants: According to CDs, they should be denied federal government grants and subsidies.

Against liberal objections that forcible deportation smacks of fascism, Pace claims that in reality it is a "compassionate" measure. This is because it will enable deportees to return, relatively cost-free, to cultures more compatible with their "true," non-American values. Pace doesn't deal with the touchy subject of how to handle DACA recipients (youngsters brought to this country as infants or children, and who know nothing about cultures or languages other than American culture and English).

A second sensitive topic concerns Jews, whom CDs approach with a combination of condescension and contempt. On one hand, they applaud the establishment of the nation state of Israel (in 1948), welcome President Trump's acknowldgment that Jerusalem is its "eternal capital," and his transfer of the American embassy from Tel Aviv to Jerusalem: all in the face of Muslim objections. They even back Israeli military aggression against those same Muslims, which some hope will precipitate the Second Coming of Christ. As a result, they find themselves agreeing with Orthodox Jews that Trump may be "Messiah bin Cyrus," or as CDs like to say, "45Cyrus."[5] The fifth-century BCE Persian Emperor Cyrus is honored in Jewish history as "a messianic figure" for having freed Israel from Babylonian captivity, and for restoring Jacob to biblical-era triumph (Trangerud 2021). On the other hand, elderly CDs who as children learned that Jews are the "spawn of Satan," hold that they deserve nothing less than God's, and by implication their own, eternal enmity.

To handle this conundrum, Pace (1985) recommends a compromise. He proposes that American Jews "who desire the continued existence of Israel" be "encouraged" to emigrate there (99, 117). Exactly how, he is reluctant to say. Other CDs favor the idea of Jews being relocated to "West Israel" on Long Island, just east New York City, or to "Jew York City" generally, where (befitting the ancient anti-Semitic canard) they can directly access banking and finance and work for the "Jews Media," especially the so-called Jew York Times. Still others recommend that Jews be resettled in "Kosher Valley" in Hollywood, near the heart of the supposedly Jewish-dominated movie industry.

As for Native American Indians and Pacific Islanders, CD consensus is that, although many are not Christian, their ancestors were already living on what is now American soil before it was occupied by "Christian missionaries." Hence, they should be provided reservations set aside solely for their own use. Ex-Ku Klux Klan leader, David Duke, who has an off-and-on relationship with the CD community, has gone so far as to suggest "Navahona" as a possible homeland for Indians, located in present-day New Mexico and Arizona (Ridgeway 1996, 150–51). Hispanic-Americans (who have been able to avoid deportation) can be relocated to "Alta California"; Black people, to "New Africa" (the states of Mississippi and Alabama); and assorted others to an unspecified "Minoria."

Slavery

The Old Testament bans the enslavement of Israelites by "abduction," and it threatens those who transgress this ban with death (Deut. 24: 7). Nevertheless, it does allow the enslavement of non-Israelite war captives (Deut. 20: 10–16). These can be compelled to labor in perpetuity, be sold to other Israelites, or be passed on as inheritances (Ex. 21: 1–4). Furthermore, the Old Testament also permits Israelites to "voluntarily" sell *themselves* to creditors or to patrons for fixed terms in order to redeem their financial debts, to right wrongs or to secure protection. (The word "voluntarily" is used advisably, considering the coercive nature of indebtedness.) Ignoring the biblical legend of "the curse of Ham" (Gen. 9: 20–27)—which is taken quite literally by many CDs—these two rulings were used by Confederate States preachers to justify the enslavement of Black Africans as "chattel," that is, as movable property like carts, furniture, and horses, and the indentured servitude of Scots-Irish immigrants. Ideally, the latter were to be emancipated after six years of service, upon making application with the proper authorities. As opposed to chattel slaves, debt servants were to be granted freedom if they were severely injured on the job (Ex. 21: 26–27); if they were killed, their masters could be criminally punished (Ex. 21: 20–21). These rulings have recently been resurrected by (primarily) Southern CDs. This is their argument:

Jesus and the Apostles were fully aware of slavery (1 Cor. 7: 21; 2 Tim. 6: 1; 1 Peter 2: 18), and of its occasionally deadly cruelties (Matt. 18: 23–25; Luke 19: 11–27), although it is not entirely clear whether they have in mind chattel slavery, indentured servitude, or both. They were also familiar with individual slaves, whom Paul in one place urges be received as "beloved brother[s]" (Phlm. 16. See also 1 Cor. 7–21; 1 Tim. 6: 1; 1 Peter 2: 18). In fact, Jesus is reported to have healed two slaves (Luke 7: 10, 22: 5). But while Jesus and the Apostles ask that masters treat their slaves justly, they never command that they be freed—even when given the opportunity to do so. This includes Paul's so-called beloved brother, the slave Onesimus. Instead, they advise slaves to accept their fate with "grace," "enthusiasm," and "humility"—even in the face of undeserved punishment (Eph. 6: 5–8; Col. 3: 22–24; 1 Tim 6: 1–2; 1 Peter 2: 18; Titus 2: 9–10). Indeed, the Apostles, all of whom were free men themselves, have the audacity to liken *themselves* to slaves, namely, as "slaves for Christ" (Rom. 1: 1, 6: 12–19). In the logic of CD, then, it follows that in an America reclaimed in Christ's name, slavery shall be permitted—not only of non-Christian foreigners and guest peoples (when appropriate), *but of Christian citizens as well.*

Section 1 of the 13th Amendment to the Constitution explicitly bans the enslavement of American citizens. However, it then adds, "except as a punishment for crimes whereof the party shall have been convicted." This is the basis of various convict-leasing programs, whereby convicts are rented by private businesses in order to lower their labor costs and enhance their output, thus increasing their profits. Viewed in this way, CD rulings are not nearly as radical as they appear at first glance. As pastor Rushdoony (1973, 286) would say, "the law here is humane and also unsentimental. *It recognizes that some people are by nature slaves and will always be so*" (my emphasis).

Two recent cases of slavery endorsement can be found in the blogs of the widely read CDs, David Barton (whom Glenn Beck once named his "favorite historian") and Stephen McDowell, the co-founders of WallBuilders.org.

Barton and McDowell insist that notwithstanding liberal opinion, in hindsight the institution of American slavery was a blessing—not only for White plantation owners but for the slaves themselves (Barton 2013). This is because it allowed them to escape "the cruelty and barbarism typical of unbelieving cultures," while enabling them "to hear the liberating message of the gospel."

True, Barton admits, "some Negroes were mistreated," but this was rare. Indeed, he continues, American slaves enjoyed "a vast increase of freedom" over what they had endured in Africa, and the relationships they experienced with their masters were characterized by "lenience," "unity and companionship" (see also Buchanan 2008). This kind of reasoning allows us to grasp the following rhetorical question posed by Arkansas CD state representative, Loy Mauch: "If slavery were [sic] so God-awful, why didn't Jesus or Paul condemn it, why was it in the Constitution and why wasn't there a war before 1861?" (quoted in Brantley 2012). From the standpoint of CD, Abraham Lincoln's Emancipation Proclamation—an anticipation of the 13th, 14th, and 15th Amendments to the Constitution—"was both inhumane and irresponsible" (BCSE 2007).

CD and Violence on the Outside

It is important to acknowledge at the outset that CD has only a tangential connection to criminal violence. In fact, Dominionists can express disbelief and horror when they learn about terrorist acts supposedly committed in their name. Neo-Nazi racists are much more likely than CDs generally, to resort to axe-handles, nooses, explosives, and guns to achieve their goals. Furthermore, they sneer at Dominionist-flavored conservatives by sarcastically pointing to the "con" in their title. William Pierce, one-time head of the neo-Nazi National Alliance, provides a striking example of this in his *The Turner Diaries* (1978). There, he rebukes CDs for being "the world's biggest conspiracy mongers ... and also the world's greatest cowards," with their cowardice "exceeded only by their stupidity." Pierce has his fictional protagonist, Earl Turner, warn that "I will listen to no more excuses from these self-serving collaborators but will simply reach for my pistol" (63, 94). Naturally, complications arise when CDs *also* extoll the virtues of Nazism. This was true for Rev. Richard Butler, quoted at the outset of this chapter, whose desktop library displayed a King James Bible juxtaposed to Hitler's *Mein Kampf*.

From 1980 to 2015, right-wing extremists were implicated in at least 433 criminal fatalities in America (Aho 2016, Appendix 1); in the half-decade after 2015, they were involved in scores more. Not all these incidents were perpetrated CDs, but many of them were. That some were not, however, underscores an observation made by sociologist Talcott Parsons (1951), and which today is accepted as standard theoretical lore by the profession of Sociology.

Parsons developed what is technically known as a "value-added" model of human behavior. Simply put, to account for *any* action one must first take into consideration the actor's verbalized intentions and unconscious dispositions (or what Parsons would call their "motivational orientation"). But in addition to this, we must also scrutinize the external circumstances in which the actor finds themselves. These include the constraints (or "conditions" [Parsons]) placed upon them by virtue of their social class, race, ethnicity, age, health, and gender; and the resources or "means" available to them to accomplish their goals. Finally, are "normative standards" that dictate which of those means the actor is permitted and/or encouraged to use. To the degree that each of these four "elements of a unit act" is met or realized, then the likelihood of a particular action will increase. Parsons goes on to write that this model applies to everything from consumer choices to the selection of marriage partners and voting preferences; and from medical therapy options to decisions regarding one's college major.

The unit act under consideration here is criminal violence. My argument is that CD increases the probability of criminal violence by: one, insisting that believers are obligated to establish "theonomy" (God's law) on earth; two, by making firearms readily available to all (male) believers; three, by hampering legal restraints that might otherwise be placed on those believers in their pursuit of dominion; and four, by advocating norms that justify and encourage the use of violence to achieve dominion. Let us examine each of these "elements" in turn.

Motivational Orientation

To understand Dominionist-related violence, we must first address its *conscious* intention. Here, it is enough to reiterate what was said at the outset of this chapter: the goal of CD is to "king [meant as a verb] in our future lives," to "become the consummate, perfect governing authorities" over mankind and earth (Clarkson 2016; Ingersoll 2015).

As to the *un*conscious way that CDs "are there" in the world, how they habitually comport themselves, let us put aside authoritarianism for the moment, a subject addressed in depth in Chapter 8. Instead, I want to focus on a factor routinely overlooked by social scientists, namely, the heroic impulse. By this, I mean an urgency to reconcile what *is* with what *should be* the case; to "realize the ideal" by "idealizing the real" (to paraphrase Hegel). Or to express it in terms that Dominionists might prefer, it is to make our sin-filled, fallen world over in a manner pleasing to the Lord: on earth as it is in Heaven.

It isn't necessary here to account for the heroic impulse. According to Ernest Becker (1973, 1975; Solomon et al. 2015), for example, it is rooted in our craving to "escape" our own mortality. To the Buddhist, David Loy (2002), on the other hand, it has more to do with there being no self to preserve. Instead, Loy says, what underlies the heroic quest is "lack," or existential void. Whatever the case, every major project undertaken by human beings can be attributed to it: compulsive money-making, the pursuit of a life-saving cure, the vain struggle to retain one's youth and vitality, the symbolic extension of one's self through reproduction, and so on. Not the least of these projects is the political-religious cause, of which Christian Dominionism (as well as Marxist-Leninism and Nazism) provide preeminent examples.

The goal of CD is not to pile up riches, to be honored as a celebrity, or to produce monumental art. It is, rather, to "save life"; to save life by "killing death." This, by extirpating death's supposed human carriers. It is this that led the Order or *Brüders Schweigen* (Secret Brotherhood) to mount an armed campaign against Jews and Black people in the middle 1980s (see Chapter 1); it is this same yearning that drove "pro-life" Army of God cadres to commit murder at abortion clinics in Pensacola, Florida; Brookline, Massachusetts; Birmingham, Alabama; and Amherst, New York from 1993 to 1998. Likewise, the person who shot to death 11 worshippers at a Jewish synagogue in Pittsburgh in 2018; the young man who murdered 22 Hispanic shoppers at an El Paso, Texas Walmart store, a year later, believing they were part of a conspiracy to "replace" White Americans with brown-skinned aliens; or, finally, the Seattle Christian patriot who bludgeoned to death a nominally Jewish family of four on Christmas Eve, 1985, believing that Black UN troops, stationed on the Canadian border, were awaiting orders from them to invade the United States.

I don't want to be misunderstood as saying that Dominionist-motivated violence is viewed by its perpetrators as being without risk. Nor am I denying that CDs sometimes feel regret at "*having to do*" what they consider God's dirty work. But fear overcome and remorse swallowed are the hallmarks of true heroism. So, after being arrested for killing the Seattle Jewish family (above), the suspect confessed to police that he felt bad about having done in the two pre-teen boys. But he went on to assure them that "sometimes soldiers have to kill" (Aho 1994, 35–49).

Rev. Jarah Crawford (1984, 395–98) elaborates on the logic of CD violence by citing the case of the biblical champion, Phineheas (Num. 25: 1–18). Phineheas "stayed the plague," writes Crawford—God's punishment for Israel having mixed with the idol-worshipping Midianites—by impaling Zimri and his Midianite lover on a spear. "It is tremendously significant," Crawford points out, that "one person took matters into his own hands…. There was no court trial, no judge, and no Supreme Court" to frustrate his labor. "Just one man who knew the mind of God and acted upon it."

"You now have a true martyr," wrote a nameless Christian patriot, following the fiery death of the leader of the Order (see Chapter 1). "A real, larger-than-life white American hero whom you can make into a folk figure. I hope that someone comes up with a really good song, written in [his] salute and named after him, just as a great song in the past was named after one who gave his life in similar circumstances a long way from America" (J.T. 1985).

Means

"Means," first of all, refers to military-style assault rifles, "bump stocks" to render them fully automatic, and high-capacity cartridge magazines. The CD preference is that these be made available to Christian men everywhere (for the most compelling scholarly argument supporting this proposal, see Lott 2010): in schools and shopping malls, in sports arenas and churches, at nightclubs and parks, and especially, in "a man's castle," his home.

One example of pro-gun partiality was recently expressed by Rev. Jerry Falwell Jr., one of Donald Trump's most fervent supporters and president of Liberty University in Lynchburg, Virginia. Liberty U. is the largest institution of higher education in the country expressly founded to propagate CD beliefs. At a compulsory campus convocation following a suspected Muslim-inspired mass shooting in San Bernardino, California (Dec. 2, 2015) that resulted in 16 deaths, Falwell Jr. urged his students to acquire guns and to purchase conceal and carry permits. He promised that Liberty U. would pay the fees (Falwell 2015). He then went on to display his own concealed .25 cal. pistol. "We could end those Muslims before they walked in [muffled] and killed them," he boasted to loud cheers and clapping. "Let's teach them a lesson if they ever show up here!"

Falwell's words reflect a belief widely shared in the CD community that a Supreme Court decision (SCOTUS 2008) striking-down provisions of the 1975 Firearms Control Regulation Act not only affirms the "natural right" of individuals to use guns in self-defense; it also validates gun usage *by the community as a whole* to defend itself against government tyranny. This view rests on a willful misreading of the Court majority's interpretation of the phrase "a well-regulated militia" (22–18). If, according to CDs, the phrase refers to "all males physically capable of acting in concert," then, because gun control laws "disable the militia," they are ipso facto unconstitutional.

The National Rifle Association, America's most powerful pro-gun lobby, was initially reluctant to have the Supreme Court hear the 2008 case, fearing that it would rule against them. Afterward, it applauded the decision, reaffirming its already close ties to the Dominionist right.[6] In doing so, however, the NRA inadvertently amplified the likelihood of armed anti-government insurrection. This was initially seen in the standoff against Bureau of Land Management officials near Bunkerville, Nevada in 2014 by hundreds of heavily armed militiamen, many of whom were Dominionists (Aho 2016, xi–xiii). Then, after the government was seen to "cave" to their demands came the much more destructive and deadly seizure of the Malheur National Wildlife Refuge in eastern Oregon, mounted by many of those same insurgents (Wilson & Rosman 2016). By 2020, the rebellion—led by one of the individuals who orchestrated both the Bunkerville and Malheur affairs, and now calling itself the "People's Rights" network—had grown to more than 20,000 members nationwide [IREHR 2021]). In response to government measures enacted to control the spread of COVID-19 that same year, several People's Rights activists were arrested for planning to kidnap, try, and execute governors whom they accused of having taken away their constitutional liberties.

"Means" also refers to the availability of "soft targets" against whom guns can be deployed: ill-protected, isolated human fetishes of Evil. Without being exhaustive, for CDs these include the "negro beasts" mentioned at the outset of this chapter, "sodomite homosexuals waiting in their lust to rape," "witches who sexually mutilate people," "seed of Satan Jews who sacrifice people in darkness," and "city-living ... 'do-gooders' who have fought for the 'rights' of these groups" (CSA n.d. This list was compiled before Muslims and Hispanic immigrants had become far-right obsessions). The vulnerable target in question might be a congregation of Black female Bible students praying at church, an unwary government official, a Jewish radio talk-show host returning home alone late one night. Or, as in another documented case, it might be a mixed-race couple strolling hand-in-hand down a Salt Lake City, Utah street, long known for its safety. Prior to their deaths, none of these individuals were cognizant that at that very moment "God's battle axe and weapons of war," as CD terrorists title themselves, were lurking nearby, awaiting a chance to redeem the world from *Them*.

Conditions

For our purposes, "conditions" denotes a legal system hampered, if not entirely crippled, in its ability to track and deter right-wing violence. Once again, the influence of CD is clear. In this case, through its airing of tales about federal and state government "tyranny," of "bureau-*rats*" scurrying about within the bowels of the "Deep State," and of alleged "false flag" operations like the bombing of the federal building in Oklahoma City, April 1995; the terrorist attack on 9/11; or the mass murder of kindergartners at Sandy Hook elementary school in Newtown, Connecticut in 2012. According to CD conspiracy theorists, all of these incidents were conducted by actors paid by the federal government, to justify and facilitate the confiscation of firearms from private citizens.

In CD fable the "Fed" is the fearsome "Beast" of Revelation (13: 1–10), still another biblical allusion to ancient Rome. Other contemporary disparagements are "Shadow Government," "Dark Command," "Hidden Hand," and "Insiders." Whichever label is used, its effect is to demoralize the officials on whom it is bestowed, thereby impeding their work. Take the case of the "crushing" of a Department of Homeland Security (DHS) report on right-wing terrorist groups (Ackerman 2012), whose number exploded after the presidential election of Barack Obama in 2008. Under pressure from far-right media, the investigating team found itself institutionally marginalized and eventually dissolved. Its disgruntled leader left the DHS to run his own private security consulting firm; the report itself was lost to memory (Office of Press Secretary 2009).

A second incident occurred when Bryan Murphy, then an undersecretary at the DHS, divulged that he was pressured by Trump administration officials to downplay "persistent and lethal" threats from domestic White supremacist groups (Dilanian 2020). This, because the report was said to have been produced by "Deep State operatives" who wanted to "make the President [Trump] look bad." When Murphy was ordered to rewrite the report saying that the real danger lay in left-wing protesters and in Mexican terrorists, he refused, arguing that "doing so would put the country in substantial and specific danger." He was subsequently demoted, although Trump administration officials denied retaliation.

Like many Christian Identity adherents who fled the declining farm economy of the Midwest in the middle 1980s, Randy Weaver and his family carried the imagery of the "Beast" with them on their way to northern Idaho (Aho 1994, 50–67). As they waved good-bye to their friends, Randy's wife is said to have warned, "you might hear of us being criminals or even being killed." This was because, through a Bible study group that met in the basement of the Weaver's Iowa home, using CD preacher Hal Lindsey's *Late Great Planet Earth* (1970), they had learned that ours are not only the End Times and that the "Beast" was out to "persecute the saints" (meaning the Weavers), but also that a Christ-like figure named Faithful and True was about to redeem their suffering. Riding atop a white horse (Rev. 19), he would supposedly lead the saints to triumph over Evil, and in so doing inaugurate the millennium, a thousand-year reign of health, liberty, peace, and prosperity. So, upon arriving in the Gem State, the Weavers set-about jerry-rigging a plywood and tar-papered mountaintop refuge armed themselves with guns and impatiently awaited the Second Coming. Through a bizarre series of missteps, they eventually stumbled into a shootout with federal marshals that resulted in three deaths, including those of Randy's wife and his teenage son.[7]

Norms

This is not the place to detail the American cultural obsession with guns. It is enough to mention "Concord-Lexington," "Revolutionary War," "Daniel Boone," "The Alamo," and the "cowboy," the latter alone on the range, fighting off Indians and pale-faced ne'er-do-wells (Schlatter 2009). There are also the cinematic portrayals of "rural radicals" (Stock 1996), of "Rambo" (based on the embellished life-story of CD lay-pastor, Bo Gritz), and of the movie-warrior, John Wayne: all of them self-proclaimed "men on white horses." With this in mind, consider the following comments, recorded at a CD gathering for God and Country held in Marble City, an unincorporated political-religious compound in northeastern Washington State, June 2018.

The main speaker was Republican Party state representative, Matt Shea (Wilson 2019a), who opened with a disclaimer: What I am about to say, he cautioned, is "a simple idea that may make you cringe a little at first." It is "that liberty must be kept by force." America is no longer a "beacon of Christianity," he went on, "because of compromise." Because good men have compromised with Evil. And more than this, because of ignorance. Ignorance of the fact "that the communists are training, they're planning, they're organizing and they are lying in wait. If you don't believe that, then you don't understand what is really wrong with America." (In CD rhetoric, "Communist" stands for the litany of fantasy foes enumerated earlier in this chapter, under subsection entitled "Means.") "Anti-fa [a loose confederation of urban anti-fascists] is kicking up and getting ready to fight, right?" The audience wagged its collective head in agreement.

Talk show host Jack Robertson, Shea's close friend, then rose to speak. "Of course, you should have an AR-15 and a thousand rounds of ammo, right?" "It's a fact that what we see on the political landscape and our cultural landscape are indicative of a coming civil war."

Shea didn't dispute Robertson's assertion but wanted to turn his attention to a different possibility: secession. Eastern Washington and Oregon, northern Idaho, and western Montana, he proposed, should all secede from their respective states and set up their own Christian redoubt, called "Liberty State." It will be dedicated to the proposition that global warming is a hoax, abortion a crime, and that those who openly flout "biblical law" should be executed. "It's either going to be bloodshed" ala Robertson, he advised, "or Liberty State."

To deter disruption by hostile non-invitees to the confab, a pistol-armed security team was positioned near the stage. Meanwhile, doing their part to further the cause, the ladies of the congregation auctioned-off pies and desserts (Sokol 2019).

It was later learned (Wilson 2019b) that Shea had distributed a document titled "Biblical Basis for War," co-authored with the pastor of Marble City. It ruminates about a future theocratic takeover of America and approvingly mentions an enterprise called Team Rugged LLC (registered in the State of Washington, 2017). Team Rugged is run by still another Dominionist preacher; its goal is to inculcate Christian "manliness," by training boys in the use of knives, pistols, rifles, and in battlefield teamwork.[8]

Notes

1 An altered and corrected version of this chapter is forthcoming by Oxford University Press.
2 At this writing, James Vincent Foxx, founder of the alt-right media collective, Red Elephants, resides in north Idaho.
3 For Identity Christianity, see Barkun (1996). For post-millennial CD, see Ingersoll (2015).
4 Texas state law mandates that this statement be written into all Texas social science textbooks (McKinley 2010).
5 "45 Cyrus" refers to the 45th President of the United States, Donald Trump, who is said by Dominionist preachers to have "restored the crumbling walls that separate us from cultural collapse." This notion was originally promulgated in the highly popular film, "The Trump Prophecy," which was first shown

during the 2018 presidential primaries. The movie was produced by professors and students at Liberty University.
6 When it was founded in 1871 by Civil War veterans, the NRA was a staunch proponent of gun-control (Winkler 2013). It sponsored marksmanship training, gun safety classes, and recreational shooting. It worked to outlaw machine guns, sawed-off shotguns, and silencers; sought to ban gun purchases by non-citizens, mail-order gun purchases, and open-carry gun displays; and it lobbied for conceal and carry permits, minimum age requirements for gun use, waiting periods between gun purchases and receipts, and the making of gun-sales records available to the police.
7 For more on this incident, see Chapter 6.
8 At this writing, Rep, Shea is being investigated for possible expulsion from the Washington State legislature for inciting violence.

5 The Big Lie
Its Model, Making, and Motive

Of the various kinds of deceptive communication, perhaps the most pernicious is the Big Lie (Ger. *Grosseluege*). This is a rhetorical device recommended by Adolf Hitler in the 1925 edition of his *Mein Kampf* (Hitler 1943, vol. 1, chap. 10). In her political history of totalitarianism, Hannah Arendt describes the Big Lie as a deliberate deception "so colossal" (Hitler's phrase) that its acceptance requires adherents to embark on "a complete rearrangement of the whole factual texture—the making of another reality" (Arendt 1967, 308–9).

Chief Nazi propagandist, Josef Goebbels, claimed that the first practitioners of the Big Lie were Jews, supposedly working in the Allied *Luegenfabrik* ("lie factory") during World War One. There, they allegedly used "their unqualified capacity for falsehood" to encourage the populations of America, England, and France to mount a "war of extermination" against Germany.[1] Goebbels points out that it was not so much the "intelligence" of the Big Liars of the time that distinguished them, but their "remarkably stupid thick-headedness." He goes on to argue that the only defense against the Big Lie would be for Aryan man to contrive his own. And so, they did. Catastrophe soon followed, particularly for Jews, but variations of Nazism's Big Lie have continued to flourish in far-right discourse. Today, it is broadcast over the air, seen on cable TV, and disseminated in cyberspace throughout Continental Europe, Britain, Russia, Hungary, and, most notably, the United States.

This chapter reviews the major features of the contemporary (American) Big-Lie, focusing on the central importance in it of a diabolic Other. It then discusses the steps involved in the social construction of this Other. The chapter closes with the question, Why? What is the attraction of the Big Lie to its adherents?

Arendt offers as one explanation, the craving for revenge by those displaced by modernization, or as we would say today, "globalization." As indicated in Chapter 2, she describes the proponents of the Big Lie as "superfluous men," those rendered redundant by technological disruption, the export of manufacturing capital to where labor is cheap, and/or the import into the home country of low-paid workers. Superfluous man's resentment at being rendered into "little men" (*Kleinmenschen*), says Arendt, is flattered by the suggestion that in actuality they are *Herrenvolk*, superior folk. In Nazi mythology, the groveling little man becomes an *Übermensch*, a blond, blue-eyed superman, upon whose shoulders the fate of Western civilization rests.

Arendt (1967, 147–57) argues that superfluous man and "superfluous capital"—a phrase she attributes to Karl Marx—emerged simultaneously after 1870 with the rise of industrialization; and they began to forge alliances with each other to advance French, British, Slavic, German, and American "pan-nationalist" colonial projects. These promised immense profits for capitalists, together with opportunities for preening patriotism to the over-educated and under-employed.

The subtext of Arendt's argument is that the still popular (liberal) narrative about believers in the Big Lie—that they are "SIC," stupid, isolated, and/or crazy—is incorrect (for a refined version of this theory, see Lipset 1960, 175). Apart from there being little evidence to support it, Arendt claims that it overlooks the discomfiting thought that "failed men" (Arendt's phrase) will find it "easier to accept" a Big Lie than they will the "old truth" of Enlightenment progress. This, they come to see as a "pious banality" that no one takes seriously anymore; or worse, as a justification for wickedness (Arendt 1967, 334).

Considerations of empirical accuracy aside, my objection to Arendt is that her explanation doesn't go nearly far enough. I argue that the Big Lie is founded on an even *bigger* lie, a self-deception that goes to the very roots of our being in the world. But before getting to this, let us review the major features of the Big Lie itself.

The Model of the Big Lie

The Big Lie has four distinctive qualities: mystery, simplicity, prophecy, and infallibility. None of these are found in academic social science, with its skepticism of mystification, its preference for complex explanations, its distrust of prophetic pronouncements, and above all, its inclination to test hypotheses against objective reality. This, of course, is precisely why the audience for the Big Lie considers conventional social science irrelevant at best. At worst, they view it as jargon-filled pomposity, a production of "pointy-headed elitists."

This is not to say that the Big Lie itself lacks the appurtenances of scholarship. On the contrary, its paper publications are often chock full of footnotes, references, indices, and appendices; the production qualities of its websites and video clips are as sophisticated as anything available from major corporations, governments, or universities. And if need be, the Big Lie can even present itself as "scientific" (cf. our discussion of the Bible sciences in Chapter 3). It can don a white lab coat, conduct "archaeological digs," and appear in public amidst beaker-equipped labs. But as Alexander Koyré (1945, 291) points out, the purpose of the Big Lie is not to account for history in accordance with scholarly standards. Rather, it is to *transform* how audiences experience the past, so as to mobilize them for political action in the future. In other words, the Big Lie "is not a light but a weapon." And its so-called truth is assessed by means of the vulgar pragmatism of whatever elevates poll numbers, sells books and online ads, or advances party interests. This explains what Arendt (1967, 333) bewails as the Big Lie's "maddening perplexity": not merely that its purveyors are cynics and its audience dupes, but that its "monstrous falsehoods can eventually be established as unquestioned facts ... and that the difference between truth and falsehood may cease to be objective and become a mere matter of power and cleverness...."

Mystery, simplicity, prophecy, and infallibility can, of course, be found in both far-left and far-right oratory. But for purposes of brevity, and given that at the present moment the dominant Euro-American political discourse leans far to the right, the following discussion draws exclusively on what I call far-right fantasy (for more on far-right fantasy, see Aho 2016, 65–81).

Mystery

In the "The Grand Inquisitor" (from *The Brothers Karamazov*), Dostoevsky writes that the average person not only hungers for bread, but also for mystery. The Big Lie satisfies this craving by positing the existence of a furtive Force lurking just beneath the surface of everyday life: a foul and loathsome conspiracy, a "breathing together" of a secret cabal whose goal is to rule the world.

This cabal goes by many names: "Freemasonry," "the Illuminati," "the Hidden Hand," "the Insiders," "Shadow Government," "the Dark Command," "the Deep State," and so on. From the standpoint of the sociology of knowledge, these and related entities represent the secularization or "humanization" of what were anciently understood to be spiritual phenomena, encompassed by terms like "fallen angels," "Satan," "demon," and "Devil." Which is to say, the cabal comprises beings in human form, but who are in contention with God. Secondarily, the names illustrate how in the melting-pot culture of post–World War II Euro-America, right-wing rhetoric has been redirected away from the mythical "Jew" toward non-ethnic sounding groupings. The word "Insider," for example, was coined by the John Birch Society, arguably the largest and most influential far-right faction in the United States during the 1950s and 1960s. *None Dare Call It Conspiracy* (Allen 1971), the definitive statement of John Birch canon, explicitly renounces any suggestion that the Insiders are Jews (39) (although the surnames Allen cites to prove the existence of the Insiders—Warburg, Lehman, Kuhn, Loeb, and Rothschild—belie his protestations. And lately, the list of alleged Insiders has been expanded to include Jews such as Henry Kissinger, Zbigniew Brzezinski, Madeleine Albright, and the considered human-Demon himself, George Soros, a onetime Holocaust survivor and billionaire financier of liberal-progressive causes).

Whatever its title, the cabal is reputed to meet at sites like the Jewish Sanhedrin in Geneva, Switzerland; in the grand ballroom of the Bilderberg Hotel in the Netherlands; behind the ivied walls of the Skull and Bones Club at Yale University; inside the headquarters of the United Nations; or intriguingly, in the dank forests of Bohemian Grove in northern California. There, it is said to make burnt offerings to the ancient Semitic fire gods Molech and Dagon, using child effigies as victims, if not live children themselves. And it devises plans to establish a tyrannical "one-world" order that will be borderless, unilingual, poly-sexual, religiously ecumenical, egalitarian, and brown-skinned.

"Bread crumbs" of these plans have purportedly been left behind by the cabal and have been ferreted out by self-proclaimed "undercover investigators," like Infowars.com conspiracy theorist, Alex Jones. Or "Qtips" about their plans have been exhumed by entirely fictitious figures such as the Internet sensation and salvific hero, "QAnon." (Supposedly, QAnon is a high-level American government official with an exclusive "Q" clearance.) The results of these so-called investigations have since been aired or released by underground presses for the edification of the masses. Or, they have been "inadvertently" leaked in pamphlets like *The Protocols of the Learned Elders of Zion*, *The Plot Against Christianity*, or most recently, in the United Nations publication, *Agenda 21*.

Simplicity

Arendt (1967, 458) tells us that "ideological super-sense [is] more adequate to the needs of the human mind than reality itself," with its fortuitousness and complexity. This being the case, the Big Lie "thrives on … escape from coincidence into consistency," into a hack historiography free of randomness or accident (352–53). It attributes every personal misfortune and public calamity, real or imagined, to a single over-arching cause: The Plot. These misfortunes and calamities include wars, recessions, plagues (like the COVID-19 pandemic), hurricanes, wildfires, earthquakes, the opioid crisis, gun massacres, and more. From the standpoint of the Big Lie, even *denials* of The Plot by liberal academicians are considered part of The Plot. Indeed, the more fervent their denials, the stronger the proof. After all, *Why, if it isn't true, are the elites so defensive about it?* Adding to this is that what might reasonably be seen as good, is invariably re-construed as bad. For instance, vaccinations are said to be "disease vectors"; equal rights for minorities, "our nightmare"; public education, "liberal indoctrination"; the Federal Emergency Management Agency, "concentration camps"; national parks, "land-grabs"; universal medical insurance, "socialized medicine," and so on. As the 17th century Puritan preacher, Cotton Mather, might have said, *the whole world is polluted!* And the reason for this is The Plot.

When people first hear about The Plot, it is understandable that they feel anxiety and dread. But this too is part of The Plot. For "they want to make you anxious and afraid." At least according to popular radio conspiracy theorist, Clyde Lewis.

Prophecy

The Big Lie represents the experience of displacement and marginalization suffered by superfluous man (as understood in Chapter 2 and in the opening section of this chapter) as nothing less than the termination of the world, the end of "everything we've grown up with, everything we've known," cries deceased right-wing radio talk show host, Rush Limbaugh. If the superfluous man in question is a fundamentalist Christian, then world collapse is pictured in apocalyptic terms as the final days of Revelation. If, on the other hand, s/he is secularized, then it gives itself to consciousness as a specter of doom. Many conspiracy-mongers leave audiences in a state of benumbed hopelessness. But at other times, the Big Lie promises them revenge, say, in the form of a "storm" (or "maelstrom") to use the phraseology of QAnon. This storm will destroy the Deep State operatives who are supposedly behind the Plot and reverse superfluous man's unhappy fortunes. Typically, this is prophesied as a "countercoup" that will arrest the "the new castrati" (one of Limbaugh's favorite foils), hold them for trial, then publicly execute them for treason. In the event that the "evil tyrants" are able to avoid prosecution—a strong likelihood given that they allegedly control the police and the courts—then their presumed locally available symbolic stand-ins are to be targeted: undocumented immigrants, political refugees, domestic minorities, and sexual deviants.

Infallibility

Alex Jones, the conspiracy theorist mentioned above, has "challenged" (his term) critics to "disprove" the lineaments of the Big Lie. Naturally, this is an empty gesture. First, as we saw in our discussion of Christian Dominionism in Chapter 3, evidence (of what quality is another matter) can be cited to support virtually any contention. For example, that Barack Obama was born in Kenya or on Mars; or that Hillary Clinton partook in a child sex-trafficking ring run out of a Washington DC pizzeria (supposedly to supply victims for the gruesome rites conducted at Bohemian Grove). On the other hand, no amount of information can ever *dis*prove that the bombing of the Murrah Federal Building in Oklahoma City (1995) or the 9/11 terrorist attack, to cite two examples, were "inside jobs," as Alex Jones maintains. Or that the Sandy Hook elementary school massacre in 2005 was "staged" by "crisis actors" to justify government confiscation of firearms. Second, and even more "maddening," to use Hannah Arendt's term, according to the logic of the Big Lie, the very *absence* of concrete evidence about Insiders, Hidden Hands, or Shadow Governments is treated as further confirmation of their existence. In other words, according to one of QAnon's Qtips, it proves that an *even more* secret society resides within an already Deep State, an *even more* insidious cell within a government that is already opaquely "gray."

All of this is to say that the most compelling rhetorical feature of the Big Lie is not its mystery, its simplicity, or its prophecy. Rather, it is its unfalsifiable, irrefutable verity. In the storm-tossed chaos of superfluous man's crumbling world, the Big Lie grants what academic social science never can: the consolation of something firm to hold on to, concrete ground upon which to stand: in other words, cognitive certitude. When "all that is solid melts into the air" (Marx), when everything one once took for granted and trusted, dissipates like mist in the afternoon sun, this is priceless.

The Chief Cabalist

The central character in the Big Lie narrative is the chief cabalist, a figure who has undergone countless name changes since John Robison (1967) first exposed its existence to Americans in his *Proofs of a Conspiracy against All the Religions and Governments of Europe* in 1798. Despite these name changes, however, its traits have remained uncannily constant. This is why Robison's depiction of the Illuminati from over two centuries ago still rings true for right-wingers today, and why his pamphlet continues to be cited as a source and guidebook for understanding what presumably is happening in the present moment.

To begin with, whatever their name, the cabalist is invariably depicted as having loathsome intentions, dirty thoughts, and a sordid soul. S/he wears a black gown (like the legendary "wicked witch," or the Jesuits of old, or like the "black-robed Mormans" [sic] of more recent vintage). Or (like the fabled Jewish banker of our day), a black suit. S/he is pictured as parading around in a black face mask, for example, or with black eye shades, seated in black helicopters or reclining in black limousines with black-tinted windows, not untypically, in the company of a black cat or some other spiteful beast.

Second are the hands of the cabalist: These are always described as soiled, sinister, or, what amounts to the same thing, as "leftist." This is in contrast to the rectal, righteous bearing of their archetypal antagonist, the "right-thinking" man. Notably, the left hand was once known as the "kackhand", that used for wiping rather than for eating or greeting. "Kack" in turn is traceable to the ancient Sanskrit noun for shit, *kakka.* "Caw-caw" is also the language of the crow. This is the preeminent totem of the Hindu Dalit or Untouchable, a status group at one time considered so filthy that their very shadow or glance could contaminate a person (Dundes 1997, 10–24). The crow was also the probable (psychological) basis of the derisive title "Jim Crow," as applied to African-Americans during the post-Reconstruction era.

Third is the tale that the cabalist is birthed from of the "bowels of the underworld," from the "dregs" (Ger. *Dreck* = feces) of society, from the muck, the mud, or *merde* (Fr.); or to quote President Donald Trump, from "shithole countries" in Africa or Central America. In contemporary American neo-Nazi fable, "mud people"—that is, Jews, aborigines, Blacks, and Hispanics—all are held up in negative contrast to "spirit folk," whose white skins are believed to signify their "delightsomeness" to the Lord, and hence their pre-selection for eternal salvation.

A related term is "gook." This is an offensive tag still occasionally applied by Americans to Asians. Originally, "gook" was invoked to depict the Japanese in World War II; nowadays, it is more often used to defame the Vietnamese, including those who collaborated with America during the recent war.

Fourth, the cabalist is mythologized as residing in decrepit gothic castles or drafty hotels, in gloomy temples, slimy sewers, or in "rat-holes" (cf. one-time Iraqi President Saddam Hussein who was captured in one during the Second Iraq war [2003–2010]). They are said to inhabit "fenian swamps," like the 19th-century Irish "monsters," who terrified the British imagination. They take up residence in fog-enshrouded redwood forests such as Bohemian Grove; or in "rat and rodent infested" cities (such as Baltimore, Maryland), where, according to President Trump, "no human being would want to live."

In sum, then, the cabalist is trash, rubbish, which explains its garbage-eating bestiary (Keen 1986): not only the crow and the rat (*Siehen der Jud!* [Behold the Jew!]), but "snakes in the grass," vermin (worms), and raccoons (or "coons," another scornful label for African Americans). There are goats (who represent Satan-worshipers), dogs (homosexuals), cockroaches, and pigs: all of them mythical compost-dwellers. In our present-day medicalized era, there are also human "cancers," "disease vectors," and "bacilli." German Nazi iconographers adopted from Martin Luther a particularly repellent creature to represent "feces-eaters like Jews": the *Schweinehund* or swine dog (Brown 1970, 225).[2]

The Making of the Cabalist

Whether we have in mind the Communist functionary, the invisible Deep State agent, the Jewish Insider, or the Shadow Government globalist, the traits attributed to the cabalist are consistently experienced by proponents of the Big Lie as inherently given. That is, they are seen, reflected on, and recalled as having *always been* that way. But in reality, these traits are the product of a long, meticulous four-step process: labeling, myth-making, embedment, and sacrifice.

Labeling

"Labeling" refers to the affixing of a pejorative tag onto a person or an out-group, one who differs from the in-group in a discernibly unacceptable way (Becker 1963). The label often takes the form of a nasty-sounding one or two-syllable expectoration like "mick," "nip," "zip," "spic," "chink," "dink," "dick," "Hun," "wop," "cunt," "fag," "slope," "kike," or "cuck," which needs little further clarification. When more abstract aspersions are at issue, however, as in the cases of "criminal," "madman," or "terrorist," the labeler may also be required to rationalize its bestowal on an out-group by staging what Harold Garfinkel (1956) calls a "public degradation ceremony": an inquisition, a trial, an official hearing, a "court of love," or a public confession, wherein the label's suitability is tested and validated.

Defamatory labels accomplish three things simultaneously. First, like all taxonomic categories they enable audiences to make sense of the chaos of auditory, olfactory, and visual stimuli with which they are inundated from one moment to the next. Or to express it more frankly, they help transmogrify human beings with all their vagaries and contradictions into specific *things*—in the case before us, things to be terrified of and loathed. Second, defamatory labels serve as short-hand and hominem arguments. In other words, insofar as the person or group in question is a swine, a pinko, a slut, or a bacterium, then whatever comes out of their mouths is ipso facto idiotic, craven, sick, or nuts, and therefore unworthy of serious attention, which takes us to a label's third and most significant achievement. It is that labels don't merely describe; they also *pre*scribe. They cognitively prepare audiences to act "appropriately." After all, what should be done with human "waste," if not to "liquidate" it and "expulse" it? With human "garbage" or "trash"? With two-legged "rats"? Or with "cancers in our midst"? In Nazi Germany, the answer was cleansing! Ethnic cleansing! *Judenreinmachen*: cleanse the homeland of Jews! As for "fags," one American editorial expressed the recommendation this way: "What we demand and ... what we expect" is "immediate and systematic cauterization." This, until "the whole situation is cleared up, and the premises thoroughly cleansed and disinfected" (Gerasi 1966, 3–4).

Myth-making

Human beings are intelligent animals; we typically demand more than slanderous labels to encourage the violation of others—even when those labels have been authenticated in the course of a defamatory rite. In other words, we also need stories about why the labeled are as supposed. Nowadays such tales are composed of a combination of pop-theology (i.e., their iniquity grows from a conscious decision to disobey God's commandments), pop-biology (their evil is due to a "demon seed" they have either inherited genetically or acquired through infection), pop-psychology (they have been abusively raised or brain-washed into a "culture of death"), and/or pop-sociology (whatever moral compass they once may have had, has been undermined by rapid social change and "anomie" (a state of normlessness that has left them without a "moral compass").

Narratives of demonization are often verified anecdotally by reference to atrocity tales. Among other things, these portray the desecration of the orifices of women and children in, say, "rape rooms" (as claimed by President George H. W. Bush about Saddam Hussein, prior to the first Gulf War [1990–1991]). When Donald Trump announced his candidacy for the presidency of the United States in 2015, one of the first things he said about Mexican immigrants was, "they are rapists." In doing so, consciously or not, he was drawing on a timeless icon of in-group peril. According to Mary Douglas (1966), the female body has always symbolized an in-group's gateways and vulnerabilities. This is one likely reason why many of the most vociferous advocates for erecting "a big, beautiful wall" (Trump's phrase) to keep Mexican "invaders" out of America, also champion campaigns to protect the purity of "our" women from them. This, by policing the invasion route par excellence, their vaginas, by imposing on them draconian anti-abortion and anti-birth control measures.

Other symbolic sites of in-group peril are the mouth (as in the kosher diet of orthodox Judaism and its contemporary attempt to ban the consumption of hamburger); the eye (one inspiration for the fundamentalist Muslim terror of "graven images," or of their evangelical Christian cousins' fear of the "modern addiction," pornography); the anus (a possible reason for the on-going hysteria surrounding male homosexuality); and the ear. Sociologist Scott Appelrouth (2001), himself a musician, has argued that unlike the mouth or eyes, one cannot shut their "aural receptors" to the "envelope" of sound. Hence, the suspicion that seductive music, an invasion route into the body politic, might be deployed by cunning aggressors to advance their evil aims. None other than Henry David Thoreau warned that the "intoxication" of music could be so great that it could "cause" (his word) the fall of entire civilizations, as it presumably did in ancient Greece and Rome. And if not policed, music could "destroy England and America" as well. This is undoubtedly one source of the dread that far-right pundits exhibit when their thought turns to the perils of syncopation, jazz, rock 'n roll, and rap.

The most revealing (and, as it turns out, dangerous) species of mythic demonization is the "The Sabbat of Orifices" (Aho 2002, 99–116). This is an elaborate tale that slanders a designated other by accusing it of ceremonially violating every bodily orifice at once, in darkness at midnight, to the scent of bewitching aromas wafting through subterranean caverns. Here, are horrifying reports of infanticide and the cannibalistic consumption of children's flesh; the feasting on forbidden drugs; and a sexual orgy involving those same children and adults of either or both genders, married and single. All of this, to the accompaniment of hypnotic music and obscene images, and overseen by a bestiary of dung-eating toads, crows, cats, snakes, and dogs.

There is evidence of the pre-Christian pagan use of the Sabbat of Orifices myth to defame various enemies. But its first use in Christian civilization was its infliction on followers of the Manichean cult by St. Augustine (345–430 CE). Since his time, it has played a central role in the Christian *armamentium* (Lat.) and used against every non-Christian confession from Islam to Hinduism, and against every considered apostasy and heresy: from the chaste, simple-living monks known as the Knights Templar in the 14th century, to the female "free spirits," as they were known, and the practitioners of witchcraft. And for centuries, the same calumny has been directed against the "international Jew" (cf. Leese 1938). After the Reformation, the Catholic Church herself fell under suspicion by Calvinists for encouraging "convent crimes" between nuns and priests (Monk 1836). And later, comparable revelations were made about the notorious (if imaginary) Mormon "seraglio" (Bennet 1842). From these and related sources, the myth has come down to us today: most recently in the form of the Satanist panic of the 1980s surrounding American child-care facilities, and in the tales about Bohemian Grove, as aired by, among others, QAnon.

If it is not already obvious, what the cross-cultural, trans-historical nature of the Sabbat narrative indicates is that it is not so much an empirical assertion, or even necessarily intended as such. Rather, it is what Carl Jung would call a psychological "archetype" (1981): a symbolic complex that expresses deep-seated "endo-psychic demons." Not merely fantasies about the commission of everyday illicitness, but repellent, consciously inconceivable repudiations of civilized order.

Embedment

Once they are composed, defamatory labels and myths must next be implanted, embedded, in the hearts and minds of the upcoming generation. Because children are not physically present when slanderous labels are coined or when atrocity tales are devised, they remain unaware of their artificially contrived nature. Instead, they receive them innocently, as common sense, what everyone always already knows about Them. In approximate order of influence, beginning with the most important, the major agents of embedment are parents, peers, propagandists, pundits, preachers, and professors. Exactly how political libel is passed on to children—whether through the content of specific lesson plans, by the example of negative role models, or by the style in which these lessons are conveyed, and whether by means of rote memorization or play-acting, or all of these at once—is a matter of endless debate that need not be addressed here. The only thing to acknowledge at this point is that by these means, hate of another becomes an element in the taken-for-granted common stock of knowledge.

Sacrifice

The culminating step in the manufacture of the cabalist is punishment (from Lat. *poena* = pain, thus the administration of pain). This is when those blamed for a misfortune, imagined or not, are called to atone for it. The crucial fact to bear in mind about sacrifice is that to be *blamed* for something is not the same as being its *cause*. To be blamed, say, for low cotton prices, and to be lynched as a result, as happened hundreds, possibly thousands, of times from 1882 to 1930 in the American Deep South (Tolnay & Beck 1990) or, during the late Middle Ages, to suffer a pogrom for allegedly "poisoning wells," as happened to Jews, means only that one is held to "respond to" it, to be responsible for it. Causality, in contrast, refers to the biopsychosocial-cultural conditions that occur prior to an event, and with which that event is highly associated, even after other preconditions are controlled for or held constant. To be sure, sometimes those held responsible for acting in heinous ways have in fact done so. But at other times, those called to account for a public calamity or a private sorrow merely have a different skin color, nose or eye shape, physiognomy, language, faith, ideology, appetite, or desire than an in-group; they may have played no role in causing those misfortunes.

The Motive of the Big Lie

From the standpoint of the protagonist (the so-called good guy), the antagonist is always *diablo*, a devil (from the Greek *dia* = away from + *bolos* = that which is thrown). In other words, its qualities are what the protagonist "throws away" from itself. And what is cast-off is a truth the protagonist cannot bear to acknowledge, a truth about its "own-most (Ger. *eigenst*) possibility" (Heidegger 1962, 24), namely, that s/he is in decay and moving inexorably toward the end; that in reality; that the protagonist is not particularly substantial or solid at all, but tenuous, fragile, and contingent. By flinging the existential fact of its own precarity outward where it attaches onto a "sin-carrier," the protagonist participates in a delusion: the conviction that it has escaped its inevitable diminishment, death, and putrefaction. This is the "bigger lie" mentioned at the outset of this chapter. And it explains why, the more emphatically the protagonist "denies" its death (Becker 1973; Solomon et al. 2015), the more vicious its slanders must be; the more extravagant its scatological fables about them; the more insistent it is on passing these tales and legends on to its children; and the bloodier are its sacrificial rites. And above all, the more relief it feels when it witnesses the antagonist's demise (as applied to war-making, see Underhill-Cady 2001).

The technical term for the casting of one's own-most possibility onto another is "negative transference." Sometimes, it is done with full awareness of what is at stake, as in the case of "political plague-mongers," as Ernest Becker (1975) calls them: preachers, politicians, propagandists, and pundits. As for the masses, however, negative transference is usually unconscious. Here, instead of seeing themselves (accurately) as co-producers of the *diaboli* (human devils) against whom they fight, they misperceive themselves as innocent, blameless victims.

Mythologist James Frazer (1951, 306, 342, 599) illustrates this in his discussion of the so-called savage mind, by which he means a way of thinking unencumbered by the insights of critical sociology. In ancient Greece, for example, a stable of slaves and degraded individuals was drawn upon during the spring equinox or amidst public *krises*, such as famines, plagues, or pestilence. These would serve as *katharmae* (or *pharmaka*), human toxins, whose ceremonial elimination (*kathairo*) was believed to have curative powers. Like the pharmaceutical cathartics we take today to relieve conditions like dyspepsia, in others words, Greek legend had it that upon witnessing the toxin's murder, the entire community would undergo its own purgative *katharsis* (Girard 1977, 286–90). (The Greek *pharmakon* is the root of the English "pharmaceutical"; the English "cathartic" is derived from the Greek term, *katharma*.)

According to accounts, as it was paraded through the public square prior to being killed, the *pharmakon's* genitals would be whipped with fig branches to symbolically render them impotent and harmless (98, 288).

A comparable rite is found in Yom Kippur (Lev. 16: 29–34), the Day of Atonement, which name comes from *kippurim*, the victim offered up for sacrifice in ancient Babylonia. Originally, in Yom Kippur, the high priest would ritually transfer the sins and adversities of Israel onto the head of a goat or a bull named Azazel. Azazel would then be led outside the gates of the village to wander in exile, allowing the community to "escape" its misfortunes.

In his letter to the Hebrews, St. Paul elaborates on the logic of the (e)scapegoat, by writing about how it "proves" that nothing can be purified without the shedding of blood (Heb. 9: 16–23). He then goes on to liken the redemptive efficacy of blood sacrifice to one's last will and testament. Such documents, he writes, only become legally actionable after the testator dies. But then, Paul adds, rites like Yom Kippur (or the Greek *pharmakon*) are in reality "useless." This is because they only "reflect" the Truth but are not true in themselves (Heb. 10: 1). For this reason, he argues, God has seen fit to substitute in place of the ancient scapegoats a more "perfect sacrifice": the unblemished "Lamb of God," Jesus Christ (cf. Heb. 9: 14). Christ's death, St. Paul goes on, not only cancels the sin-debts of the tiny nation of Jews (or an exclusive Greek polis), but those of the entire human race. Furthermore, it is enough that it occur only once in history; it need not be repeated.

Had the Christian narrative of redemptive sacrifice been implemented in everyday life, perhaps it could have averted subsequent efforts at human riddance, rendering wars, terrorist insurrections, and executions superfluous and unnecessary. Or at least it might have tempered their ferocity. It hardly needs to be said, however, that history has not turned out this way. On the contrary, first, under the influence of Zoroastrianism, with which Israel came into contact during the Babylonian Exile [ca. 599 BCE], Azazel, the sacrificial goat, began transforming into the figure of Satan, eventually becoming the now familiar hairy, horned, cloven-hoofed goat-*man*, reputed head of the so-called fallen angels (Pagels 1995). In Genesis 6: 1–4, Azazel-Satan is described as having "lusted" after the "daughters of men," and through them brought forth a race of giants. These are the supposed "Sons of Darkness" who would later be vilified in popular Jewish, Christian, and Muslim legend (1 Enoch 6–8; cf. Jubilees 5). They are the Antagonists against whom the "Sons of Light" struggle and subdue in the End Times.

The first suggestion of Christianity's appropriation of the reconfigured Azazel is already evident in the epistle just cited where St. Paul lauds the efficacy of Christ's execution. Here, he reiterates the lesson that Christ's sacrifice "perfects all whom he is sanctifying." But he then follows this comment with a warning: *unless the person in question "deliberately sins"* (my emphasis). In that case, there can be no merciful forgiveness by a loving Father, but "only the dreadful prospect of judgement and of the raging fire that is to burn rebels" (Heb. 10: 14). Like the brambles and thistles of the field, in other words, the deliberate sinner shall "end by being burnt" (Heb. 6: 6), with "far severer punishment" to come later (Heb. 10: 14).

It isn't necessary to recount the parade of others upon whom the title "deliberate sinner" has been bestowed. It is enough to repeat what we have observed already in earlier chapters: they become repositories of every imaginable crime, from sexual perversity and cannibalism to child murder and vampirism. The paradigmatic example, of course, is the "International Jew," the so-called left (or, sinister)-hand of Christianity (Ruether 1979). But there is also the Satan-worshipping witch and the Christian crusader of enduring Muslim legend. Which is to say nothing of the so-called Great Satan herself, modern America. And, of course, there is always an available Muslim jihadi. It is enough to remind ourselves of Pascal's contention, quoted in the Introduction to this book, that "Men never do evil so completely and cheerfully as when they do it for religious conviction." This is because the phrase, "Sons of Darkness," stands for everything that is refused by the Jew, Christian, and Muslim: their refuse. And what they refuse is what they fear most and frantically (if futilely) flee: their own existential fragility and precariousness, their own death.

Those upon whom the projective strobe of the Jew, Christian, and/or Muslim falls are everywhere subject to the most terrifying biblical commandment of all: the ban (Heb. *herem*. From the Babylonian *hrm*): "As regards the towns of those peoples which ... God gives you as your own inheritance," goes the commandment, "you must not spare the life of any living thing. You shall utterly destroy them" (Deut. 20: 16; 13: 13–19; 17–17). Failure to carry out this commandment, the passage continues, is itself punishable by death. The biblical category "those peoples," originally referred to the natives of the land "promised" to the Jews by their tribal God, Yahweh. To legitimize their extirpation, the scribe and prophet Ezra (who flourished in 5th century BCE) associates them with the most revolting impurity he can envision, *nidda*: the menstruant and her blood (Ezra 9: 11). And he characterizes the Promised Land as having been made "unclean because of the foulness (*niddat*) of the natives ... and of the abomination with which their impurities have infected it from end to end." Which, as just indicated, means that it must be cleansed. By fire.

Conclusion

We may give thanks that the Jewish, Christian, and Muslim *ethoi* (ethics) of extermination have been compelled to adapt to the conditions of modernity in the approximate order of their arrival in history. Crucial among these conditions are laws that require synagogue, church, and mosque to be administered separately from corporations (where they exist) that claim monopolies over the legitimate means of violence in their respective territories: the state. One result of this has been that the "savage mind" (James Frazier's term, mentioned above) of the Abrahamic faithful has found itself institutionally restrained from acting out its worst instincts. Predictably, it has balked at the imposition, calling the separation of church and state a "liberal lie," an "infringement on religious liberty," a loser's appeal to "women of both sexes," or as "an affront to our manly dignity". Or, to borrow from our discussion of the Big Lie, it is viewed as one more step in the diabolic Plot to "satanify" the world.

Nor has the institutional splitting off of sacred affairs from matters of state come without a price. For if the 20th century has taught us anything, it is that the only thing worse than violence perpetrated in the name of a God, is violence undertaken without it. When Martin Luther demanded that the Church free itself from her corrupting entanglements with the state, he also inadvertently liberated states to pursue their naked power interests unencumbered by moral scruples (Luther 1974, 102–3, 130). The outcome has been "pure war" (Virilio 1983), machine-generated mega-death (Wyschogrod 1985).

Still, it seems that there is no going back. A globalizing world beckons us to acknowledge that the them, the Other, whom we earlier mistook as wholly different from us, is in large measure a product of our own troubled imaginations. It is our own selves "seen as through a glass, darkly" (1 Cor. 13: 12). To become aware of this, of course, is a wounding. And furthermore, it does nothing to protect us from those who continue to insist on projecting their garbage outward onto us. Additionally, even when there is little risk to us in eating our own shit, this does little to address our shared existential problematic, the fact of our ultimate groundlessness and mortality. Nevertheless, it may cause us to momentarily hesitate before mindlessly embarking, one more time, on an armed quest to "kill death." The point is that the conviction of our own innocence is an illusion. It is a cognitive privilege accorded exclusively to the ignorant. The Big Lie doesn't so much expose the truth about history. Rather, it reveals how insistent we are in remaining unconscious about it and ourselves.

Notes

1 Nazism and its contemporary derivatives hold that the most important product of the Jewish Lie Factory is "Spinozism" (a derogatory term, named after the Dutch Jew, Baruch Spinoza [1632–1677]). Today, it is reviled as liberal Enlightenment philosophy, which maintains (1) that there is an objective reality, (2) that this reality is accessible to every human being by means of reason, and (3) that reason is predicated on individual civil, political, and social rights.
2 The reverse is also true: In-groups are known to rape vanquished females and males to put the final stamp of approbation on their conquests. Or in a perverse form of "excremental assault" (DePres, 1984), they will force the vanquished to "eat shit": drink from filled toilets, clean latrines without hand tools, and/or demand that they eat from bowls soiled by non-scheduled latrine breaks, a particular torment for dysentery sufferers.

6 The Danse Macabre

Deadly Miscommunications

Social life is an ongoing conversation, a turning together, a dance. There are a variety of dances, many of which end on happy notes. But there is one dance that leads its partners unwittingly to their mutual destruction, the *danse macabre* (Fr. dance of death). This chapter briefly reviews the steps in the *danse macabre* and then illustrates them with three encounters between federal law enforcement officials and right-wing extremists: Ruby Ridge, Idaho (1992); Waco, Texas (1993); and Oklahoma City (1995). The chapter concludes by examining dance moves that have been undertaken by the South African government to avert such tragedies: The Truth and Reconciliation Commission (TRC). It compares the relative successes and failures of the Commission's moves and ruminates on the ethical and political challenges that remain.

Mutual Diabolization

The *danse macabre* follows a preprogrammed script; it results in the unconscious transfer of each party's unassimilated garbage onto their partners (Abrams & Zweig 1991). The script consists of the four steps recounted in the last chapter: name-calling (or labeling), demonic mythologizing, embedment, and sacrificial riddance (or murder). And it is devised and mediated through all the familiar vectors of slander and defamation: from priest, preacher, policeman, and pamphleteer, to pundit, parent, politician, professor, and peer.[1]

Because the steps in the *danse* enable each party to imaginatively discard their own precariousness, contingency, and mendacity and place it in the hands of their partner, each enjoys the momentary experience of blamelessness. Thus, their eventual, inevitable, victimization at the hands of that partner comes to them as a horrifying, undeserved surprise. This, naturally, adds to their rage, motivating them to generate still filthier labels; meaner, more gruesome myths; and calls for bloodier vengeance. On and on, without end, until each party is destroyed, or until boredom and fatigue set in, and the *danse* comes to a temporary halt.

Naming or Labeling

As we saw earlier, names and labels allow speakers and writers to differentiate among objects, including people, and to group together those who share likenesses, while excluding others (Becker 1963). Which is a short way of saying that they are essential for cognitive functioning. Without them, we would be overwhelmed by meaningless noise and rendered effectively blind and deaf.

Pejorative labels accomplish three additional tasks. This is why every society has a virtually bottomless thesaurus of aspersions from which it can draw. "Terrorist," "liptard," "gook," "fascist," "commie," "idiot," "nut," and "liar" are merely some of the less vulgar. Whatever the case, negative labels first enable protagonists to identify an antagonist as a diabolic *thing*: as an object "thrown apart," and thus wholly different-from, or other-than, themselves.[2] Second, they also serve as implicit ad hominem arguments against anything that comes from the mouth of the antagonist who is a "very bad man," a "blind sentimentalist," "a loony-bird," or "he who always lies." Third, and most importantly, defamatory labels never just *de*scribe; they also *pre*scribe. That is, they prepare a protagonist to act maliciously toward an antagonist. To anticipate our discussion of the Waco incident, it was never merely a matter of theoretical salience whether David Koresh was "the wacko from Waco" (as officials called him) or "the Lamb of God" (the honorific title bestowed on him by his followers); whether his children were "hostages" (as the government claimed) or "my babies" (to use Koresh's words); or whether Mt. Carmel was an "armed compound" (as the government insisted) or "our home" (to quote Koresh). Each side was cognitively readying themselves to act "appropriately," that is, to attack and/or to defend themselves from their *danse* partner (Sanford & Comstock 1971).

Nasty words baffle and hurt, which is, after all, their intent. But hurt can occasion anger, and angry people strike back. When they do, this can validate the original label, proving to the protagonist in question that the antagonist *is truly* as supposed. And yet in a Kafkaesque way, if the label is not disputed, this too can lend it credence. In other words, labels can be as sticky as the tar baby from which B'rer Rabbit hopelessly tries to extricate himself. Whatever the labeled party does effectively reconfirms their mendacity.[3]

Myth-making

Human beings rarely are satisfied merely to cast aspersions. We also want explanations for why the defamed *are* as claimed: biographies and histories. Is it because of their genes? A disease that they contracted as children? Their religious convictions? Or is it the lack thereof? Maybe they were discriminated against, abused, or raised in poverty. To say, as we have here, that such accounts are mythical is not to deny that they are also at least partly true. In fact, usually every mythical narrative of reputed evil-doers is supplemented with discursive and non-discursive "proofs." The first typically take the form of written documents, and these in turn can be either secular (i.e., "scientific") in tone, or they can be posed in religious language. Examples of discursive proofs, routinely invoked by federal agents at both Waco and Ruby Ridge, included *The Diagnostic and Statistical Manual of the American Psychological Association*, Cult Awareness Network profiles, and crisis management textbooks with their pop bio/psycho/social theories. The prototypical religious text, on the other hand, repeatedly cited by the residents at both Ruby Ridge and Waco, was the Bible, especially, the prophecies of Amos, Daniel, Jeremiah, and "John" (Revelation). There were also non-canonical biblical Apocrypha, most notably the book of Enoch, which finds favor on the far-right because of its depiction of a cosmic war between the Sons of Perdition (the presumed anticipation of today's Illuminati, International Jew, or Deep State agent.) and the Sons of Light (themselves). The Apocrypha are said to contain knowledge so esoteric that they can only be understood by spiritual adepts, not by outsiders.

Whether written documents have a scientific-sounding tenor or are posed in quasi-religious terms, one essential feature they tend to share is what we described in the last chapter as "atrocity tales" (as applied to Waco, see Docherty 2001). These report on the evils that have allegedly been committed by the antagonist in question. Such tales simultaneously announce, one, the protagonist's status as a victim, and two, their innocence. (Again, for what I mean by 'protagonist,' see endnote 2.)

Myth-makers typically rely on more than just written documents to validate their stories; they also conduct direct observation or "espionage." Here, we see a second Kafkaesque factor at work. For now, the outward law-abidingness, piety, intelligence, and/or emotional balance of a particular antagonist may be retrospectively reinterpreted by the protagonist from the standpoint of the antagonist's negative "master status," that is, as indicators of their "actual" (from the standpoint of the protagonist) intransigence, heresy, stupidity, and/or madness. For example, the antagonist's outwardly peaceful gestures might be taken as "tricks"; their family relations as "abuse"; their offers to surrender, a "ruse"; and their willingness to negotiate, a sign of their "weakness."[4]

Both the protagonist and the antagonist seek to "get their stories out" by limiting the public's access to alternative narratives. This is because, to paraphrase W. I. Thomas, those who define a situation, can control it. Other things being equal, state actors normally are given the benefit of the doubt by the public when its mythic accounts are compared to those generated by designated deviants. As a result, the latter are often compelled to air their messages via underground outlets: short-wave radio broadcasts, Internet blogs, Tweets, and desktop book publishing. But this too may be offered as proof of the doubtfulness of their claims. The standoffs at Ruby Ridge and Waco were either "routine confrontations gone bad" between "law-abiding officials" and "religious fanatics" (as the police contended) or they were "struggles" between the Sons of Light and the Sons of Darkness in these, the Last Days (according to the antagonists in question). It all depended on which information sources the audience consulted.

Embedment

As we saw in Chapter 5, "embedment" refers to the implanting of demeaning labels and slanderous myths in the hearts and minds of the upcoming generation. This can occur in the course of dinner table discussions with mom and dad, through Sunday school preaching, classroom lessons, professional punditry, and/or through afterschool gossip between peer-group friends. For the most part, children are not present when pejorative tags are coined; they almost never witness the labors undertaken by political ideologues as they concoct their genealogies and atrocity tales: editorialists, TV producers, theologians, and social scientists. Thus, they don't receive them as mature adults might, as socially contrived. Rather, they give themselves to youthful consciousness as what "everyone always already knows to be true" about *Them*. In this way, they become virtually unassailable components of the child's stock of knowledge.[5] The technical term for the end result of this process is "political socialization."

Riddance

The proper treatment for social malignancy of any sort involves some combination of political *medicamenta*: the burning, poisoning, and/or the surgical excision of the evil-doer (Duncan 1962). Often this is done in the course of what Emile Durkheim and Joseph Ward Swain (1969) call "piacular rites" (after the Latin *piaculum* = sin offering). These in turn can take the form of intricate, solemn ceremonials or as rampaging lynch mobs. In either case, they entail the unconscious projection or negative transference of an in-group's own ills and shared anxieties onto an out-person or an out-group. To repeat an observation made earlier, the enduringness of piacular rites through time and across cultures demonstrates that human beings rarely learn the most important truths—namely, about their cultural *thema*—that is, their shared values and collective identity—without the shedding of blood by an *ana-thema*. And the bloodier their riddance, the more gleeful are those who witness it; the harder its executors must labor to overcome their own doubts, fears, and revulsion; and as a result, the more heroically they are viewed.

A Grand and Terrible Ball

What follows are sociological reconstructions of three episodes of *dansee macabre* from recent American history, using the four-step model just depicted. From a distance, each episode appears as a sui generis, an event unique unto itself. Close-up, however, it becomes clear that each is inextricably bound up with the others; each providing impetus for the next, culminating in what was (until September 11, 2001 [i.e., 9/11]) the deadliest domestic terrorist attack in American history: the destruction of the Murrah federal building in Oklahoma City. Our reconstructions are based mainly on secondary accounts by relatively neutral commentators. These are enriched by a variety of primary documents composed by the participants, whose biases are more transparent: newspaper letter snippets, ideologically driven pamphlets, courtroom testimony, novels, official government pronouncements, Bible quotations, and partisan book-length treatises. To avoid losing ourselves in polemics, for the most part we cite these sources without questioning their accuracy. Rather, they are presented here as expressions of the mindsets of their respective authors.

One: Ruby Ridge, Idaho, August 21–22, 1992. In a failed attempt to arrest a purported neo-Nazi, the suspect's 14-year-old son and his wife, plus a US Marshal, are all shot to death near the suspect's wilderness cabin; the boy's best friend is critically injured.

Two: Waco, Texas, April 19, 1993. Seventy-six Branch Davidians, including 23 children, fearful of ending up like the victims at Ruby Ridge, are immolated in their tar-paper and plywood church barracks, known as Mt. Carmel. This, after FBI tanks try to insert CS gas through its walls following a shootout that had occurred seven weeks earlier between the reputed "cultists" and a regiment of Alcohol Tobacco and Fire Arms (ATF) officers. In full combat gear, they ride to Mt. Carmel in a convoy of 80 military vehicles and 3 National Guard helicopters. The original shootout resulted in at least 10 deaths, 4 of them federal agents, with many more injured.

Three: On the same date as the Waco incident, two years later, in a fiendish memorial to its victims and to those at Ruby Ridge, a gigantic fertilizer bomb shears the front wall off the Oklahoma City Federal Building, killing 19 children and scores of mostly female clerks. The per-terrorist murder rate of 128 is comparable to that of the attack on the Twin Towers in New York City on 9/11.

Apocalypse at Mt. Carmel

The portrait of David Koresh and the Davidians by the *Waco Tribune-Herald* in a seven-part series, "Sinful Messiah" (as well as in an official Bureau of Alcohol Tobacco and Firearms [ATF] affidavit) issued just prior to the shootout, was painted with bold strokes of hyperbole and seasoned with a sprinkling of truth (BATF, n.d.)

Both profiles were based on accounts provided to government officials by a one-time rival and disaffected protégé of David Koresh. They alleged child rape and polygamy, the manufacture of automatic weapons, a "drug nexus" of methamphetamine labs and convicted dealers, "coercive mind-control" and "brain-washing," and heresy: in short, all the lurid imagery associated with the label, "cult."

Both portraits overlooked contrary reports that "no one familiar with [Koresh] ... associates him with drug use.... He [even] distrusted medicines that came in injectable [sic] and even pill form" (Reavis 1995, 126). The portraits also ignored reports that rumors of weapons violations—including one in which the Davidians are supposedly armed with a .50 caliber machine gun—were outrageously misleading. (One undercover agent confessed under oath that he never saw a prohibited weapon or any explosive devices at Mt. Carmel, which is to say, nothing to justify a search warrant. His colleagues, however, "took him for a dupe." "Nobody at the ATF wanted 'to listen to it'" (Reavis 1995, 73). The ATF refused a personal invitation from Koresh himself to search the facilities for weapons violations.

Finally, the portraits failed to mention that child-welfare officials had found the Davidian children to be healthy, well-mannered, and seemingly content. Instead, the ATF report described Koresh as the illegitimate son of a single mother; that he was a stubble-bearded, jeans and jogging shoe-wearing working class transient with a stutter and a learning disability; that he was a megalomaniac and self-anointed "third Christ" (after the first two, Melchezidek and Jesus), who believed himself sent to do the Messiah's work of restoring the greatness of Israel; and, finally, a self-admitted "greatest of sinners."[6]

Added to this were claims that Mt. Carmel was populated by race-mixing couples who danced together to "mean guitar-playing" and intimations of worse. Rick Reavis believes that Koresh's self-promoting braggadocio about "winning the bedroom" (Koresh's words) was "the most radical and costliest doctrine ever preached at Mt. Carmel," scandalizing as it did the puritanical ethos of Waco's Southern Baptist community, where dancing at the time was still frowned upon and race-mixing, an anathema.

The newspaper series and ATF report both granted that all the families at Mt. Carmel had private apartments. But they went on to add that the apartments had no closets or doors. Furthermore, the families were said share their meals communally, the implication being that there was little actual privacy: again, an affront to local mores.

These, then, were the core features of the canonical texts, so to say, that informed the way by which the ATF and FBI approached the Davidians. But the Davidians had their own, equally provocative, texts by which they understood the world: most notably, the Book of Revelation. This had earlier been given warrant by the Seventh-Day Adventist Church of which the Davidians considered themselves an un-corrupted "branch."[7] The storyline of Revelation is that seven wax seals from an arcane manuscript are opened by a "Lamb," each seal illuminating a particular mystery about the Last Days: the Rapture, Tribulations, the Beast, the Whore of Babylon, the Battle of Armageddon, the Judgment of the Living, and so on. The calling of SDA Church authorities—whom David Koresh considered himself to be—is to decipher the hidden meanings of these mysteries in light of contemporary events. This enables them to date, and prepare for, the Second Coming of Christ. To the Davidians, for example, the "Beast" signifies the "Great Satan," the United States government, in particular its purportedly non-constitutional statutes and agencies, such as the Federal Reserve System, the Bureau of Land Management, and the Internal Revenue Service; the Beast's so-called whore is Roman Catholicism and other unenlightened faiths; and the Lamb "wounded for our transgressions ... [and] bruised for our iniquities ... is none other than the 'third Christ' himself, David Koresh."

Koresh predicted that ordinary people, blinded as they are by the "Deceiver," would be unable to grasp his messianic stature. They would diagnose him as suffering a persecutory complex and would go on to "despise and reject" him. Nevertheless, he promised that he would "not fail nor be discouraged," till He "have set judgment in the earth" (quoting Isaiah 42: 4). Unlike orthodox Christians who picture Jesus as meekly turning the other cheek, in other words, Koresh saw Jesus as a muscular warrior. "He that hath no sword," Koresh quoted Jesus as saying (Luke 22–26), "let him sell his garment, and buy one." "For, behold," he went on (from Isaiah 66: 15–16), "the Lord will come with fire, and with his chariots like a whirlwind, to render his anger with fury, and his rebuke with flames of fire. For by fire and by his sword will the Lord plead with all flesh: the slain of the Lord shall be many" (quoted in Reavis 1995, 100–101). Koresh was especially intrigued by the minor prophet, Nahum, who preaches about the necessity of bloodthirsty vengeance and plunder. And he interpreted Nahum's talk of "chariots ... with flaming torches" (Nahum 2: 3–4) as a metaphor of federal government armored vehicles.

Several of Koresh's followers anticipated being "Raptured" bodily into Heaven, prior to the prophesied confrontation with the government, and they expressed disappointment when this failed to occur. Others at Mt. Carmel predicted that they would be duly arrested and only *then* be delivered into freedom by the Lord. Still others hoped that "we would all get killed" and see their reward in heaven (Reavis 1995, 185). This is to say that far from being frightened of imminent imprisonment and death, they ostensibly looked forward to it. Courtroom testimony by one survivor revealed that after promising to surrender peacefully, the Davidians planned to file out of their barracks and fire on the arresting officers, drawing fire, and then being killed themselves. "The plan involved taking as many of 'the beast' with us as we could" (Reavis 1995, 216).

This, then, was this mindset that the Davidians assumed when they pondered the prophesied encounter with the US government. And it was the disposition of the state to accommodate them. In anticipation, the Davidians cut holes into the barracks' walls to provide themselves clear lines of fire. Then they "waited around" for the End Times to commence, "looking forward to their role" in it. One witness confessed that when agents began disgorging from their trucks, "fear was not the Davidians' foremost thought ... we believed prophecy was being fulfilled ... That thought can be quite elating. To see ... [the] fulfillment of God's words ... was very exciting" (Reavis 1995, 185).

After the shootout, the so-called FBI "fighters" (as opposed to the much-maligned "talkers" in FBI lore) became increasingly frustrated with the slow pace of negotiations. "And then what's next?" they began sarcastically asking each other, "He's [Koresh's] going to write his memoirs?" (Reavis 1995, 257). At first, the FBI promised the public that "we're prepared to do whatever it takes to stay here as long as it takes to settle this matter without any further bloodshed" (Reavis 1995, 258). But when Koresh failed to deliver on his promise to come out peacefully with the children after Passover, this was the proverbial straw that broke the camel's back. At that point, the head of the FBI ordered the tanks carrying CS gas to be deployed.

"War Is Upon the Land. The Tyrants Blood Will Flow"

Even before the shootout at Mt. Carmel, the Davidians had become increasingly paranoid. There were fly-overs by black government helicopters, discoveries of telephone pole surveillance cameras on the property; and supposed "Bible students" were discovered to be undercover investigators or state welfare authorities. Above all, there was a sense of distrust arising from the Ruby Ridge incident that had occurred less than a year earlier. "Well, I do remember ... the Weaver story," said one spokesman, "and ... you know, it definitely unsettles a person" (Docherty 2001, 201).

That Randall Weaver, his wife, and children showed up in Idaho in 1983 was not by accident (see also Chapter 4, under the subsection, titled "Conditions"). In right-wing newspapers throughout the country, Idaho at the time was being advertised as a haven for victims of the declining Midwestern farm economy, who saw in their plight one more sign of the Last Days. Having received a heavy dose of apocalypticism from Hal Lindsey's wildly popular *Late Great Planet Earth* (1970), a handful of them sought escape from the coming Tribulations in the northern Rockies.

It is important to acknowledge that the Weavers were far from being Seventh-Day Adventists (or Branch Davidians). SDAs are in sympathetic identity with Judaism, honor the Jewish (Saturday) sabbath, and celebrate all the major festivals in the Jewish lunar calendar. Furthermore, the SDA (and Davidian) diets are modeled after the Jewish Torah, which discourages the consumption of sugar candy, pork, white flour, milk, alcohol, and caffeinated drinks. The Weavers, by contrast, were Identity Christians and they despised Judaism and everything it supposedly represents, especially what the Weavers considered its "fraudulent" claim that Jews are the Lord's Chosen People. The Weavers, supposing they were the "white sons of Isaac" or the Saxons, viewed *themselves* as the true inheritors of the biblical promise made by God to rule earth; their Judeophobia was evident in their preoccupation with "ZOG" (Zionist Occupation Government), a fictional entity supposedly hatched from a "cons-piracy" of "International Jewish bankers" headquartered in "Jew York City," together with "Jews media" magnates and "Kosher Valley" movie moguls.

As it happened, at the very moment that the Weavers were disembarking to the Rockies, northern Idaho was attracting a virulent strain of Identity Christians. Just down the highway south from Ruby Ridge, where the Weavers would erect their forest refuge, the *Brüders Schweigen* (Secret Brotherhood) was conducting live-fire paramilitary exercises, using "runnin' nigger" targets for practice, and readying themselves to firebomb porno shops and synagogues. Within weeks of its founding the *Brüders Schweigen* was already boasting about "liberating" other people's money from banks and using it as their own (Flynn & Gerhardt 1989). With allowances for exaggeration, the Justice Department judged the Secret Brotherhood, "without a doubt the best organized and most serious terrorist threat that this country has ever seen" (Bock 1995, 56). Following the prosecution of the Secret Brotherhood, as recounted in Chapter 1, police attention began to focus squarely on Idaho, and on families like the Weavers.

We need not reiterate the slanders and myth-making efforts undertaken by the government to understand what the Weavers were about, except to mention that by smearing them with the moniker "Nazi," it was stigmatizing them with one of the two most incendiary titles in modern American culture (the other, being "Communist"). To be sure, the Weavers were occasionally seen at Aryan Nations Church gatherings, where I met them. But evidently, they never joined the Church itself. And, yes, like the Davidians, they renounced the IRS, the Forest Service, the Bureau of Land Management, and the like, but at least in my presence they disclaimed any accusation of being race supremacists.

In any case, believing Randall Weaver to be a neo-Nazi, the ATF entrapped him on a misdemeanor weapons violation. It then offered to suspend the charges if he agreed to spy on members of the Aryan Nations Church. Being in his view an honorable person, Weaver refused, telling himself that the government was acting just as the Bible said it would. The family then penned a letter to the Church warning them of the situation. Predictably, the ATF reacted by threatening the family with the confiscation of their plywood cabin. Still Randall refused; in the end, he was formally charged, and a date set for a court hearing.

Somehow the published court-ordered date was in error—conspiracy theorists believe, purposively. As a result, Randall missed the hearing and was declared a fugitive; the US Marshals Service was charged with his arrest. Weaver's wife, Vickie, angrily responded to the news by threatening the head of the Marshals Service. "You are on the side of the One World Beastly Government," she wrote. "Whether we live or ... die we will not obey your lawless government" (Bock 1995, 49). The government's response to Vickie's words was to commence a "threat assessment" of what they were now facing. In the course of this, suspicions were raised about the Weavers cultivating marijuana; that their cabin was supposedly equipped with an "arsenal" of "heavy-caliber guns on tripods"; that Randall himself had once threatened the President; that he would "shoot on sight" anyone who tried to seize him; that he had planted explosives in the nearby woods; and that his children were "hostages," "brainwashed" into "anti-ZOG robots" to obey orders "on command." While each of these assertions had questionable veracity and at worst were complete fabrications, the Marshals Service treated them as true. As a result, the situation on Ruby Ridge was formally classified as a "major case." This permitted them to install electronic listening devices and solar-powered motion-activated cameras in the surrounding forest and to periodically surveil the family by means of helicopter fly-overs.

For 18 months the government sought to enlist intermediaries to persuade Randall to surrender. When these efforts failed, it deployed foot patrols to stake out the Weaver cabin. On an otherwise routine reconnaissance mission, a combat-ready elite team surprised Randall's son, his son's best friend, and *his* dog as they were hunting. The dog was fired upon and killed; the son returned fire and received a bullet to the arm. While fleeing from the scene, crying in pain, one of the marshals shot him in the back; he died on the spot. The son's friend fired back and killed the marshal, who was later revealed to be the most decorated officer in the history of the service.

Enraged at what had befallen one of its own, the government deployed sniper teams to "neutralize" the Weavers. The following day, Randall himself was wounded. Bleeding, he ran back to the cabin. And as he stumbled through the cabin door, held open by Vickie who was also holding her baby, she was inadvertently shot in the head. Fragments from her skull struck her son's best friend in the chest, critically injuring him.

The Last Dance

Mt. Carmel and Ruby Ridge confirmed what many right-wing tacticians had already concluded following the fiery shootout with the *Brüders Schweigen* a decade earlier on Puget Sound, Washington (see Chapter 1), and the surrender of the Covenant, Sword, and Arm of the Lord sect to federal agents in Arkansas earlier that same year.[8] It is that bluff and swagger, camouflage outfits, black-face, and semi-automatic rifles are not sufficient for a group of aggrieved citizens to withstand the armed might of the United States, especially if that group allows itself to be surrounded in its bunker. Thus, as has happened countless times in the past, here and elsewhere, the thinking of the rebels turned to guerrilla war, "little war," using mobile units, unknown to each other, acting independently from a central command, sharing little more than a general hostility toward the state, taking matters into their own hands (Beam 1992).

The Turner Diaries (Pierce 1978), the so-called Bible of the extremist right, recommends doing exactly this; it became a best seller on the gun show circuit following the Mt. Carmel incident. It became so pivotal to Timothy McVeigh, the eventual bomber of the Murrah federal building, that he slept with a copy of it under his pillow. He also memorized some of its pithier adages and marketed it at discount prices to his fellow malcontents. One of the novel's chapters details the obliteration of FBI headquarters in Washington, DC, by a guerilla unit. They pack fertilizer and diesel oil into the backend of a panel truck, drive it into the basement parking lot, and detonate it.

While there were notable theological differences between the Davidians and the Weavers, as mentioned above, both honed their anti-government bona fides through Bible study. This is a far cry from the crowd around McVeigh. First of all, while the Davidians (perhaps) and the Weavers (for sure) abstained from illegal drug use, several of McVeigh's followers were self-admitted crystal meth users, an "elixir" known to enhance paranoia and to occasion outbursts of rage. Second, McVeigh's followers were only episodically employed, and mostly unmarried. Third, McVeigh's ultimate concern, at least according to Mark Hamm (1997), wasn't God. It was guns. And his bedtime reading consisted of articles in *Shotgun News*, *Guns and Ammo*, and *Soldier of Fortune* magazines. Evidently, the highpoint of his life had been the few hours he served as a gunner on a Bradley Fighting Vehicle during the first Gulf War (1991), after which he was decorated for killing Iraqi troops. Following the intoxicating rush of battle, he suffered from bouts of "postwar hangover" and became increasingly depressed, withdrawn, and even more obsessed with guns (Hamm 1997, 150–51). In short, unlike the Davidians and the Weavers, who appear to have accidently stumbled into violence as a consequence of their faiths, McVeigh offers a counterexample of a person predisposed to violence, and looking for a justifiable way to express it. This, he found in the vituperative right-wing radio broadcasts of the day and in the scurrilous racist propaganda issued after the tragedies at Ruby Ridge and Mt. Carmel.

The conflagration at Mt. Carmel shattered McVeigh. He had worked for a short time with the chief patron and financier of the Davidians; he was witnessed several times in Waco during the siege. When he saw its barracks crumble in flames on TV, "he screamed in horror. Then he began to cry" (Hamm 1997, 165). So much for the legend that he had no feelings. Later, on his fake driver's license he inscribed "April 19," the day of the Mt. Carmel fire, as the date of his "birth," that is, the day of his awakening.[9]

After Mt. Carmel, the BATF (the Bureau of Alcohol Tobacco and Firearms) was rechristened by the far-right as "Burn all toddlers first!" In other words, it became an object of scorn. And as fate would have it, its Midwest regional offices were situated on the ninth floor of the Murrah federal building in Oklahoma City. This meant that in order to reach it, McVeigh first had to go through the day-care center, America's Kids, stationed on the second floor. Of course, the children were oblivious of what was about to befall them that bright Spring morning as they snacked on crackers and juice. But rites of riddance are often accompanied by "collateral damage," as it is called in military euphemism, the deaths of noncombatants. And after all, McVeigh already had stenciled on his sweatshirt the incendiary phrase: "The tree of liberty must be refreshed from time to time by the blood of tyrants and patriots."

Truth and Reconciliation

Readers may be wondering how encounters like those just described can be averted? Is there no way to break through the logic of mutually escalated loathing? Or is it the fate of human beings to go 'round and 'round in *dansee macabre* to the bitter end? As a way to think ourselves out of this conundrum, ponder for a moment The TRC that conducted several tribunals in post-apartheid South Africa, about the same time that the tragedies at Ruby Ridge, Mt. Carmel, and Oklahoma City were unfolding (Villa-Vincencio & Doxtader 2003).

Before beginning, however, some clarifications are in order. First of all, as hideous as the events just described were, they hardly measure up to what was inflicted on the "Bantu" (Black) population of South Africa during apartheid. Second, I don't want to be misunderstood as suggesting that in armed encounters between state actors and private militias, there is an equivalency of power resources or of moral culpability for what ensues. A state, after all, is an institution that monopolizes the means of legitimate coercion within a society. Thus, as a matter of practical justice (where 'justice' implies a kind of balance), the state will almost always have a greater burden of responsibility to defuse inflammatory situations. Third, it is clear from the handful of encounters between the government and right-wing extremists that have taken place since Oklahoma City, such as at the Bundy Ranch outside Bunkerville, Nevada (2014), at Justus Township, Montana (1996), and at the Malheur National Wildlife Refuge in eastern Oregon (2016), state officials have shown they can handle armed insurgencies firmly, largely non-violently, yet effectively. (Although the participants in these three stand-offs numbered in the hundreds, if not thousands, collectively they resulted in only a single fatality, that near the Malheur Refuge: a likely suicide-by-police, after the victim's car attempted to evade a road-block and nearly ran over several Oregon state patrolmen.) With these caveats in mind, let turn now to the TRC.

When South African government officials and White citizens were given opportunities to confess in public to the misdeeds they had committed against the Black population in exchange for amnesty, and their victims were permitted to recount what they had endured at their hands, something odd and seemingly unpredictable occurred. While critics at the time framed the tribunals as enterprises in liberal naïveté and expressed fears that they would only inflame an already volatile situation, in fact, they had the opposite effect: They helped mollify antagonisms that had been simmering between the White and Black communities of South Africa for decades; rates of retribution between the two declined precipitously. This, despite the fact that most of the seven thousand individuals who petitioned to confess their misdeeds were denied the opportunity to do so, due to their considered unreliability or because they appeared insufficiently remorseful.

The TRC proceedings demonstrate how confessions (and pardons) can disrupt hostile communications: that is, *dansee macabre* in which each opponent is initially convinced of the exclusive truth of their own partisan view of reality, and where the self-identities of each participant contradict what others believe them to be. They accomplish these effects in four ways: First, they weaken the adhesive on the labels that each party has heretofore bestowed on the other, disclosing the reality of their contrived, fictional nature. Second, they enable each party to understand that they are not simply victims of the encounters in question. Rather, the hearts and minds of *all* the participants harbor hateful, murderous intent. Third, by casting doubt on the basic theme of the prototypical atrocity tale—that I (we) am wholly innocent; you (them) are evil—they interrupt the embedment of those labels and tales in the psyches of children. Fourth, by being forced to acknowledge, swallow, and then digest what previously they had transferred (or projected) onto a convenient them, the "dance" partners come to realize the futility of escaping from their own duplicity, brutality, and greed. In other words, by undermining each of the steps in the *danse macabre*, space is created for the possibility of reconciliation.

Archbishop Desmond Tutu (d. 2021), who attended several of the tribunals, says that they provide an alternative way to rectify a major injustice. Instead of having the state, standing in for the victim, inflict an equal degree of pain on the persecutor—call this, justice through retribution or pay-back—the tribunal restores moral balance by having *victim* grant their persecutor(s) a pardon, a "gift" (from Fr. *pardonne* = gift). In this way, the victims are momentarily transformed into the morally superior party; and by accepting their pardon, the persecutor is humbled. When this occurs, "there seems to be something spiritual, even sacramental [that occurs]," Tutu continues, "a sign that moves and touches those who are [its] witnesses" (Gobodo-Madikizela 2003, 95). But make no mistake: in the tribunal, pardons are granted *only after* the persecutor has freely confessed *in detail* to the wrongs they have committed, and only after they have *heard* the recitations of what their victims have suffered. By humbly accepting the gift (the pardon), the evil of what they have done is not forgotten, but reconfirmed.

Because Tutu himself uses the word "sacramental" to describe the effect of the tribunal, we are reminded of the similarity between it and, say, rituals like the Roman Catholic sacrament of Penance (or as it is popularly known, oracular private Confession). The difference, of course, is that in Penance, it is supposedly God—acting through the person of an ordained priest—who absolves the penitent. In the reconciliation tribunal, the gift of a pardon is conferred by a wounded human being. But regardless of this, what transpires is not merely a transactional this-for-that. Rather, it is a granting of something *more* to the persecutor than what the injured party has suffered: a merciful, gratuitous offering whose value can never be repaid.

Both Penance and the TRC hearings enact at a public level what can often be seen in face-to-face encounters, when one partner's trust has been betrayed, say, by adultery (Tavuchis 1991). At first, the victim may demand that the betrayer "account for" or give good reasons (or a good story), for their misdeed. What may then follow is a litany of excuses (I didn't really do it, i.e., the cause resides outside, *ex-*, myself) and/or justifications (No real harm was done anyway, or What was done was right). In the event that the betrayed party rejects this litany, then assuming the betrayer desires to maintain the relationship, he or she is encouraged to honestly acknowledge the harm they have done, and of their responsibility for it: in short, an apology. The final step in this informal rite is the conferral by the betrayed of forgiveness, followed by a humiliating acceptance of forgiveness by the betrayer.

In closing, what is important to keep in mind are not the nuances of these and related ceremonies (cf. Reid 2000). Nor need we address how they can be exploited by perpetrators of horrible acts to evade their rightful due or used to inflict even more pain on their victims. (Or for that matter, how victims can psychologically torture their persecutors by withholding from them the gift of atonement.) Instead, it is the cognitive/emotional alterations that participants report experiencing after having undergone them (cf. Gobodo-Madikizela 2003). These include the victims sobbing in grief, *not only for themselves but for their tormentors.* It is conversions like these that make it difficult, if not necessarily impossible, to accept further invitations to a *danse macabre*.

Notes

1 Joel Best (1995) offers an accessible anthology of case studies that illustrate these steps.
2 Here, by "protagonist," I am referring to any person or group that sees or experiences themselves as the "good-guy(s)," or as peace-loving, intelligent, and sane devotees of truth. The "antagonist," by contrast, is any person or group identified as "bad." The implication of these designations is that *any* individual or group, say the police, may be an antagonist from the point of view of a perpetrator, but a protagonist from the standpoint of the general public; or vice versa.
3 In ethnomethodology (the study of the "methods" that group's use to construct and secure their realities), this is known as the "principle of reflexivity" (Mehan & Wood 1973).
4 Ethnomethodology titles this the principle of "indexicality."
5 Ethnomethodology refers to this as the "rule of economy," the resistance of any grand narrative to self-correction.
6 'Koresh' is the Hebrew name of the Persian emperor Cyrus, who is said to have freed the Jews from exile from 535 to 515 BCE.
7 The Seventh-Day Adventist Church promulgates a brand of Christianity that can be highly problematic for orthodox Christians, including Southern Baptists. For example, it permits females to serve as clergy. In fact, the founder of the SDA was a prophetess, Ellen White (d. 1925). The Davidians in turn are rumored to worship both male and female deities. (In 1978, a woman named Sister Roden had a vision of the Holy Spirit as female.) And Davidians believe that males, not females, are the cause of mankind's Fall.
8 Ironically, the lessons learned from the peaceful surrender of the CSA were used as guidance by the ATF when it planned its raid at Mt. Carmel.
9 The date, "April 19," enjoys mythical stature in the world of the American far-right. April 19, 1995, was the day of the CSA siege, mentioned earlier. On April 19, 1992, Operation Northern Exposure, the stakeout of the Weaver cabin, commenced; and it was that day in 1775 when Lexington was burned to the ground by the British. April 19 is also known as the "Day of the Rope" in *The Turner Diaries*, when Jews are hung in public, as well as the day when Richard Snell, a CSA terrorist, was executed for murdering a state patrolman and a store clerk he mistook as a Jew. Snell is alleged to have recommended to McVeigh that he bomb the Murrah federal building.

Interlude 2 God and Guns

On June 23, 2022, one day before the announcement of *Dobbs v. Jackson Health Center* (see Interlude 1), the Supreme Court of the United States (SCOTUS) issued a decision striking down a century-old New York State gun control law (that had since been implemented in a number of neighboring states). The old gun control law limited licenses to carry firearms outside one's home to target shooters, hunters, and/or to those who have jobs that require them to carry cash. It is not yet certain whether the 2022 SCOTUS ruling will now permit firearms in public schools, at sporting events and at rock concerts, in places where alcohol is served, at polling locations, in legislative bodies, in courthouses, or on airplanes. Whatever the case, to deter potential court challenges to its now null and void gun control law for being discriminatory, New York State had previously required that gun licensees pass "objective criteria" before being allowed to open-carry weapons. This included being fingerprinted, submitting to a background check and a mental health clearance, and undertaking training in firearm safety.

Much like the Dobbs decision on abortion, the SCOTUS gun ruling is anticipated to shake up gun control laws across the country. In this case, however, the ostensible aim of the Court is not to enhance the safety of unborn children, but quite the opposite: to affirm the right that many adult American men already claim, to openly carry guns in public, as a God-given and "natural" right. This, of course, comes at the price of potentially imperiling those same unborn children, their parents, and others. For as SCOTUS says, the constitutional right to open-carry is not and should not be limited to people with demonstrable "special needs," such as messengers. There is no little irony in the fact that the Supreme Court's gun ruling was announced just one month after an 18-year-old White man, motivated by racial hatred, murdered 10 Black shoppers at a Tops Friendly grocery story in Buffalo, New York, while armed with a military-style semi-automatic rifle.

In an angry dissent, the Governor of New York, Kathy Hochul, who had been raised in Buffalo, said that SCOTUS's latest gun ruling is "not just reckless"; "it is irresponsible." It is another sign, she went on, of the "insanity" of the gun culture that permeates American life. Other critics went even further, arguing that the ruling demonstrates the fallacious logic that underlies the Court's "hyper-originalism." That is, its attempt to derive contemporary legal conclusions on the basis of a fatuous analogy (or similarity) between contemporary circumstances and those of a distant, some say imaginary, past. By using this kind of reasoning, critics contend, a variety of other gun laws have now become subject to Court review and possible rejection as unconstitutional. Among them are "red flag" laws that allow guns to be confiscated from certifiably dangerous individuals, laws that restrict the marketing of high-capacity cartridge magazines to the public, laws that ban the sale of military-style firearms to private citizens, or laws that deal specifically with domestic violence.

Several of the justices defend themselves from the charge of hyperoriginalism by claiming, without citing empirical evidence, that in today's America, it is already the wild west, and that men, as always, have had a right to protect themselves and their loved ones from harm by having access to firearms. Evidently, the justices have given little thought to the role that their *own* rulings have played in promoting a wild west-like world. More importantly, if SCOTUS continues to rule in favor of religious liberty on the ground that it is a "disfavored right" in the minds of most Americans (as they have done previously in decisions involving religious discrimination against minorities, and with the right to abortion), then it is surely on the way to de-legitimizing itself, opening the door to public ridicule, and possibly worse.

7 The Case of the Minor Family[1]

As we shall see in the next chapter, high levels of personal authoritarianism are positively correlated with various measures of bigotry, xenophobia, and racism. But even high authoritarianism scores are insufficient to turn one into a practicing extremist. In part, this is because many authoritarians are self-isolating and hence among the last and least likely to join *any* kind of movement. Thanks to field research on contemporary far-rightists, we also know that authoritarianism may not be causally necessary either. In fact, many of today's right-wing extremists were probably not true believers at first. Rather, they appear to have become so only after their initial efforts at dressing and posturing the part, espousing the movement's "truths," and clumsily performing its casual cruelties; won them Facebook "likes," political votes, back-slaps, money, or promises of romance (Blee 2002). At the outset, however, they were likely closer to opportunists.

This chapter illustrates these and related observations by examining the case of an outwardly average Idaho family, one of whose members became deeply involved with the Church of Jesus Christ Christian-Aryan Nations and later renounced it. The story begins with Lisa.

Getting into Hate

Lisa Charles-Minor (an alias), now in her sixties, is the youngest child of Jim and Mary Charles (also aliases), a Roman Catholic family from a northern Idaho logging town named after the river that meanders through it, located near Ruby Ridge (see Chapter 6). Lisa has two older sisters, Sheila and Alice (both aliases). When I first met Alice, she described Lisa to me as "attractive, popular, 5 foot 2, dark, long hair, very pretty smile, arched eyes, well-built, no need to stuff her bra." Her senior yearbook sums up her high school career: Lisa Charles—JV and varsity basketball; cheerleader 1, 2, 3, 4; homecoming queen; queen of hearts; carnival princess; class president, class representative; pep club; drill team; pep band; regular band; student body secretary; chorus; journalism staff; yearbook staff. In short, Lisa was an all-American girl.

By the time the three sisters were adolescents their mother, Mary had long since resigned herself to a life of tedium and helplessness and was unable, or at least unwilling, to encourage them or to offer them much guidance regarding how to negotiate the world outside their small town. Mary's husband, Jim, the sisters' father, was a lower level Forest Service official, whom Alice characterizes as "distant and passive-aggressive." "He took the silent route," says Alice, and spent his off-hours alone in the nearby woods, fishing and hunting. In other words, all three girls were compelled by circumstances to forge destinies largely independent of their parents. Alice somehow ended up going to college hundreds of miles away in Pocatello, Idaho; for her part, Lisa climbed on the social track, took pride in her appearance, wore make-up, and assiduously avoided drinking and drugs. But at eighteen she traveled to Moscow, Idaho, to study physical therapy at the state's land-grant university, joined a sorority, and "got into guys, going out a lot." Before two years passed,

DOI: 10.4324/9781003391265-10

she dropped out of college (for financial reasons) and moved to Portland, Oregon. There, according to Alice, she got involved in the local drug scene and before long had evolved into a "full-blown hippie," "eating acid by the handfuls." "Stoned most of the time," Alice continues. Lisa endured a series of dead-end relationships with local drug users. One was a bearded friend of her cousin named Craig (an alias). Craig liked to compare himself to Charles Manson, head of the notorious Los Angeles Manson family gang, which was still in operation at the time. He was heard bragging to friends about how he "controlled Lisa."

Whether Craig's hold over Lisa owed itself to an absence in her life of a positive father-figure is a question best left to psychoanalysts. But realizing that if she did not pull herself together and soon, hers would be a short, senseless, brutal life, she returned home to Idaho and began to pray for redemption. How this solution came to her is not clear, except for the fact of her Catholic background. What is known is that she was eventually "born again," joined a local evangelical church, and found employment as a clerk in its bookstore. It was there that she met Ed Minor (an alias).

For many years Ed's cause had been the Aryan Nations Church, an extreme form of Christian Dominionism that preaches the doctrine of Christian Identity. Ed was introduced to Identity through friends while working as an electrical engineer at Lockheed Aircraft in Lancaster, California. Among those friends was an Identity lay-minister, later presumably ordained, named Richard Butler. Butler was a highly respected aeronautic technician, having patented the procedure for repairing flats on airplane tires without having to remove them from their rims. Furthermore, he had long been associated with various "fascist" groups such as the Silver Shirt Legion and, after World War II, with the right-wing militia known as the US Rangers. When Ed met Butler, Butler was attending services at an Aryan Nations church in Hollywood, California, then overseen by a preacher named Rev. Wesley Swift, a one-time Methodist minister and Ku Klux Klan Kleagle, or organizer.

According to a disaffected few in the congregation, after Swift died, Butler "stole" the Church's mailing lists and Swift's taped sermons, and somehow "finagled" his way into the pulpit. Before long he found himself (self-appointed?) as its national leader. And when Butler moved the church's headquarters to Hayden Lake, in northern Idaho in the late 1970s, a contingent of the Hollywood congregation went with him, settling in the surrounding pine woods.

Speculation still persists about what might have induced Butler and his followers to migrate hundreds of miles from Los Angeles to a region known for its lingering dampness and frigid winters. Some say it was its striking beauty. Others contend that it was the fact that local property taxes at the time were comparatively low. Still others, that Idaho's gun laws were (and still are) extra-ordinarily lax. But perhaps the most straight-forward answer is that area around Spokane, Washington, and Coeur D'Alene, Idaho, have been a haven for far-right fanatics for decades, possibly traceable to the presence there of Confederate states loyalists who arrived after the Civil War to work in the nearby silver mines.

We will never know for certain whether Butler personally encouraged Ed Minor to join the Aryan Nations Church, but it could hardly have been his turgid sermons, which fail to measure up to Rev. Swift's blistering oratory. But whatever the reason, Ed was among those who traveled with Butler's caravan on their way to the Gem State. When he arrived near the shores of Hayden Lake, a new Aryan Nations chapel and outbuildings were already being erected; Ed volunteered to install the utilities.

Ed Minor is about a decade older than Lisa, comparatively well-educated and sure of himself. In other words, he was the kind of man, stable and Christian, that Lisa had been looking for when, as was his practice, he made a recruitment visit to her bookstore. They soon began dating. However, almost immediately, a problem arose. Having been raised Catholic, Lisa had learned as a child that ancient Israel was a Jewish nation (not: Aryan or Caucasian), and that Jesus himself had been a Jew. But this conflicted with what Ed was now telling her. How could they ever find common ground? Perhaps never, Lisa feared.

Nevertheless, bit by bit, with Ed's help, Lisa began to adopt Ed's Christian Identity dogma for herself—including what must have been intriguing to an unmoored young woman from a tiny, isolated logging town, the consolation of a new, more noble, way to understand her place in the world. For she learned from Ed that after Israel escaped from exile in northern Persia (i.e., Iran) during the 6th and 7th centuries BCE, they fled over the Caucasus Mountains, hence, their presumed racial type: Caucasian.

Ed went on to tell Lisa that after crossing the Caucasus Mountains, the tribes of ancient Israel migrated further north and settled in what today are various European countries, several of which allegedly bear the names of their tribal associations, or the titles of singular events in Israelite history. For instance, Ed related that the ancient Hebrew words *b'rith* (covenant) and *ish* (man) are the roots of the modern term "British," which therefore supposedly means "men of the covenant" (for more on this mythical connection, see Chapter 1). Or again, Ed went on, "Iberia," the name of the peninsula on which Spain and Portugal are located, is a short-hand version of the term "Hebrew"; and that the Iberian seaport of Cadiz was the place where the Israelite tribe of Gad allegedly settled. He also taught Lisa that the tribespeople of ancient Judah were the reputed ancestors of the German Jutes, as well as the source of the name given to *their* first European homeland, "Jutland." Finally, Ed claimed, the name of the biblical tribe of Dan is the supposed etymological root of countless European place-names, such as Don, Danube, Dnieper, Dniepro, Donetsk, Donbas, and Danzig, as well as *Dan*mark, Mace*don*ia, and Scan*din*avia (for these and related Identity legends, see Haberman 1932). All of this meant that Lisa could trace her personal lineage back to ancient Israel.

Lisa and Ed spent hours together pouring over the Bible, Lisa struggling against what she later described as her "prideful resistance" to the Identity message. During one late-night session, however, she suddenly saw the light. She remembered that she had once heard in Sunday school that Jews were "Christ killers." Now, as an adult, she began to question how the Jews could *really* be God's chosen people if they hate Christ? Happily, Ed had the answer: The Jews, he told her, are not really the chosen people at all, but imposters. In fact, according to Ed, they are not even Semites (i.e., descendants of the patriarch Shem), but offspring of Cain, mankind's first murderer who, after being exiled "east of Eden" by God, mated with the witch women of Nod, producing the forerunners of the Canaanites. Those who truly deserve the title "chosen," Ed told Lisa, are Aryan White people like herself. And the Bible was written for them.

In the end, Lisa and Ed were married in the newly built Aryan Nations chapel, flags from various Aryan nations blowing in the wind, with Rev. Butler officiating. Before 13 years passed, they produced seven children; when I was conducting this research, the oldest was already a teen.

The children attended public schools haphazardly, at best. This is because Ed and Lisa believed that public schools teach the satanic pedagogy of "secular humanism." Nor were they financially able to send their kids to a private church academy, given Ed's irregular employment and the family's status on welfare rolls. Nor, evidently, were they formally taught much at home. As a result, all seven kids (who are now grown-ups) are only marginally literate. Nonetheless, each of them can expound on who is at fault for the world's ills: It's "Them," the Jews.

Let us pause for a moment to reflect on what the story of Lisa and Ed tells us about how people can get into hate groups. The most popular explanation, mentioned several times in earlier chapters, is that they must have been "SIC": stupid, isolated from the ordinary channels of community belonging, and/or simply crazy. But in regard to Ed and Lisa, this theory doesn't appear to hold much water. In the first place, Ed and Lisa were both at least smart enough to have attended accredited colleges, from which Ed earned a degree—and in a notably challenging field: Engineering. Second, both of them appear to have been relatively well integrated into their communities of origin: Ed in Lancaster, California, and the "all-American girl," Lisa, in her Idaho logging town. Finally, to my knowledge, there is no documented evidence that either of them was ever diagnosed as having a mental illness.

This being the case, it seems we are forced to fall back on an alternative theory of why people join hate groups. In short, it is that however people acquire hate-filled beliefs in the first place, as adults they simply seek out groups congenial with their outlooks, say, the KKK, the Christian Anti-Communism Crusade, or the Silver Shirt Legion, and so on. But once again, there seems to be a problem. For the tale of Ed and Lisa suggests that the reverse is more likely the case. Which is to say, people come to hate Blacks, Communists, Jews, and the like, only *after* they have first bonded with—met and established ties with—espousers of hate whom they respect and admire. In regard to Ed, this was Rev. Butler and the Hollywood Aryan Nations Church; for Lisa, it was her love of Ed. Once these ties were established, Lisa and Ed both commenced to alter their worldviews so as to nurture and sustain those connections, in the end coming to despise the same outgroups as those reviled by their sponsors. Furthermore, as the examples of Ed and Lisa also illustrate, social ties like these are often in large measure due to chance. In other words, they emerge from where people just happen to work, the towns in which they happen to reside, and/or the churches they happen to be affiliated with, and so on.[2] Had Ed Minor not met Richard Butler at Lockheed Aircraft, the likelihood of his ever hearing about, much less joining, the Aryan Nations Church would have been nil; had Lisa not been reborn, joined a nearby Bible church, and found employment in its bookstore, she never would have crossed paths with Ed. Her life would have assumed some other, altogether different, trajectory. As for the seven Minor children, happenstance has fated them to be born to and raised by parents who instilled in them the Identity tenet that as Saxons, Sac-sons, or sons of Isaac, they are "God's battle axe and weapons of war," which means that they were trained by mom and dad not merely to loathe specific peoples, but to act on their feelings.

This is not to say that Lisa, Ed, nor even their kids were helpless victims of external forces over which they had no control. An illustration of this last point is provided by the example of another Idahoan by the name of Tara Westover (2017), who was raised just down the freeway from the town where I raised my own children. By sheer dint of her own will, the encouragement of an older brother who had earlier graduated with a Chemistry degree from Idaho State University, Tara—home-schooled in circumstances almost identical to those of the Minor children, but in her case by renegade Mormon parents—went on to earn a Ph.D. in political theory from Oxford University in England. Of the many humiliating moments that she recounts in her autobiography is one relating to her quest to attain a formal education: In front of her classmates at the Mormon Church's Brigham Young University, she confessed that she had never before heard of the Jewish Holocaust.

Getting Out of Hate

As the years passed, Lisa became increasingly annoyed with Ed. Apart from his know-it-all sanctimoniousness, Ed discouraged Lisa from maintaining contact with her birth family, whom he considered "weird." From Ed's standpoint, this makes sense. After all, Lisa's oldest sister, Sheila, is an acupuncturist and a New Age healer. And when I met her, Alice was a liberal college student working on a Sociology degree at Idaho State U.

There were other sources of irritation as well. For example, Ed and Lisa had opened a bed and breakfast in their home, but there were few customers. Then, Ed's aging father moved in with them, and all the work fell on Lisa's shoulders. It was around this same time that Lisa and Alice began meeting, furtively at first, at a restaurant in their old home town, just up the highway from Hayden Lake. Their initial encounters consisted mostly of small talk, gossip, and reminiscences. But one afternoon, Lisa revealed to Alice that she was depressed, lacked energy, and had no desire to go on. At that point, she suddenly stood up in a huff and left. Nevertheless, Alice felt that an "invisible line" of intimacy had been broached; the ice between them had broken; other contacts would follow.

Alice told me that despite Lisa's racism and bigotry, she saw something of herself in her little sister. For she too once had been married to a religious zealot, we'll call him Bob, whom she describes as a "sex-obsessed" fundamentalist preacher; she went on to say that on their wedding night he "raped" her. Yet, following their divorce, it was *she* who was adjudged the wrongful party and who lost legal custody of the kids. In the course of their secret encounters, Alice began encouraging Lisa to see her situation with Ed as analogous to her own with Bob, namely, as "abuse," and as "unacceptable."

Like her older sister, Sheila, Alice too has long considered herself a New Ager of sorts. While taking my Sociology of Religion course she volunteered to lecture on auras and on mind-control over matter (telekinesis). Her business card reads: "Specializing in lightness, wholeness practitioner, channel for the ascended masters, ecology, technology and business consultant, readings and long distance healings, seminars." In final her final letter to me, she gushed:

> Guess what! I can channel and I mean, really, really channel others now. I've been doing it for some time, but now I've decided to do something with it. In a few years, I will be publishing my work. I'll be on the radio in California ... I've been locating places all over the world and I can do this. This guy [she was then involved with] is a very clairvoyant person and we sit around channeling information about companies and stream problems and how to solve them ... He and I are on the same wave length. I can do this. He can do this. He wants to make money. I want to make money. He channels. I channel. This is it! I am going to be channeling how to solve all the world's environmental problems on this planet.[3]

This is the outlook that Alice began bringing to the table in the course of her café-rendezvous with Lisa. She gave Lisa New Age literature, read Lisa's aura, and even conducted a "chakra analysis" on her spine. She aided Lisa in "guided memory recovery"—to help her overcome her depression and fatigue. Then, Alice reports, "it" happened. "Lisa's world is beginning to crack for her." Or to say it sociologically, Lisa began to reconfigure her life story in terms of the new vocabulary that Alice was providing her.

During one afternoon encounter with Alice, Lisa recalled a pivotal event that occurred when she was 18 years old, the evening of her high school graduation. She remembered going on a date and returning home "totally changed." As she described it to Alice, there had been an "entity." It came to her and requested that she relinquish control over her existence. Lisa went on to say that she allowed the entity to "implant instruments" in her body: one in her pelvic area, a second one in her neck. Later, she altered her story to say that the devices were actually implanted in her aura. Whatever the case, the entity told Lisa that "we have come to help you end your species problems."

Over the next few months, Lisa related to Alice how she had had other encounters with the so-called entity, and that she now feared that it had used her womb to carry its fetal products (a storyline that will be familiar to readers of reports of "demon sperm" and "incubi"). Her own children, she tearfully confessed, might be "cyborgs," half-human aliens.

To invoke a little psychology at this point, it seems that on the night of her graduation from high school, Lisa "dissociated": she disjoined her subjective self from her flesh and allowed her body to be used—by what or by whom, we'll never really know. But now, with the help of her *oldest* sister, Sheila, she told Alice that she was enjoying a "full recovery." Sheila's own guru, Lisa said, had consoled her with news that after removing the instruments, he found that they were already "dysfunctional."

After each visit with Alice, Lisa brought news of these happenings home to Ed; he was not pleased. What Lisa told him confirmed every suspicion he already had about the Charles family's weirdness. One evening, after Lisa returned home from a visit with Alice, Ed and Lisa angrily fought: first with words, then with fists. After this came "wrestling," during the course of which Lisa fell down the stairs. The sheriff was called and a restraining order was issued; Ed ended up in jail, charged with domestic battery. The predictable end was not long in coming: Ed and Lisa divorced after 23 years of marriage.

The important thing to note at this point is that now, without Ed in her life, Lisa had little reason to retain her affiliation with the Aryan Nations Church. At first, of course, she was reluctant to abandon the racist cosmology that up to that point had given her life so much meaning and direction. But at Alice's urging, she began to broaden her views. "There are no secrets," she now tells Alice. "No accidents, no victims." "Peace is achievable." Thus, "there is nothing to fear." Alice tells me that during the Democratic Party presidential primary election of 1988, Lisa voted to support the Black candidate, Rev. Jesse Jackson.

Conclusion

Let us reflect once again, this time on how people can gravitate out of hate groups. The prevailing theory is that they do so only after having lost faith in its tenets. Finding these either implausible or morally repugnant, they become disillusioned with the group itself. And after realizing that they share little with its members, they leave. As with the SIC-ness theory of conversion, this sounds credible. However, a closer examination of Lisa's and Ed's life stories tells us something different. It is that leave-taking or defection from a religious group is in essence a "mirror image" of conversion to it (Stark & Bainbridge 1985). Which is to say, it generally happens only *after* people become alienated from the bonds they once had with the group's members. When these relationships fracture and crumble, the individual in question loses the social structure that had earlier lent plausibility to their faith; they abandon what was, until that moment, central to their lives.

There are a number of policy implications that follow from the "mirror-image" theory of disaffection. One is that no amount of hectoring by preachers, police, parents, professors, or pundits is likely to occasion defections from hate groups. On the contrary, minds and hearts change only after personal relationships do. In fact, disparaging another's beliefs can backfire, hardening an individual's attachments to the group that espouses them, and of which they are a part. For example, in response to liberal media claims that he and his comrades were fascists, a Ku Klux Klan Kludd (or chaplain) once told me that "*We're* not the haters; we're the lovers." "We love our race." Pointing vaguely to the distant hills, he went on to say, "*They* [the "Jews-media"] are" the real haters. Hence, it wasn't he who needed to change, but them.

In the end, if we are truly serious about putting an end to hate and to the violence that sometimes sprouts from it; we first must reach out to those with whom we disagree, fear, and even detest and bind them to us. How to do this is a challenge for which I have no clear answers.[4]

Notes

1 With the exception of Revs. Richard Butler and Wesley Swift, plus Tara Westover, all the names in this chapter are fictitious. The interviews and written correspondence on which the chapter is based took place over a period of several years, beginning in the early 1990s.
2 The classic sociological analysis of the process of religious conversion is Lofland and Stark (1965, 1977). In it they describe tactics like "hooking" and "love-bombing" that were used to beguile unwitting people into joining Rev. Sun Myung Moon's Unification Church (the "Moonies"). Similar observations have since been made about the radical evangelical group known as the Children of God and its use of "flirty fishing" (i.e., sex) as a recruitment tactic (Richardson & Davis 1983); as well as recruitment to Scientology and to Satanist cults. For recruitment to far-right groups in particular, see Aho (1991, 196–209).
3 I was so alarmed after having received this letter that I permanently broke off communications with Alice.
4 For a possible clue, see the "love story" involving a Jewish cantor (singer) and an anti-Semitic Klansman (Aho 1994, 139–51).

8 Revisiting Authoritarianism

After being banned from teaching in Nazi Germany and subsequently exiled, a group of Jewish social scientists associated with the Marxist-leaning Frankfurt University Institute for Social Research (hereafter, the "Frankfurt School" or "FS") undertook several research projects (Jeffries 2017). One of the most important was the authoritarian personality (hereafter, "the AP").

The question guiding the AP project was: why did German citizens, who were fully, if only recently enfranchised, and among the world's most literate and technically skilled populations, not only fail to resist Nazism, but actively collude with it? This was amidst an unprecedented economic crisis after World War I that saw hyperinflation, mass unemployment, and ravaging poverty. According to Marxist canon, these should have been the preconditions for socialist revolution. But what happened is that many of those hit hardest by the crisis—blue-collar workers and the old middle class of small shopkeepers, clerks, artisans, farmers, and independent professionals—consented to the loss of their political rights and the enhancement of their misery (Worrell 2008, 7–10, 18). The FS believed that what lay behind this shocking outcome was authoritarianism. Evidently, in ways to be examined more closely below, early 20th-century Germans had become accustomed to fawning over big power men while inflicting pain on the marginalized and weak; Nazism provided them the perfect vehicle to act out their proclivities.

We now know that variations of authoritarianism can flourish under virtually any circumstance: in liberal democracies like Sweden, France, and Britain, in the nominally Christian countries of south and central America, in Buddhist Myanmar, within the dominant political party in India, the pro-Hindu Bharatiya Janata (BJP), in one-time Communist nations, and even in the so-called exceptional land of America. This is to say nothing of "Islamo-fascism" and Zionist fanaticism. All of which suggests that the observations of the FS, once restricted to early-twentieth-century Germany, have relevance far beyond their original focus. Consider the United States.

After witnessing President Donald Trump's invocation of hackneyed fascist tropes, as in his description of the liberal media as "enemies of the people"; his threat to jail political opponents like "crooked Hillary" Clinton; his diatribe about how America has been "infested" by dark-skinned immigrants from "shit-hole countries"; his plaudits of tough-guy violence; his advocacy of dog-eat-dog nationalism and lamentation of American innocence and victimhood; and especially, his displays of obsequiousness toward ruthless, murderous strongmen—Vladimir Putin, Rodrigo Duterte, Mohammad bin Salman, Kim Jong-un (to whom Trump has professed his "love")—pundits have wondered: Can what happened years ago in Germany occur here? (cf. Applebaum 2018; Browning 2018; Ross 2016; Snyder 2018; Sunstein 2018). And this was before Trump refused to concede to having been fairly defeated in the 2020 presidential election (see Chapter 2).

While we may never fully know Trump's motives (but see McAdams 2016), what is of interest to Sociology is not so much the mindset of a single individual, but the enthusiastic reception that Trump's behavior has garnered from the American far-right, most paradoxically from White evangelical voters (Newport 2020). White evangelical support for Trump (at this writing) hovers at around 75 percent and 81 percent for the men (Burton 2018), this is a staggering 33 percent difference from the attitudes of the overall public. And it is in spite of the fact that many of Trump's economic policies run counter to the practical interests of his supporters, and in the face of confirmed stories about Trump's womanizing, a supposed "sin" that "values voters" like themselves claim to stand against.

Some of Trump's support, of course, can be attributed to partisanship. Since the Reagan era, white evangelicals have backed GOP presidential nominees over Democrats by a ratio of around 4:1, this includes their support of the decidedly non-evangelical Mormon candidate for President in 2012, Mitt Romney. Yet one wonders whether other factors might be at play as well. Matthew MacWilliams (2016) and Robert "Bob" Altemeyer (2016), the latter of whose work on the AP is discussed below, hypothesize that one of these factors is authoritarianism. John Dean, who was initially complicit in President Richard Nixon's Watergate scandal, has written a book that entertains just this possibility (2006). He was so taken by Altemeyer's prescience regarding Republican Party authoritarianism, that Dean encouraged him to compose a layperson's version of his 1996 book (Altemeyer n.d.).

There exists a massive social psychology on the contemporary American far-right. With no attempt at being exhaustive, the books alone published in just the last decade or so include Aho (2016), Hedges (2006), Niewert (2017), and Wolf (2007). Each of these alludes to authoritarianism, and some to the FS in particular. But in my view, none plumb authoritarianism in a manner faithful to the FS's psychoanalytic/phenomenological thrust. The goal of this chapter is to correct this oversight. I begin by revisiting the origins of the concept of "the AP" in post–World War I Germany. I then offer a precis of how, according to the FS, the AP has come to be. I cover the criticism surrounding the measurability of "the AP" as originally conceived. I then critique this criticism by summarizing the FS's portrayal of the inner-life of the prototypical AP. I close by addressing the usefulness of this narrative for Sociology today. Throughout this chapter, my intention is to drink deeply from the stream of the FS (as well as from that of its critics), without drowning in it.

The tacit objective of this chapter is once again to destabilize the notion that right-wing extremists are "SIC": stupid (ill-educated), socially isolated, and/or crazy (for a statement of this theory by the once-celebrated liberal sociologist, Seymour Martin Lipset, see Lipset 1960, 175). In my view, the abiding significance of the FS is its insistence on empathetically understanding the "action orientation" (the motives, cognitions, and emotional posture) of the AP from the *inside*, from its own standpoint, rather than from the objectifying gaze of the outsider. In other words, instead of viewing the AP as an "other," a stupid, lonely, mentally disturbed individual, the FS pictures them as a "normal neurotic," a living human being, whose admittedly disturbing way of existing emerges from concrete, possibly rectifiable, conditions.

Authoritarianism and the F-Scale

Erich Fromm's *Escape from Freedom* (1965 [1941]) is conventionally considered the foundational text of the AP project. However, an anticipation of his argument (in Fromm 1984)—largely unknown in America as it was not published in English until a half-century after the fact—shows that years earlier Fromm was already struggling to understand how presumably leftist-inclined German workers of the Weimer era (1919–1933) could vote to support anti-Semitic candidates. His conclusions were based on data gathered from a survey conducted by the FS from 1929 to 1931. Not only was this the first survey in history to use a facsimile of "modern" (in this case, psychoanalytic) methods to account for political behavior (Brunner 1994, 632), it was arguably the most ambitious enterprise ever undertaken by the FS. It involved over 3000 respondents, answering 271 open-ended questions on everything from their political opinions and attitudes toward Jews, to their musical tastes and art preferences, how they decorated their homes, and whether or not they collected stamps or attended church.

A second FS study that also went unpublished was conducted from 1944 to 1945. It too was focused on the issue of anti-Semitism, but this time among (mostly union) workers from seven of the most populous cities in America. Mark Worrell (2008, 11) considers it "the single most important" research "in the history of Marxist sociology." Among its "startling" findings is that 30 percent of the sample expressed outward hostility toward Jews; 11% favored their extermination (86–87, 315–16). One wonders what the figures might have been had the sample included rural Americans and southerners.

As for *Escape from Freedom*, it clearly evinces the influence of Freudian psychologist Wilhelm Reich's *The Mass Psychology of Fascism* (1980 [1933]). But reflecting Fromm's evolution away from classical Freudianism, it rejects Reich's explanation for fascism in thwarted sexuality (in addition to Reich's devotion to Soviet Communism [Burston 2017, 4]). Fromm borrows the phrase "sado-masochism" from Reich—which Freud had earlier taken from sexologist Richard von Krafft-Ebing (1922 [1892])—but he subtly alters its meaning. To Fromm, it is no longer a simple *sexual* pathology, but "a new anthropological type," a character structure with "so to speak ... two sexes," each of which is "aroused" by power (190). The first is what one might call the "manly-man," a person who is enchanted by the use of force. The second comprises "women of both sexes," whose feebleness and fragility evoke manly man's contempt. According to Fromm, the source of each so-called sex is to be found in a "fictitious"—or as we would say today, "alienated" or "neurotic"—attempt to rid oneself of the "unbearable" aloneness that plagues modern existence (173–75). Manly man does so by "swallowing" its victims; women of both sexes, by making themselves tiny, quiet, and edible. Fromm grants that both of these tendencies likely have been with our species since the beginning of time. What is different today is their "symbiotic fusion" into a psychological hybrid. One that exhibits growling aggression toward considered inferiors and dog-like cringing in the presence of superiors: the AP.

Although Theodor Adorno, the lead author of *The Authoritarian Personality* (Adorno et al. 1950), was still invoking Oedipal terminology at the time, he would go on to distinguish between different types of AP (762–71). First is the "semi-erudite," conspiratorial "crank" who resides on the "lunatic fringe." Then there is the bureaucratic "manipulator" who can be "the most merciless of all." And finally, there is the "nihilistic" rebel, the most extreme of whom are "retrogressive sociopaths" who fantasize about wreaking vengeance on civilized order. As examples of the latter, Adorno cites the Freikorps (paramilitaries) of the Weimer period, who later would become standard bearers of the Nazi SA and SS.

During its exile in America, the FS devised what came to be known as the F (fascist)-scale, a way to assess an individual's propensity to authoritarianism without appearing to do so. This was done by systemically culling and refining items drawn from a prior E (ethnocentrism) scale, a political-economic conservative scale, and an AS (anti-Semitism) scale (Adorno et al. 1950, 222–79). Each item in turn was selected for its reliability, readability, and suitability on samples of White, non-Jewish, mentally fit, adolescent, and middle-aged American subjects drawn from various social statuses. The result was a 30-item Likert-like questionnaire,[1] believed capable of scientifically assessing several dimensions of authoritarianism (228): One is the tendency of the respondent to project what is most intolerable about themselves onto available targets. Second is a tendency to identify with brash tough guys. Coupled with this, third, is a fascination with high-powered weaponry. Fourth, an attitude of cynical destructiveness. Fifth, a distrust of art and artists, intellectuals, and science. And finally, sixth is conspiracy-mongering, superstition, and cognitive rigidity.

Helping make *The Authoritarian Personality* accessible to nontechnical readers are "genetic analyses" (i.e., psychoanalyses) of two of the project's most voluble interviewees, "Larry" and "Mack" (787–816). They are selected to illustrate the differences in character between an average non-authoritarian and a high-scorer on the F-scale. Larry, the non-authoritarian, is pictured as passive, effeminate, well mannered, other-directed, and as exhibiting a positive-mother complex. Mack, by contrast, is described as virile, crude, self-absorbed, subservient, and misogynistic: a spitting image of the manly man.

Following its issuance, American academics gave the F-scale a less than full-throated endorsement. Among other problems, they noted, was its anti-conservative bias, a concern shared by Fromm, and a major reason why he broke from Adorno (Burston 2017, 5). (The FS returned the insult by accusing Fromm of being "too Marxist" [Brunner 1994, 634].) The anti-conservative bias of the F-scale is evident in the following sample of items drawn directly from the questionnaire. Do you agree or disagree, the questionnaire asks, that "Obedience and respect for authority are the most important virtues children should learn?" Or that "The true American way of life is disappearing so fast that force may be necessary to preserve it?" Or that sex criminals "ought to be publicly whipped, or worse?" and so on. If you do, goes the theory, then supposedly you have a penchant for authoritarianism.

But critics began to ask, what about *left*-wing servility, the mindless devotion that progressives sometimes exhibit toward leftist tyrants? Conservative American sociologist, Edward Shils (1954), even proposed that a second authoritarian questionnaire be composed to assess this possibility and playfully suggested a title: the R-scale (with "R" standing for "red").[2]

Bob Altemeyer (Altemeyer 1996, 219) eventually took up Shils' challenge and devised a left-wing authoritarianism scale. If it is true, Altemeyer reasoned, that left and right-wing college students are psychologically alike, then they should be equally attracted to authoritarian leaders who share their respective ideological biases. He was (I think, happily) taken aback to discover that in fact they are not and concluded that "the idea that authoritarian personalities are equally drawn to communist and fascist movements is clearly false" (216). He went on to deride the idea of left-wing authoritarianism (LWA) as "the Loch Ness monster of political psychology," "something as scarce as hens' teeth" (for a contrary conclusion, however, see Conway et al. 2017).

A second problem with the F-scale is its "response set," the fact that all of its questions are posed the same way so that if a respondent can figure out how to answer the first handful in a politically correct (in this case, liberal progressive) way, they can conceal their real (possibly reactionary) attitudes.

After administering the F-scale to about 2100 subjects (mostly from California), and generalizing their findings to the larger US population, the FS researchers estimated that up to 30 percent of Americans harbor pro-fascist, authoritarian tendencies. This not only comports with the conclusion of the 1944–1945 FS survey of the American working class (mentioned earlier), it agrees with Altemeyer's own estimate, made four decades later.

I suppose one can take comfort in knowing that 30 percent is but a fraction of the American public. However, as Max Weber warns (1958a), numbers alone (or, as he would say, "gunpowder") rarely determine the outcome of a political struggle. Rather, it is organizational discipline: the inclination of followers to march in lock-step when so commanded. As recent history demonstrates, America's far-right is more than capable of mounting intricately planned, methodical, and sustained campaigns.

The Frankfurt School Account of Authoritarianism

What I want to focus on here, however, is not the validity of the F-scale nor the accuracy of its predictions. It is instead, why? Why, according to the FS, are some people drawn like moths to bloviating demagogues and to political cruelty? Having been trained as neo-Freudians, we are not surprised to learn that the FS traces authoritarianism back to childhood (including elementary school) experience. While not formerly associated with the FS, clinical psychologist and author, Alice Miller (1984) and psychiatrist, Morton Schatzman (1973) have become late proponents of this notion. Miller bases her argument on Katharina Rutschsky's untranslated book, *Schwarze Pädagogik* ("Black Pedagogy"); Schatzman bases his in part on the memoirs of the hospitalized son of a Dr. Moritz Schreber (whom we will be introduced to, shortly).

According to Miller and Schatzman, Germans were beguiled by Nazism, not because of their stupidity, insanity, inherent evil, or economic insecurity, but because of the "poisonous pedagogy" that had been inflicted on them as youngsters by their parents, teachers, and priests. This, in turn, presumably owed itself to advice proffered in late 19th-century German childcare manuals. The most notorious of these was one authored by Dr. Schreber (1806–1861), which was reissued multiple times. Schreber became so popular that *Schrebervereine* (Schreber clubs) were established throughout the early modern Fatherland. His methods were subsequently insinuated into "medical indoor gymnastics" facilities (Schreber's phrase) which today have become virtually ubiquitous (Pronger 2002); into the "concentration camp" regimens of Nazi public schools (Ziemer 1941); into the routines of the male "finishing schools" of imperial Germany (Theweleit 1987, 1989, 2: 143–53); and finally, into the empire's "nihilistic rehearsals" (Amidon & Krier 2009) in colonial Africa and China.

Why Schreber and his ilk enjoyed such a wide audience, Miller and Schatzman answer tautologically (if not incorrectly) that German parents, educators, and preachers had themselves been raised the same way. A more expansive explanation is offered by Max Weber (1958b), which greatly influenced the FS (cf. Fromm 1965 [1941], 67–68, 81–122). It is that the manuals gave German bourgeoisie guidance on how to instill in their children the habits of self-renunciation, obedience, stoicism, and orderliness: aptitudes thought necessary for laboring in the factories of the emerging rational bureaucratic enterprises of the early modern period.

Weber's argument is that neo-Calvinist sects—in the case of Germany, Pietism; in England, Wesley-ism; and in America, Presbyterianism, Methodism, and Baptist assemblies—introduced congregants to a salvific technology of "inner-worldly asceticism" (from Gr. = "exercise"). Modeled after the *other*-worldly practices of medieval monasticism, inner-worldly asceticism provided believers surety about their postmortem fates. Now, their methodical work, silence, and compliance could be taken as "signs," if not exactly proofs, of their eternal salvation. In other words, according to Weber, the Protestant Ethic transformed what had once been considered markers of monastic virtue into signifiers of grace. This idea was further secularized when inner-worldly asceticism became a marker of *bodily health*. Here, the old exercises remained, and if anything were harshened, but they were reframed as cures for disease, rather than as remedies for sin.

On these lines, Schreber urges parents and teachers to seek out and "ruthlessly" extirpate the ignoble "weeds" of wickedness in children, lest they fester into vice. "*Suppress everything in the child ...*" so that their "true nobility" can spring forth (Miller 1984, 60 her emphasis). For as Proverbs (3: 12) teaches, "Those whom the Lord loveth, He correcteth."

The goal of Schreber's child-care philosophy was to "habituate" the child to an attitude of rectitude, as exemplified, among other ways, by a visibly righteous, correct, erect, rectal bearing, or as "that most German of cultural tropes" expresses it: *Gehorsamkeit* (submissiveness) (Theweleit 1987, 1989, 2: xi. For elaboration, see 2: 43–61). This would require three things: First, verbally scolding them for being a *Schlappschwanz* (a spineless sissy, or literally, a "limp penis"). In other words, don't permit them to shuffle, sag, slump, slouch, slop, smack, or slurp. *Man tut das nicht!* ("One does not do that!"). Second, use folklore to warn them about the fate that awaits mischievous, absent-minded, slovenly children. This, for example, by reading them either Dr. Heinrich Hoffmann's *Der Struwwelpeter* ("Shaggy Peter") or Wilhelm Busch's *Max und Moritz*. The latter culminates in Max and Moritz being ground into flour, baked in an oven, then fed to geese. Third is the administration of pain: the rapping of hands, the "pedagogy of the whip" (to quote Theweleit), and/or immersion in ice-water baths. In this regard, Schreber recommends that hand manacles and leg fetters be affixed to bed posts to avert the child from assuming a fetal position, or worse: thumb-sucking or masturbating. He suggests that steel back braces be attached to chairs, placed next to desks with sharp steel edges to keep them from curling over their school work; chin straps to hold their heads straight, and so on.

Perhaps Weber's "iron cage" (1958b, 181–82) (*stahlhartes Gehaus* = "steel-enclosed house") was not intended merely as a metaphor for high capitalism, but as a literal reflection of his own upbringing in a typical, prosperous Prussian household (Mitzman 1969, 107). As was standard for his class, Weber also endured the mandatory "inanities of Prussian military discipline" for a year in Strassburg (Mitzman 1969, 24).

Schatzman (1973, 42–47) provides illustrations of Schreber's disciplinary instruments, taken directly from his text. He goes on to speculate that it was their deployment that occasioned the suicide of Dr. Schreber's youngest son. The eldest, a once esteemed judge, was committed to an insane asylum, horrified that God was turning him into a woman. Freud (1943 [1911]) famously interpreted the eldest son's paranoia as a psychological "defense" against his budding homosexuality. Schatzman, however, offers an alternative, "transactional" (i.e., "sociological") explanation, namely, that the eldest son was a victim of his father's "sadism."[3] But forbidden (out of fear of suffering even greater pain) from entertaining the "dangerous thought" that his father had abused him, he "misconstrued" his anguish and attributed it instead to "God" and to His "divine miracles" (*Wunder*). There was the hot/cold ablution "miracle," for example; the "extremely painful" (the eldest son's words) "coccyx miracle" that resulted from the father inflicting on him the "bridge" and the "*geradhalter*" (straight-holder); the "head-compression machine miracle" that left the son with excruciating headaches into adulthood; the *Kopfhalter* (head-holder) "miracle"; and the chin-band, a helmet-like device that the son described as the "being tied to earth miracle".

The Authoritarian Personality in Anglo-American Hands

To her satisfaction, Miller (1984, 147–97, n.d.) confirms her causal account of authoritarianism anecdotally, by citing the child-rearing traumas suffered by leading Nazi figures like Rudolf Höss, Hermann Goering, and Adolf Hitler; Susan Griffin uses Miller's theory to explain the authoritarianism of the fastidious SS mass murderer, Heinrich Himmler (Griffin 1992, 115–83). Likewise, Theweleit, in his account of the inner lives of leading Freikorps figures. The problem is that as plausible as these narratives seem, they are not really testable (i.e., falsifiable). This is because they are posed in such vague terms that virtually anything can be cited to verify them. It is this, in part, that has given impetus to an alternative, call it an "Anglo-American," way to approach the subject of authoritarianism. This involves the devising of more accurate and less transparently biased ways to measure authoritarianism, and a refocus away from the social-cultural context out of which authoritarianism is said to have emerged, to matters of individual psycho-genesis.

The prime example of this newer approach is the research program undertaken by now-retired Canadian political psychologist, Bob Altemeyer (1988, 1996, n.d.). After a decade of painstaking labor, Altemeyer formulated his own 30-question RWA scale. It is purposively structured to discourage a "response set," the technical problem mentioned earlier (which Altemeyer confesses, "was much easier said than done"). And he is "surprised" (his word) that the questions in his revised RWA scale enjoy such a high degree of inter-item consistency. This suggests to him that the RWA scale is indeed accessing something real. Altemeyer relates that it was the lack of inter-item consistency in the original F-scale that drove him to concoct an alternative to it in the first place. After all, he asks rhetorically, what do superstition, cynical destructiveness, and hostility toward minorities (three of the factors enumerated earlier in this Chapter) that the FS alleges are components of the AP, have to do with one another? According to Altemeyer, not much.

The RWA scale measures a subject's "pre-fascist potential" by means of their responses to questions that relate to three "attitudinal clusters": their expressed willingness to obey political and/or religious authorities, their agreement with written expressions of hostility toward authoritatively identified enemies, and their willingness to comply, at least on paper, with popular conventions, especially those dealing with sex.

Altemeyer (and by today, scores of other researchers) have administered the RWA scale to college students from across Canada, the United States, and Western Europe. They find that high scores on the three clusters correlate with, among other things, support for government malfeasance (such as illegal wiretaps and searches, judicial torture, and military trials of political dissenters); intolerance of crimes committed by minority people, coupled with tolerance of crimes committed by high officials (e.g., by Richard Nixon, after Watergate); and a readiness to administer mock electrical shocks to peers who fail at designated tasks (modeled after the notorious Stanley Milgram experiments [1974]). High RWA scores also correlate with racism, ethnocentrism, anti-gay hostility, misogyny, dislike of the homeless; and hatred of abortionists and religious "cultists"; as well as with religious orthodoxy and adherence to conventionally accepted political outlooks.

As to why some subjects score high on the RWA scale, Altemeyer and his co-researchers reject the original FS theory, described in the previous section, because of what they see as its obscurity. In several places, Altemeyer insists that before one can scientifically assert anything, they first must have "clear, precise, and well-delineated" definitions of the terms they are using (Altemeyer 1996, 47, 48). And for all its richness and subtlety, the FS psychoanalytic approach provides little of this. So, Altemeyer and his followers opt instead for a variation of behavioral learning theory (78–82). One *learns* to be a proto-fascist (or the opposite), he says, through negative and/or positive "reinforcement," that is, from a calculus of punishments and/or rewards administered for behaving in acceptable or unacceptable ways. These reinforcers can be administered directly or indirectly (i.e., by watching what happens to others when they speak or act in unacceptable or in pleasing ways). And they can be given out either by parents, pedagogues, preachers, politicians, professors, or peers.

According to Altemeyer, if what our significant others convey is authoritarian, then the longer we spend time under their tutelage the more likely we are to exhibit authoritarian inclinations ourselves. The reverse is also true. As an educator, I am struck by Altemeyer's finding that regardless of their majors, the *more* semesters that young people spend in college, the lower are their RWA scores. During matriculation, initially high RWA scorers and liberal arts majors in particular evince precipitous declines in authoritarianism (Altemeyer 1988, 91–5). This, of course, will raise all kinds of suspicions in the minds of authoritarian conspiracy theorists, not the least of which is that the students have merely been brainwashed by liberal professors. I'll ignore that concern here, except to say that, tongue in cheek, Altemeyer smilingly confesses that his student respondents "were well served by their university experience" (Altemeyer 1996, 85).[4]

The FS School Responds

A more telling objection to the Altemeyer approach is this: the learning theory of authoritarianism may indeed be clear, precise, and well delineated, but this comes at what the FS would likely consider an unacceptably steep price, namely, the "de-eroticization" of the concept of "the AP" (Marcuse 1964, 73). By "de-eroticization," Herbert Marcuse means the "reduction" (in the pursuit of efficiency) of any institution or practice, or in our case, any concept, to its supposed function.[5]

Reduction in this sense is most easily accomplished by excising from the institution or practice in question its overlays of aesthetic valance and sensual pleasure. In regard to war-making, for instance, it is the elimination of "militarism"—flag waving, be-medaled uniforms, marching bands, goose-stepping troops, and martial music—from the "military way," its major purpose: the removal of an enemy from the battlefield. Or again, it is the displacement of the lived experience of embodiment (*Leib*) by considerations of organismic functioning (*Körper*), as assessed by lab tests and high-tech electronics. To take eroticism proper, reduction involves the equating of eroticism with sexuality, and sexuality with sex: that is, to the "bringing of one's own genitals into contact with those of someone" else (Marcuse 1962, 187). It is genital contact period, shorn of the arts of flirtation and seduction, sex without romance, and with neither commitment nor love.

On the face of it, it would seem that the de-eroticization of authoritarianism would be *its* operational reduction to items on something like Altemeyer's RWA questionnaire. But if that were true, then the FS would be guilty of the same thing with its F-scale. (In fact, Meloen, Van Der Linden, and De Witte [1996] find that in regard to predicting ethnocentrism, anti-Semitism, misogyny, punitive-ness, and the like, "it does not matter much which one of the authoritarianism scales is used" [651].) The real concern that the FS has with Altemeyer, then, is not just this. It is, rather, that the Anglo-American approach to authoritarianism overlooks the very quality that lends the FS theory its critical "magic": its *phenomenology* of authoritarianism. To be fair, Altemeyer does allude at places to the "psychodynamics" of authoritarianism, but he dismisses consideration of these dynamics as scientifically "obsolete."

To say it differently, the Anglo-American approach to authoritarianism emphasizes the *what* of authoritarianism, what it is as an objective thing. In contrast, the FS deals with the *how* or the *way* by which the AP "is there" in the world. In other words, its *Dasein* or its "being there," to use Martin Heidegger's neo-logism: how the AP sees, thinks about, remembers (historicizes), and feels about things, including other people and itself.

The phenomenological posture assumed by the FS toward authoritarianism owes its itself to the cultural-historical context out of which the FS emerged. Whereas the inquiries of Altemeyer and his followers are rooted in the Anglo-American empiricist tradition, the goal of which is to causally *explain* problematic things in parsimonious ways (with a mind to controlling or eliminating them), the FS reflects the impact of Wilhelm Dilthey and German historicism (*Geisteswissenschaft*), the goal of which is to sympathetically *understand* (*Verstehen*) human actions as deeply and as profoundly as possible (for more on these two methodologies, see Fay 1996). This is in hope of offering a critique of the *Volkgeist* (or culture) from which those actions arise. Fromm's Ph.D. mentor, recall, was the celebrated Diltheyan historian Alfred Weber, Max's younger brother. For his part, Marcuse studied under the founder of modern phenomenology himself, Edmund Husserl, and he wrote his dissertation under Husserl's most celebrated student, Martin Heidegger. Theodor Adorno was still another Husserl protégé. He received a doctorate on the basis of his psycho-biography of the Danish existential phenomenologist, Søren Kierkegaard.

So how, then, according to the FS, *is* the AP "there" for the most part?[6]

To start with, the AP takes sensual delight in taunting, teasing, titillating, and tormenting a vulnerable target. S/he "trolls" the victim, watches it squirm, weep, and rage, and then cites its distress as proof of the need to inflict on them an even more exquisite pain. *For your own good!* as Alice Miller might say. Think of the wicked Timothy Gedge in William Trevor's *Children of Dynsmouth* (1976, made into a BBC Screen Two TV series in 1987). Timothy spies on his most defenseless neighbors—elderly veterans, lonely widows, and distraught orphans—lies about what he witnesses, then uses "our little secret" to blackmail them. After bringing them to tears, near madness, and homicidal fantasies, he grins with satisfaction.

Stephen Miller (no relation to Alice), President Trump's major speech writer and policy adviser, provides another telling example. Naturally, Miller doesn't call what he does "sadism." Rather, he characterizes it as "triggering the libs" or "melting the snowflakes," referring to those unable to stand the heat of his smirk. He advocates vindictive policies and then uses liberal outrage as confirmation of their mental illness (namely, as "Trump derangement syndrome") or as proof of their lack of patriotism (Coppins 2018). It is Miller who proposed that to deter Hispanic immigration to America, refugee children be taken from their parents and caged in detention centers. He is also said to have composed the administration's first ban on travelers from Muslim countries, which led to mass demonstrations and chaos at American airports, just days after Trump's inauguration. Full implementation of these measures was averted only by means of court-ordered injunctions.

The flip side to sadism is masochism. The AP not only tyrannizes the helpless; they are animated by abasing themselves to a higher authority. Here, three phenomenological facts are at play.

At the most superficial level, self-degradation and submission are transactional. They win from the authority his/her smiling indulgence. A case in point is a Trump campaign speech: pointing derisively to mainstream media videographers who were recording the scene, Trump told the audience, "they think they are the elite." "But they're not the elite," he assured them. "*You're the elite!*" The audience roared its approval. At last, they seemed to say, someone sees us, understands us, and speaks for us.

Trump "was not afraid to say" about ranks of torch-bearing neo-Nazis, who chanted "Jews will not replace us!" (in Charlestown, Virginia, summer, 2017) that some were "very nice people." This came just hours after one of them had murdered a liberal protester and seriously injured several others "Thank you," tweeted David Duke afterwards. "Thank you for your honesty and courage to tell the truth…" (Lemon 2017). (We will meet Duke again in Chapter 9.)

At a deeper level, self-abnegation and submission gain the AP a sense of ethical certainty, a conviction that their sadism (as just described) is right and just. To paraphrase Fromm, they earn one an "escape from freedom," liberation from "decidiphobia," from the dread of having to choose for themselves, and therefore be morally responsible for, how they are in the world. For now, their private envies and petty aversions become those of the Leader; they in turn experience themselves as the Leader's "battle axe and weapons of war." In a sense, it is not *they* who act, but the Leader acting through them. "*By defending myself against the Jew, I am fighting for the work of the Lord*" (Hitler 1943, 249 and 65. His emphasis. see also Miller 1984, 71). Hitler's pretensions earned perverse confirmation when one of America's leading Christian Dominionist preachers, Rev. John Hagee (pastor of San Antonio's 19,000-seat Cornerstone Church), declared that the Holocaust was part of God's plan (Huffingtonpost 2008). The technical term for the merging of an AP's intentions with those of a putative authority is "participation mystique." Fromm (1965 [1941], 163) describes this as the "fusion" of oneself with somebody independent from themselves, so as to acquire what they themselves lack.

Third and most telling, from the standpoint of the "infantilized psyche" of the AP, the Leader represents the super-critical parent/teacher/preacher/pundit/peer whose attention and affirmation they crave. Haunted by the possibility that they are in fact what this other has told them—that they are losers, worthless, ugly, and alone—they "split-off" their detestable parts and transfer them, unconsciously, to someone or some group "out there." *This* now becomes their sin-carrier, a "goat" who can be hospitalized, tortured, forced into exile, imprisoned, or killed, taking with them the AP's "ontological insecurity" (Perera 1986, 16).

Alice Miller (1984, 188) relates the story of a one-time member of the *Bund Deutscher Mädel* (League of German girls [Ziemer 1941, 123–44]). After the war, the woman confessed to Miller her relief upon learning from the Nazi Party about a group upon whom she could heap her doubts, fears, and resentments. Now in good conscience she could project the bad weakling self she had always feared she was, onto the "bad," "weakling" Jew, thereby experiencing herself as upright, strong, and pure.[7] Miller interprets the otherwise inexplicable Nazi command that the homeland be thoroughly "cleansed" of Jews (*Judenreinmachen*), as a symbolic expression of the terror that the split-off parts of Party members might someday return. In other words, to the Nazis the Jew was a fetish (a fiction); its extermination a perverse, if consoling, magical rite.

Summary and Conclusion

It is easy to denounce the AP and turn it into something other than ourselves. This is especially true when one has been on the receiving end of their cravenness and mendacity. But the nearer we approach them, talk with them, and listen to their conversion stories, the more familiar they become, the harder it is to fit them into our pre-set categories. We begin to see ourselves in them. This can be unsettling, but as Georg Simmel (1977) in his explication of Diltheyan methodology tells us, being unsettled in this way is precisely the purpose of social-historical research. It is to "remember" (as opposed to *dis*member) what it is we share as human beings.

What Simmel is describing, of course, is *Verstehen*. While earlier I translated this as "sympathetic understanding," Simmel renders it more precisely as the act of imaginatively putting oneself in the other's place, and trying to think, see, remember, and feel about the world as *they* do. One implication of this is that the more impoverished our imaginations are—or to say it differently, the more destitute our lived experience—the less well suited we will be to grasp the mindset of another. This is why Simmel can say that "whoever has never loved will never understand love or the lover; someone with a passionate disposition will never understand one who is apathetic; the weakling will never understand the hero, nor will the hero ever understand the weakling" (65).

The same is true of authoritarianism: Whoever chooses to remain blind to their *own* propensity to sado-masochism—how we pleasure ourselves in the torments of our foes, how beguiling we find our superiors, and how willing we are to abase ourselves before them—will never understand the AP. To be sure, we can condemn it, campaign against it, and even attempt to police it, but it will remain elusive. Like the mythical Hide-Behind, it will hover just beyond our reach. In this way, it will continue to haunt us, surprise us again and again, and use *us* to do its dirty work. Like the neo-Freudian tradition from which it emerged, the abiding gift of the FS is instruction about the darkness that lurks in each of us. It is an invitation to transcend the "false consciousness" (Geuss 1981) of our own innocence.

Notes

1. A Likert scale offers subjects four or more ways to respond to a questionnaire item: Do you strongly agree? Somewhat agree? Somewhat disagree? Strongly disagree? Or do you have no opinion?
2. One of the most ironic examples of what seems to be left-wing authoritarianism occurred in 1969 at none other than Frankfurt University itself. Like thespians re-enacting the myth of Oedipus, graduate students, several of whom were budding sociologists, rebelled against their intellectual forebears. They occupied seminars, disrupted lectures, and even forced some professors to undergo ritual self-criticism (Jeffries 2017, 241–50). During one incident, the *Busenaktion*, three young women bared their breasts in front of a dismayed Adorno. A second victim was Herbert Marcuse who had earlier been welcomed back to Germany like a conquering hero. He was publicly shamed for allegedly being a sell-out to corporate capitalism and militarism. (During World War II, Marcuse had worked for the precursor of the CIA.) "Flower power and erotic liberation," says Stuart Jeffries, appeared to have mutated "into their own kind of oppression" (347).
3. Arthur Mitzman (1969) argues, analogously, that Weber's off-and-on mania, his melancholia, and his periodic mental hospitalizations owed themselves to his struggle to free himself from his father, a "genuine despot," upon whom he was financially dependent (20), and his rigid neo-Calvinist mother.

4 Surveys conducted in 1978–1979 (Lederer 1982) found that the authoritarianism scores of German youth had declined so steeply since 1945 that they were now a bit lower than those of their American compeers. Whether or how much this can be attributed to the adoption by post-war West German parents and pedagogues of progressive American child-rearing practices remains an intriguing, still open, question.
5 Marcuse likely got a sense of the *sociological*, apart from the strictly Kantian, significance of "instrumental rationality" (*Zweckrationalität*) from Max Weber (cf. 1964 [1947], 115, n. 38).
6 For a riveting phenomenology of the prototypical AP that goes far beyond the following discussion, see Theweleit (1987–1989). It is based on his close interpretation of 250 Freikorps novels and memoirs from the 1920s. While Theweleit agrees with the psychoanalytic orientation of the FS, he lambasts it for its unwillingness to face the "attraction of fascism itself," which is to say, its "passionate celebration of violence" and rape-infused misogyny.
7 For more on the concept of psychological projection or "negative transference," see the section titled "The Motive of the Big Lie" in Chapter 5.

9 "Fascism" Reconsidered

Introduction

Alexander Reid Ross, a geography lecturer at Portland State University (in Oregon), has written a comprehensive social history of what he calls "fascism" (Ross 2017), primarily in Europe and America, from around 1900 to the present.[1] I want to spend some time with Ross's book because it challenges my approach to the subject of American right-wing extremism (without mentioning my name), particularly in regard to the role that I believe the Christian church has played in its recent American upsurge. But first, some preliminaries.

Ross's main thesis is that fascism "creeps along" by insinuating itself into mainstream cultures and institutions through a "syncretic" appropriation of traditional conservative narratives; reactionary populist, anarchist, and liberal-progressive ideologies; together with selected (if bastardized) passages from biology, ecology, demography, and "race science." Because of this, it is not so much a static thing or a clearly delineated product, but a never-ending "process," a "drift," or a "contagion" that today reaches across national boundaries to touch on virtually the entire world.

Two "primal emotions" underlie this process of fascist "hybridization," says Ross: (1) resentment at modernization (or globalization) by those it displaces, whom Ross (after Maurice Barrès) calls "superfluous men,"[2] and (2) cravings for revenge against those considered responsible for it, such as liberal arts professors at prestigious universities; transnational corporate executives and their spokespeople in the oil industry, banking, hi-tech communications, and drug manufacture; and finally, government bureaucrats.

The explanatory theme of marginalization or "disenfranchisement," as just characterized, runs throughout the book. But it is easy to get lost in Ross's (admittedly unavoidable) reportage on countless, minute "groupuscules," or factions that fracture and then reconstitute themselves under a blur of new titles.[3] What makes Ross's account doubly challenging is that he seems to breeze past developments conventionally viewed as pivotal to fascist history, while doting on relatively minor figures and on insignificant, if momentarily newsworthy, happenings. The word "Nazism," for example, is cited only four times in the index (although both Hitler and the Holocaust are more thoroughly discussed). Meanwhile, multiple pages are devoted to entities like the French Nouvelle Droite (New Right), the Italian Ordine Nuovo (New Order), the French OAS (Organisation de l'Armée Secrète), Autonomous Nationalism, the Greek Golden Dawn, Gladio (the Sword), and to obscure figures (at least to most readers), such as Julius Evola (developer of the post-war mythos of the Aryan Superman), Alexander Dugan (Vladimir Putin's so-called brain and the Russian apologist for "national Bolshevism" which emerged after the fall of the Soviet Union. Dugan is a critic of what he calls Jewish cosmopolitan "Atlanticism"). There is also Troy Southgate (a British proponent of national libertarianism) and Savitri Devi (fascism's putative "spiritual leader"). But in Ross's defense, his book *is* a history of fascism across the world, not just in America.

Then there is the matter of omission. Ross has done a masterful job of bringing together a mass of material from different cultures, historical moments, and countries, but perhaps inevitably—after all, no one can examine everything—he overlooks two scholars whose work is essential for grasping the peculiarities of the *American* far-right: Hannah Arendt and her unparalleled study of the subject, *The Origins of Totalitarianism* (1967 [1951]), and Michael Barkun's classic, *Religion and the Racist Right* (1996). Among other things, Barkun characterizes the ways by which American-made Christian Identity (CI) differs from British Israelism (BI), two theological orientations that Ross inaccurately conflates. Ross appears to be unaware that BI was created and carried primarily by professional academics housed at exclusive universities in England, whereas CI is a product of comparatively ill-educated amateurs, most of whom are fully absorbed in the lay Protestant evangelical world.

Part of the problem here is that the word "fascism" is, at best, only loosely defined. Is the fascist, asks Ross, a "personality type," as the Frankfurt School supposes?[4] Or is it an "attitude," as Wilhelm Reich (1980 [1933]) argues? Is it, as conservative sociologist Robert Nisbet says, the outcome of a "quest for community" in the face of the community-shattering consequences of modernization (Nisbet 1953)? Or, to borrow from Marxist-Leninist phraseology, is it a movement that seeks "a third way" between the stultifying political options of corporate liberalism and the conservatism of the *ancien régime* which flourished before the French Revolution (ca. 1798)? In the end, Ross opts for Robert Griffin's characterization (Griffin 1992), that fascism is "palingenetic ultra-nationalism," or a "mythopoetic" resuscitation of ancient origin stories, plus the birth announcement of a new man.[5] I sympathize with Ross. "Fascism" is exceedingly hard to pin down, which is one reason—but not the only one (see Chapter 2)—why I forego using the word in my own analysis of the contemporary American far-right.[6]

Fascist Creep in America

After sketching the roots and trajectory of fascism in Europe, Ross turns to the United States, to flesh out what he really means by "fascist creep" or "contagion." He begins by offering a standard review of the role played by the American Legion and several major corporations in the promotion of ultra-rightism during the interwar period of the 1920s and 1930s. For instance, there was the DuPont family business, which became a major producer of gunpowder, rayon, and nylon. (The patriarch of the family had earlier fled France for the United States during the French Revolution.) The list also includes Standard Oil, Texaco Oil, the National Association of Manufacturers, the Ford Motor Company, and Henry Ford himself. (Ford received the Grand Cross of the Order of the German Eagle, personally from Hitler, partly for his invention of the moving assembly line, but no less so than for his book-length screed, *The International Jew*, which was distributed in Dearborn, Michigan, near the Ford motor company factory.) To these names, Ross adds those of several of the individuals mentioned in Chapter 2: Huey Long, Rev. G. L. K. Smith, and the Catholic priest, Father Coughlin. (Coughlin openly accused Jews of "persecuting" hapless Christians; under auspices of the Christian Front, he helped organize platoon-sized units, comprised military veterans and off-duty policemen in Boston and New York City, to fend off the threat). After briefly discussing William Dudley Pelley (of the Silver Shirt Legion), and the German-American Bund, Ross goes on to devote a sentence each to the Black Legion (a White terrorist group that also arose in Michigan during this period), the Silver Battalion, and the Gold Shirts.

The Great Sedition Trial

Because he fails to provide much more than a list of names and dates of political developments during the interwar period, Ross largely ignores the larger question of how the American far-right acquired the prominence it enjoys today, which is another way of saying that he avoids mentioning Revs. Carl McIntire, Fred Schwarz, and Billy James Hargis, who, together with Francis Schaeffer, Rousas Rushdoony, and the right-wing radio and TV preachers of our era, played pivotal roles in the emergence of Christian Dominionism.[7] Another factor that Ross overlooks is passage of the Alien Registration Act (or Smith Act) in 1940. This has been used by the federal government to persecute and prosecute Nazi sympathizers but has ended up inadvertently igniting even more ferocious right-wing, anti-government hostility.

The most notable example of this took place during what turns out to have been the largest sedition trial in American history. This commenced in April 1944 and ended abruptly a year later, following the death of the trial judge, Edward Eichner (Piper & Hoop 1999). All of the charges filed against the defendants were subsequently dismissed, and a number of the trial's critics attributed Eichner's fatal heart attack to the impossibility of the situation in which, as an inexperienced jurist, he found himself: trying to discourage far-right beliefs, which he found repugnant, without compromising the defendants' constitutional right to express them.

All 30 of the defendants (reduced from the original 42), say Piper and Hoop, were "fanatic Roosevelt haters," devoted anti-Communists, and in some cases, vicious anti-Semites. Without being exhaustive, they included George Viereck (a German-American poet, suspected Nazi secret agent, and Roosevelt critic); Lawrence Dennis (a former State Department official and publisher of various pro-fascist books and magazines); and the so-called Jayhawk [Kansas] Nazi, Rev Gerald Winrod. (It is worth mentioning that Winrod's most famous protégé at the time was a young Southern Baptist minister by the name of Billy Graham.) Finally, there was Elizabeth Dilling. An outspoken anti-war isolationist, under the pseudonym "Rev. F. Woodruff Johnson," Dilling authored *The Octopus*, a book-length trashing of Roosevelt's New Deal. Earlier, she had gained notoriety for conducting the paid research on which Henry Ford based his *International Jew*. There were also handfuls of little known, non-influential followers, several of whom were virtually penniless. At the same time, a number of nationally prominent anti-war American Firsters were able to avoid indictment altogether, such as the famed airman, Charles Lindbergh (who was a personal hero of Hitler's), Senators Robert Taft (R-Ohio), and Burton Wheeler (D-Montana), along with more than 20 other congressmen. This lent credence to public suspicion that the sedition trial had less to do with internal subversion than it did with ordinary American political antagonisms.

The immediate spur of the sedition trial, of course, was World War II, which was just then nearing an end; and with it the American alliance with Joseph Stalin and the Soviet Union. Added to this, was Roosevelt's anger at having been unfairly accused of introducing Americans to what conservative critics labeled, his "Soviet-style" New Deal reforms. There was also widespread conservative opposition to pro-war lobbying efforts undertaken by the Jewish Anti-Defamation League of B'nai B'rith (the ADL); and conservative hostility to what was being excoriated in far-right circles as the "*Jewish*-owned" *Washington Post*.

The case against the defendants revolved around allegations that they had surreptitiously conspired with Hitler to imperil the morale of American troops overseas (and had thus impeded the war effort). As proof, prosecutors drew parallels between Nazi propaganda messages and the content of some of the literature authored by the persons just mentioned. Dilling's argument in the *Plot Against Christianity*, for example, is that Talmudic Judaism was the "progenitor" of modern Communism, as well as its reputed "father," Karl Marx (whom Dilling claims was descended from a long line of rabbis (Honoreff n.d.). This is to say nothing of her diatribe against the supposed "Jewish sympathizer," President "Rosenfeld" himself.

That the prosecutors were unable to offer empirical evidence that the defendants had in fact planned, much less acted, to overthrow the government, was cited by the defendants as proof that the trial was essentially an attack on their right to free speech and was therefore unconstitutional. And in the end, the "Great Sedition Trial," as it is now known, fell to pieces under the weight of ridicule from the mouths of progressive civil libertarians and conservatives alike. This, for being a supposed "farce," "a joke," "a [Soviet-style] show trial," "a fraud," and as "a black page in American jurisprudence" (Piper & Hoop 1999).

This is not the only instance in recent American history when a criminal court proceeding against ultra-rightists has backfired. A second, more recent, case was the failed prosecution of those who instigated the 41-day siege of the Malheur National Wildlife Refuge, Oregon, in 2016 (Templeton, Wilson & Haas, 2016) which is now celebrated in far-right circles as a "dress rehearsal" for the January 6, 2021, attack on the US Capitol (which is detailed Chapter 2).

Another, more telling, example took place in Ft. Smith, Arkansas in 1988 when 14 White supremacists were tried for plotting to overthrow the government. When all the defendants were acquitted by an all-White jury, Klansman Louis Beam, who previously had served as head of the Aryan Nations prison ministry, chortled that Zionist Occupation Government suffered "a terrible defeat here today." What makes the Ft. Smith trial particularly salient for this book is that several of the defendants played important roles in the rise of Christian Dominionism: Rev. Richard Butler (and his Church of Jesus Christ Christian-Aryan Nations), affiliates of the *Brüders Schweigen* (or Order), Rev. James Ellison, pastor of the Covenant Sword and Arm of the Lord (or CSA), and Tom Metzger, whom we will meet later.

The point is that in America, to criminally prosecute right-wing extremists (or for that matter, left-wingers) for seditious conspiracy can be risky; not just for the defendants, but for the government that brings charges against them. For in both of the trials just mentioned, their effect was to besmirch the legitimacy of the state, while enhancing, if not exactly validating, the hate-filled claims proffered by the defendants. This may be the unavoidable peril of granting American citizens, on paper, the right to free speech, and the right to peaceably assemble, but then prosecuting them when they *do* speak out and peaceably assemble. Liberal TV talk-show host, Rachelle Maddow, has gone so far as to argue that *every* sedition trial brought by an American government is doomed to fail, for the simple reason that the government that is supposedly imperiled is still healthy enough to prosecute the alleged the seditionists.

"Fascism" During the Cold War

Following his discussion of the American far-right during the three decades between the early 1920s and the late 1940s, Ross turns his attention to figures and developments after 1950. One of the most important is William Potter Gale, a now-deceased Army veteran who "fought a guerilla war in the Philippines," and who, after World War II, founded a right-wing militia known as the U.S. Rangers. According to Ross, Gale was enthralled by the 19th-century American romance legend concerning the "settler-colonial pioneer posse." Ostensibly, this is why he encouraged the Rangers to set up their own tiny enclaves, largely independent of state control, and against whom they could file (occasionally fraudulent) lawsuits, liens, and checks, while holding themselves accountable "only to themselves" (Ross 2017, 113).[8]

Ross relates how Gale "inspire[d]" Robert DePugh (who founded still another far-right militia, the California Minutemen) and later "join[ed] with" Harry Beach of Portland, Oregon, to create Posse Comitatus (PC). "Posse Comitatus" or "power of the county" is a phrase from English common law, wherein the "shire-reeve" (or sheriff) of a particular "shire" (a town or a district) is appointed by the monarch to stand in for his or her authority. In theory, the Gale-Beach PC was to be a movement comprised small cadres of self-styled "sovereign citizens" or "freemen" who consider their local county sheriff to be the "supreme law of the land."

After it was founded, PC began to "grow though contact with Christian Identity and Klan networks," during which it gained "an intense following" in the Pacific Northwest. Ross writes that this was partly due to Gale's friendship with Richard Butler who, at the time, was running his own parallel political program, he called "the Northwest Imperative (NI)."[9] The goal of the NI was to create a racially pure White Christian province along the northern stretches of Pacific coast by having small tactical units, like those just described, harass local non-White populations into abandoning their homes and moving elsewhere.

In addition to Gale, Beach, DePugh, and Butler, a fifth figure mentioned by Ross as pivotal to the growth of contemporary American "fascism" (remember, this is Ross's term, not my own) is David Duke, the founder and one-time Grand Wizard of the Knights of the KKK. Duke marketed his KKKK as a business-suited version of what a Klan Klavern could and should be—in short, something far different from the popular impression of the group as a motley crew of barely literate back-country hicks (or to repeat the portrait drawn by satirist H. L. Mencken, following the infamous "Monkey Trial" of the early 1920s, as "gaping primates of the upland valleys" "where learning is too heavy a burden to carry"). Defiantly, Duke took pains to present *himself* as a born-again, college-educated, racket-ball-playing poet, and he rode his impression management skills to a seat in the Louisiana State House of Representatives in 1989. Eventually, he even ran for US President on the Populist Party ticket, a group then headed by a former American Nazi Party commander.[10]

Ross tells us that Duke was forced to "resign" from his leadership of the KKKK after his underlings discovered that he had tried selling its membership rolls to outsiders. But more scandalously, that he had authored (and self-published) *Finders Keepers*, a sex manual intended for women of the Klan (Ross 2017, 114). Its subtitle reads, "How to Find and Keep the Man You Want." Following his resignation, Duke set about retooling himself into what he considered a "respectable racist," by helping establish a conventionally acceptable organization he named the National Association for the Advancement of *White* People. The NAAWP was explicitly modeled after the NAACP, a highly thought of, politically adept Black civil rights organization. And just as the NAACP had done in behalf of its Black clientele, the NAAWP portrayed *White* people as victims of "discrimination," in this case, by "anti-White racists." It also lobbied for racial separation or apartheid, "cloaked," says Ross, "under the banner of equality." In sum, then, it was in these ways that a more fashionable fascism began to "creep" or "drift" into mainstream American culture.

The process of "marginal, murky hybridization" was further enhanced by what came to be known as the Wise Use (WU) movement, which Ross contends was a "front" created by resource industry magnates to battle private citizen advocates of environmental preservation and their supposed allies: the "bureau-*rats*" who man federal government agencies like the Forest Service and the Bureau of Land Management.

Wise Use grew out of the same milieu of disenchantment that PC had earlier. And in fact, Ross argues that after it was founded, PC "used" WU as its "primary recruiting ground" (Ross 2017, 121). But whereas PC worked to mobilize down-on-their-luck farmers and small business people in the Midwest, during the farm crisis of the 1980s—think of the Randy Weaver family, for example, as portrayed in Chapter 6—WU focused on marginally employed loggers, miners, grazers, and resource workers in the Pacific Northwest, with "a thinly veiled 'anti-capitalist,' anti-Semitic message."

While the assertion that WU was a "primary recruiting ground" for PC is debatable, it is undeniable that the ideological concept of "wise use" is traceable to Ron Paul's brand of libertarianism, as popularized by the CATO Institute, an organizational product of two of America's leading natural resource company CEOs, Charles Koch and his brother, David. With help from far-right ideologue, Paul Weyrich (Ross 2017, 237), the CATO Institute subsequently spun off two significant so-called conservative lobbies, FreedomWorks and Americans for Prosperity.

Wise Use maligns the federal government for undermining "private property rights" by what WU calls "land grabs," "seizures," and "takings." This, for example, by declaring "eminent domain" over private acreage for wetland restoration, reforestation, and reclamation projects, and/ or by imposing on logging and mining companies a morass of land-use restrictions. While doing this, WU simultaneously portrays private citizen environmentalists and "rewilding" proponents, like Earth First! and its so-called wealthy [college student] elitists, as street fighters for the "green establishment," which WU accuses of being linked to the United Nations, to transnational corporations, to the Rockefeller family, and intriguingly, to liberal pro-immigration groups. Ross says that this partly explains how WU came to the attention of White nationalists in the first place. "White nationalism," he warns, "remains a significant problem that conservationists tend to ignore, again exposing how the fringes of combative movements like the Patriot and the militant environmental movements can cross over in a murky, marginal area of hybridization and fascist creep" (Ross 2017, 124).

Still another pathway followed by post-1950s "fascist creepers" into the American cultural heartland involved Tom Metzger and his WAR (White Aryan Resistance) movement, which he founded in 1983.

When he was younger, Metzger served as a campaign organizer for Barry Goldwater, and later for George Wallace, in their failed presidential campaigns. But he was introduced to "fascism" while working as a lieutenant for David Duke in the KKKK. After witnessing Duke's electoral success in Louisiana (mentioned above), Metzger sought out a similar congressional seat for himself, representing the state of California. And when this failed, he turned his full attention to WAR, with the goal of harnessing violently inclined, but ideologically vacuous White youth, by providing them an "entryway" into the White nationalist cause.

Apart from publishing the usual assortment of Holocaust denial and "race science" literature, what brought Metzger to the attention of a wider public was his adoption of what were at the time several novel recruitment and commitment gambits. One, was his use of WAR telephone message boards to maintain regular contact with his fickle young recruits. A second was his production of *Race and Reason* videos, which were intended for airing on free public access TV stations. *Race and Reason* enabled Metzger to "creep over to issues [here-to-fore] 'owned' by the left, [by using] anti-Wall Street rhetoric" and by verbally attacking the twin "Jewish monsters" of globalism and consumerism. "It isn't the blacks who are the problem," Metzger would argue. "It's the creeps on Wall Street and Washington of our own race" (Ross 2017, 145–46).

Still a third ploy utilized by Metzger was his willingness to appear on afternoon commercial TV talk shows (such as those hosted by Larry King, Sally Jessie Raphael, Geraldo, and Oprah Winfrey). There, he would "debate" various liberal guests by scoffing at practices like "voting or writing to your congressman," "being non-offensive," and/or by playing the game of "meet, eat, and retreat" politics.

Fourth and most significant was Metzger's enlistment of *his own* skinhead son and his friends as advertising agents for the Aryan Youth Movement and the White Student Union (two fronts of the WAR), in high schools and colleges across the country. From this, WAR gained further notoriety by staging fights with anti-racist skinheads at local bars and in mosh pits to the "music" of racist skinhead punk bands like Skrewdriver, Lockjaw, and Poison Idea. This all reconfirmed to Metzger how easy it was to mold "plastic" pubescent White boys into full-blown racists.

WAR briefly rose to prominence in the Pacific Northwest. Then it financially collapsed when Metzger was bankrupted in lawsuits, after several of his "WARskins" were tried and convicted for murdering an Ethiopian immigrant in Portland, Oregon (Ross 2017, 156).

According to Ross, then, Metzger should not only be credited for being one of the few American far-rightists of our era open to the possibility courting new audiences; he was also technically adept enough to do so successfully. Yet, there was one potential "recruitment ground" that Metzger appears to have overlooked, namely, the Christian church. This is not to say that Metzger was unaware of the religious demographic, or indifferent to it. On the contrary, through his involvement with the WARskins, Metzger became acutely aware of how enthralled young people could be with religious organizations like the World Church of the Creator, for example, by Nordic Odinism, by Anton LaVey's Church of Satan, and even by Charles Manson and his murderous Manson Family cult-gang. This provides a clear window into how different fascism is, from the groups and doctrines under consideration in this book.

Satanism and Fascism

Satanism explicitly rejects Christianity and its Christian Patriot adherents, both of whom it accuses of representing the "anti-White mainstream." Anton LaVey, for instance, has gone so far as to argue that fascism is "*a heroic and admirable form of Satanism*" (my emphasis, Ross 2017, 158). Ross agrees with this, if not with the sentimental judgment that lies behind it. In one place, he writes that "LaVey's Satanism and fascism, certainly [*do*] seemed made for one another" (158). And as proof, he quotes LaVey as arguing that if one follows 19th-century German Marxist, Ludwig Feuerbach, and reverses the biblical assertion (in Gen. 1: 23–27) to say that *man created God in mankind's image and likeness*, then one will end-up by affirming a core satanic tenet. Or, as LaVey clumsily expresses it, "if you are going to create a God in your own image, why not create that God as yourself?" For "any man is a god if he chooses to recognize himself as one" (158).

The trouble that LaVey has with Christianity, Ross tells us, is that LaVey considers Christianity to be a "Jewish contrivance" (Ross 2017, 150). This supposedly explains why Christianity repudiates "manly virtues" like pride, strength, money-making, and violence. In the Sermon on the Mount (Matt 5: 3–9), for example, Jesus promises believers worldly and heavenly blessings, but only if they are *meek* peacemakers, and *poor* (in spirit). Not: if they are strong, healthy, and wealthy. But the evidence of our own eyes, LaVey continues, proves that it is the strong, healthy, and wealthy who are the truly "blessed ... for they ... possess the earth." And it is the "weak [who] are cursed ... for they ... inherit the yoke" (Ross 2017, 158).

Ben Klassen, the founder and first "Pontifex Maximus" of the (Satanic) World Church of the Creator, who has since taken his own life, will go even further. Klassen maintains that Christianity has imbued its believers with "suicidal virtues" like meekness, love of one's enemies, simplicity, and poverty. For this reason, its adherents have forfeited their primordial right to rule earth and earthlings (Ross 2017, 150). This being the case, he offers his version of Satanism as a "cure" for Western mankind's ultimate problematic: its crippling sense of personal inadequacy, its overweening helplessness and sense of victimhood, and its unremitting shame and guilt. Klassen goes on to attribute the collapse of Western civilization as a whole to this mindset.

This is not the place to debate Klassen or LaVey. Instead, we want to discern what it is that Ross appears to have taken from them, which is this: American "fascists" (again, this is Ross's term) have failed to mine the potentially rich recruitment ground of the Christian church. Not: because they are unaware of the Church's existence but because they both believe that Christianity harbors a Jewish-inflected timidity. I leave it to readers to determine whether this judgment is based on an empirically accurate assessment of how Christians (or for that matter, Jews) are in reality, or it is an unconscious *projection* (or transference) onto Christians and Jews of Klassen's and LaVey's own personal flaws, fecklessness, frailties, and fears.[11] But if we can believe what has been exhibited time and again in the previous chapters, it seems clear that the latter is more likely the case. That is, at least when it comes to Christians who harbor *Dominionist* ambitions. For in the course of *their* struggle against Them, their own diabolic other(s)—Blacks, homosexuals, females, Jews, Muslims, transsexuals, environmentalists, liberals, Hispanics, progressive educators, and the like—Christian Dominionists display few, if any, signs of doubt, hesitancy, meekness, trepidation, or for that matter, mercy.

Conclusion

Ross does a thorough job of tracing the fascinating permutations of "fascism," as it has adapted to the American life world after 1990: moving from the TEA Party, whose antics beginning in 2009 "gained publicity through FOX News," to the financial nourishment provided by outlets like FreedomWorks and Americans for Prosperity; achieving a "spur" from the oratorical outrages of Glenn Beck, Bill O'Reilly, and Ann Coulter (Ross 2017, 237–38). Then, "[d]riving the radical message into the heart of the Republican Party," have come countless lessor commentators, like Jared Taylor and his American Renaissance movement, the "race realism" of *The Bell Curve*, and Pat Buchanan. According to Ross, the outcome has been "extensive and complex," "a crucial element of the modern fascist creep" (Ross 2017, 246, 247).

And all of this is to say nothing of J.T. Ready (the court-martialed Marine, Mormon convert, mass murderer, and suicide victim, who played a pivotal role in turning Arizona from a relatively moderate state into a hotbed of right-wing fanaticism); ALEC (the American Legislative Exchange Council, still another product of Weyrich and the Koch brothers, which composes model far-right legislation and policy recommendations); the siege of the Bundy ranch in Bunkerville, Nevada (see Aho 2016, xi–xiii); the hi-tech Silicon Valley billionaires, Balaji Srinivasan and Peter Thiel (who advocate that wealthy people secede from the United States and reestablish themselves in sovereign, self-sufficient floating Pacific Ocean island city-states); the violent Men's Rights movement (which maintains that *women* are not the real victims of the Zionist conspiracy, but White males); and Richard Spencer (the putative "defender" of White children, who plaintively asks, "don't they have rights too?" And if so, "who stands for them?"). And, finally, are cynical nihilists like Steve Bannon and Donald Trump. To reiterate what Ross had already concluded: fascism is not a definitive, stable thing, but a never-ending process of becoming. Like a phoenix, it reemerges time and again from its own ashes.

As noted earlier, what Ross calls fascism shares a "family resemblance" to traditional conservatism (of the *ancien regime*), with its myth of "organic solidarity" and its preference for "natural [i.e., inherited] hierarchical arrangements" over individual achievement, and above all, its suspicion of claims concerning universal human rights, or "Spinozism."[12]). But to market itself to contemporary White American middle-class audiences, it has found it necessary to veil its conservative roots and draw more and more on left-wing imagery and memes. To win over young people, it has adopted punk, heavy metal, and hip-hop music styles. And for their parents and grandparents, UFO conspiracy-mongering, line-dancing, and alternative medicine. Today's "fascist" movement supports "(White) worker's rights," while decrying "discrimination" against Whites (by non-Whites). It speaks to the need for "White pride worldwide," and for "(White) consciousness-raising"; for "racial justice" ("Equal rights for Whites!"), and for "gender equality" (for White men). And it advocates "multiculturalism" and "biodiversity" (in this case, meaning the need to ban non-Caucasian immigrants from America and to re-segregate the races already here, so as to avert White man's imminent "extinction"). And it has replaced the old fascist canard, "international Jewish cabal," with the more palatable leftist slander, "Zionist."

Black and Brown interests are advanced by the NAACP and recognized on American college campuses with Black and Latinx studies programs. In perverse mimicry, the far-right demands its own *White*-ethnic studies institutes to honor the contributions of *its* ancestors. And it mounts resistance campaigns against anti-White discrimination through a National Association for the

Advancement of *White* People. It softens the unsavory Nazi appeal to *Blut und Boden* (blood and soil) by organizing liberal-sounding "anti-consumerist" and "buy local" campaigns, together with "pro-life" advocacy, veganism, and no-smoking recommendations.

Progressive-liberals may dream of an environmentally sustainable, egalitarian Ecotopia whose matriarchal-friendly, free-love citizenry defend themselves by means of Gandhian non-violence (Callenbach 1990). But not to be outdone, the American far-right fantasizes about erecting *White Christian Citadels*, ruled by born-again patriarchs willing to protect *their* prerogatives with guns (cf. Aho 2016, 137–38). Which, if either, of these alternatives will be America's future remains to be seen.

Notes

1 Unless otherwise specified, all the page numbers cited in this chapter refer to Ross's book.
2 For more on "superfluous man," see the opening section of Chapter 5.
3 For examples of this from the present era in America alone, see the opening section of Chapter 2.
4 See Chapter 8 for support of this idea.
5 "Palingenetic" is a technical term in biology, referring to the repetition in a single organism, say a human being or a worm, of the stages in the evolution of its own species during embryonic development.
6 For my full objection to the term "fascism," see Chapter 2, under the section titled "Status Displacement."
7 For much more on these figures, see Chapter 3.
8 For two different examples of recent attempts to implement this idea in practice, see my portrayals of Justus Township, Montana, and the Christian Citadel, in Idaho, respectively, in Aho (2016, 107, 137–38).
9 For more on Richard Butler, see Chapter 7.
10 For more on David Duke, see Chapter 8.
11 For more on the concept of psychological projection or "negative transference," see my discussion under the section titled "The Motive of the Big Lie" in Chapter 5.
12 For more on Spinozism, see Endnote 1 to Chapter 5.

References

Abrams, Jeremiah & Zweig, Connie (eds.) (1991). *Meeting the Shadow*. Los Angeles, CA: Tarcher.
Ackerman, Spencer (2012). *DHS Crushed This Analysis about Far-Right Terror*. Available at: https://www.wired.com/2012/08/dhs
Adorno, Theodor (2020). *Aspects of the New Right Extremism*, trans. by Wieland Hoban, afterword by Volker Weiss. London: Polity.
Adorno, Theodor, et al. (1950). *The Authoritarian Personality*. London & New York, NY: Routledge.
Aho, James (1991). *The Politics of Righteousness*. Seattle, WA: University of Washington Press.
Aho, James (1993). "The Recent Ethnogenesis of 'White Man'." *Left Bank* 5: 55–64.
Aho, James (1994). *This Thing of Darkness*. Seattle, WA: University of Washington Press.
Aho, James (2002). *The Orifice as Sacrificial Site*. Hawthorne, NY: Aldine de Gruyter.
Aho, James (2015). *Far-Right Fantasy*. New York, NY: Routledge.
Aho, James (2020). *Political Extremism and Radicalism in the Twentieth Century: Right-Wing America*. Andover, England: Cengage Learning (EMEA) Ltd.
Aho, James & Aho, Kevin (2008). *Body Matters*. Lanham, MD: Lexington Books.
Allen, JH (1930 [1902]). *Judah's Sceptre and Joseph's Birthright*. Boston, MA: A. A. Beauchamp.
Allen, Gary (1971). *None Dare Call It Conspiracy*. Seal Beach, CA: Concord Press.
Altemeyer, Bob (1988). *Enemies of Freedom*. San Francisco, CA: Jossey-Bass.
Altemeyer, Bob (1996). *The Authoritarian Specter*. Cambridge, MA & London: Harvard University Press.
Altemeyer, Bob (2016). *Donald Trump and Authoritarian Followers*. Available (consulted August 3, 2018) at: https://theauthoritarians.org/org/donald-trump-and-authoritarian-followers/
Altemeyer, Bob (n.d.). *The Authoritarians*. Winnipeg, CA: University of Manitoba. OCLC 191061722.
Amidon, K & Krier, D (2009). *On Rereading Klaus Theweleit's Male Fantasies*. Available (consulted December 10, 2018) at: https://journals.sagepub.com/doi/abs/10.1177/1097184X0832611
Appelrouth, Scott (2001). "The Discourse of Jazz, Art, Class, and the Body." In *Pacific Sociological Association Annual Meetings*, San Francisco.
Applebaum, Ann (2018). "A Warning from Europe: The Worst Is Yet to Come." *The Atlantic*, Oct.: 53–63.
Arendt, Hannah (1967). *The Origins of Totalitarianism*. Cleveland, OH & New York, NY: World Pub. Co.
Augustine, St (1960). *Confessions of St. Augustine*, trans. by John Ryan. Garden City, NY: Doubleday & Co.
Banfield, Edward (1967). *The Moral Basis of a Backward Society*. New York, NY: Free Press.
Barkun, Michael (1996). *Religion and the Racist Right*. Chapel Hill, NC: University of North Caroline Press.
Baron, Bruce (1992). *Heaven on Earth: The Social and Political Agendas of Dominion Theology*. Grand Rapids, MI: Zondervan.
Barton, David (2013). *The Founding Fathers and Slavery*. Available at: https://Wallbuilders.com/bible-slavery-America's-Founders/
Batchelor, Steven (2004). *Living with the Devil*. New York, NY: Riverhead Books.
BATF (Bureau of Alcohol and Firearms) (n.d.). *Government Reports on Branch Davidians*. Available at: https://www.atf.gov/our-history/remembering-waco
BCSE (British Centre for Science Education) (2007). *In Extremis: Rousas Rushdoony and His Connections*. Available at: http://www.ocseweb.org.uk/index. Php/Main/rousasrushdoony

Beam, Louis (1992). "Leaderless Resistance." *Concerning the Killing of Vickie and Samuel Weaver by the United States Government*. Laporte, CO: Scriptures for America Ministries.
Becker, Howard (1963). *The Outsiders*. Glencoe, IL: Free Press.
Becker, Ernest (1973). *The Denial of Death*. New York, NY: Free Press.
Becker, Ernest (1975). *Escape from Evil*. New York, NY: Free Press.
Bennet, John C (1842). *History of the Saints: Or, an Expose of Joe Smith and Mormonism*. Boston, MA: Leland & Whiting.
Best, Joel (1995). *Images of Issues*. Hawthorne, NY: Aldine de Gruyter.
Blee, Kathleen (2002). *Inside Organized Racism*. Berkeley, CA: University of California Press.
Bock, Alan (1995). *Ambush at Ruby Ridge*. Irvine, CA: Dickens Books.
Bowler, Kate (2019). *Everything Happens for a Reason: And Other Lies I've Loved*. New York, NY: Random House.
Brantley, Max (2012). *Loy Mauch Update: The Republican Rep Is on Record on Slavery, Too*. Available at: http://www.arkansastimes.com/ArkansasBlog/archives/2012/10/6/loy-mauch-update-the-republican-rep-is-on-record-slavery-too
Bringhurst, Tracy (2022). "Idaho Pastor's Anti-LGBTQ Comments Go Viral." *Idaho State Journal*, A4.
Brown, Norman (1970). *Life against Death*. Middletown, CT: Wesleyan University Press.
Browning, C (2018). "The Suffocation of Democracy." *New York Review of Books*. Available (consulted October 8, 2018) at: https://www.nybooks.com/articles/2018/10/25/suffocation-of-democracy
Brunner, J (1994). "Looking into the Hearts of Workers." *Political Psychology* 15: 631–54.
Buchanan, Pat (2008). *A Brief for Whitey*. Available at: https://buchanan.org/blog/pjb-a-brief-for-whitey-969
Burghart, Devin (2014). *Status of the Tea Party Movement: Part Two*. Available (consulted 27 January 2015) at: http://IREHR.org/issue-areas/tea-party-nationalism
Burston, D (2017). "'It Can't Happen Here': Trump, Authoritarianism and American Politics." *Psychotherapy and Politics International*. Available (consulted August 4, 2018) at: Https://voxpopulisphere.com/2016/10/24/daniel-burston-it-cant-happen-here/
Burton, T (2018). *White Evangelical Support for Trump Is at an All-Time High*. Available (consulted 2 August 2018) at: https://www.vox.com/2018/11/5/18059454/trump-white-evangelicals-christian-nationalism-john-fea
Callenbach, Ernest (1990). *Ecotopia: The Notebooks and Reports of William Weston*. New York, NY: Bantam Books.
Chapman, Lee Roy (2012). *The Strange Love of Dr. Billy James Hargis. The Best of This Land*. Available (consulted Nov. 13, 2022) at: https://thislandpress.com/2012/11/02/the-strange-love-of-dr-billy-james-hargis/
Clarkson, Frederick (2016). "Dominionism Rising: A Theocratic Movement Hiding in Plain Sight." *The Public Eye* Summer, 12–26.
Colby, Gerard & Dennett, Charlotte (1995). *Thy Will Be Done*. New York, NY: Harper/Collins.
Conway, L, et al. (2017). "Finding the Loch Ness Monster: Left-Wing Authoritarianism in the United States. *Political Psychology*. DOI:10.1111/pops.12470.
Coppins, M (2018). *Stephen Miller: Trump's Right-Hand Troll*. Available (consulted July 20, 2018) at: https://www.theatlantic.com/politics/archive/2018/05/stephen-miller-trump-adviser/561317/
Crawford, Jarah (1984). *Last Battle Cry*. Middlebury, VT: Jann Pub.
CSA (Covenant Sword and the Arm of the Lord) (n.d.). *Prepare War*. Pontiac, MO: Covenant, Sword and the Arm of the Lord.
Deace, Steve & Horowitz, Daniel (2023). *The Rise of the Fourth Reich*. New York, NY: Post Hill Press.
Dean, John (2006). *Conservatives without a Conscience*. New York, NY: Viking.
Dean, John & Altemeyer, Rob (2020). *Authoritarian Nightmare*. Brooklyn, NY: Melville House.
Decker, Ed & Hunt, Dave (1984). *The God Makers: A Shocking Expose of What the Mormon Church Really Believes*. Eugene, OR: Harvest House.
DePres, Terrence (1984). *The Survivor: An Anatomy of the Death Camps*. New York, NY: Oxford University Press.
Diamond, Sara (1996). *Roads to Dominion: Right-Wing Movements and Political Power in the United States*. New York, NY: Guilford Press.

Dilanian, Ken (2020). *National Security Whistleblower Says TOP DHS Officials Distorted Intel to Match Trump Statements Lied to Congress.* Available (consulted Sept. 20, 2020) at: https://www.nbcnews.com/politics/national-security/whistleblower-says-top-dhs-officials-distorted-intel-match-trump-statements-n1239685

Docherty, Jayne (2001). *Learning Lessons from Waco: When the Parties Bring Their Gods to the Negotiation Table.* Syracuse, NY: Syracuse University Press.

Dorrien, Gary (2009). *Social Ethics in the Making.* Malden, MA: Wiley-Blackwell.

Douglas, Mary (1966). *Purity and Danger.* London: Routledge & Kegan Paul.

Duncan, Hugh D (1962). *Communication and Social Order.* New York, NY: Bedminster Press.

Dundes, Allen (1997). *Two Tales of Crow and Sparrow.* Lanham, MD: Rowan & Littlefield.

Durkheim, Emile & Swain, Joseph Ward (1969). *The Elementary Forms of Religious Life.* Glencoe, IL: Free Press.

Elmer, Slaisier & Elmer, Evelyn (1984). *Sociology and Immigration: The Grim Forecast for America.* Monterey, VA: American Immigration Control Foundation.

Falwell, Jerry Jr. (2015). *Jerry Falwell Jr. Calls for Liberty Students to Carry Guns.* Available at: https://www.youtube.com/watch?v-PyVj6dsEfF8

Fay, Bryan (1996). *Contemporary Philosophy of Social Science.* Hoboken, NJ: Wiley-Blackwell.

Flynn, Richard & Gerhardt, Gary (1989). *The Silent Brotherhood: Inside the American Racist Underground.* New York, NY: Free Press.

Frame, Randy (1989). "The Theonomic Urge." *Christianity Today*: 38–40.

Frazer, James (1951). *The Golden Bough*, abridged & edited. New York, NY: Macmillan.

Freud, Sigmund (1943 [1911]). *The Schreber Case*, trans. by A. Webber. London & New York, NY: Penguin Books.

Fromm, Eric (1965 [1941]). *Escape from Freedom.* New York, NY: Holt, Rinehart & Winston.

Fromm, Eric (1984). *The Working Class in Weimer Germany.* Cambridge, MA: Harvard University Press.

Gardell, Mattias (2003). *Gods of the Blood.* Durham: North Carolina. Duke University Press.

Garfinkel, Harold (1956). "Conditions of Successful Degradation Ceremonies." *American Journal of Sociology* 61: 420–24.

George, Wesley (1962). *The Biology of the Race Problem.* New York, NY: National Putnam Letters Committee.

Gerasi, John (1966). *The Boys of Boise.* New York, NY: Macmillan.

Gerson, Jeanne Suk (2022). "Keep Out." *The New Yorker*, June 27.

Geuss, Raymond (1981). *The Idea of a Critical Theory.* Cambridge, UK: Cambridge University Press.

Girard, Rene (1977). *Violence and the Sacred*, trans. by P Gregory. Baltimore, MD: Johns Hopkins University Press.

Gobodo-Madikizela, Punla (2003). *A Human Being Died That Night: A South African Story of Forgiveness.* New York, NY: Houghton-Mifflin.

Goldberg, Jonah (2007). *Liberal Fascism: The Secret History of the American Left.* NY: Doubleday.

Goldberg, Michelle (2007). *Kingdom Coming.* New York, NY: Vintage Books.

Grant, George (1987). *The Changing of the Guard: Biblical Principles for Biblical Action.* Ft. Worth, TX: Dominion Press.

Griffin, Susan (1992). *A Chorus of Stones.* New York, NY: Doubleday & Co.

Gusfield, Joseph (1986). *Symbolic Crusade*, Edition: 2nd ed. Urbana, IL: University of Illinois Press.

Haberman, Frederick (1932). *Tracing Our Ancestors.* Metairie, LA: New Christian Crusade Church.

Hamm, Mark (1997). *Apocalypse in Oklahoma: Waco and Ruby Ridge Revenged.* Boston, MA: Northeastern University Press.

Hedges, Chris (2006). *American Fascists.* New York, NY: Free Press.

Heidegger, Martin (1962). *Being and Time*, trans. by J. Macquarrie & E. Robinson. New York, NY: Harper & Row.

Herbst, Jurgen (1965). *The German Historical School in American Scholarship.* Ithaca, NY: Cornell University Press.

Hitler, Adolf (1943). *Mein Kampf*, trans. by R. Manheim. Boston, MA: Houghton-Mifflin.

Hofstadter, Richard (1963). *Anti-Intellectualism in American Life.* New York, NY: Vintage.

Honoreff, Zach (n.d.). *Who Is Elizabeth Dilling and Why Is Glenn Beck a Fan?* Available at: https://historynewsnetwork.org

Huffingtonpost (2008). *McCain Backer Hagee Said Hitler War Fulfilling God's Will (Audio)*. Available (consulted November 30, 2018) at: https://huffingtonpost.com/2008/05/21/mccain-backer-hagee-said_n_102892.html

Ingersoll, Julie (2015). *Building God's Kingdom: Inside the World of Christian Reconstruction*. New York, NY: Oxford University Press.

IREHR (Institute for Research and Education on Human Rights & Montana Human Rights Network) (2021). *Ammon's Army Marches On: People's Rights Network*. Available at: https://www.irehr.org/reports/ammons-army-marches-on/

Jeffries, Stuart (2017). *Grand Hotel Abyss: The Lives of the Frankfurt School*. London: Verso.

Juergensmeyer, Mark (2000). *Terror in the Mind of God*. Berkeley, CA: University of California Press.

Juergensmeyer, Mark, Moore, Kathleen & Sachsenmaier, Dominic (eds.) (2023). *Religious Othering: Global Dimensions*. London, England & New York, NY: Routledge.

Jung, Carl (1981). *The Archetypes and the Collective Unconscious*, vol. 9, part 1 of *The Collected Works of C.G. Jung*, trans. by R.F.C. Hull, ed. by William McGuire, et al. Princeton, NJ: Princeton University Press.

Kaplan, Jeffrey (1997). *Radical Religion in America*. Syracuse, NY: Syracuse University Press.

Keen, Sam (1986). *Faces of the Enemy*. San Francisco, CA: Harper & Row.

Koyré, A (1945). "The Political Function of the Modern Lie." *Contemporary Jewish Record* 7(June): 290–300.

Krafft-Ebing, R (1922 [1892]). *Psychopathia Sexualis*. Brooklyn, NY: Physicians and Surgeons Books.

Lederer, G (1982). "Trends in Authoritarianism: A Study of Adolescents in West Germany and the United States Since 1945." *Journal of Cross-Cultural Psychology* 13: 299–314.

Leese, Arnold (1938). *Jewish Ritual Murder*. London: International Fascist League.

Lemon, J (2017). *Trump Defended White Supremacists ....* Available (consulted August 1, 2018) at: https://www.stepfeed.com/trump-defended-white-supremacists-these-muslims-shot-back-9505

Lepore, Jill (2023). "The American Beast." *The New Yorker*, Jan. 16, pp. 58–64.

Lindsey, Hal (1970). *The Late Great Planet Earth*. Grand Rapids, MI: Zondervan.

Lipset, Seymour Martin (1960). "'Fascism'—Left, Right, and Center." In SM Lipset (ed.) *Political Man*. Garden City, NY: Doubleday-Anchor.

Lipset, Seymour Martin & Raab, Earl (1970). *The Politics of Unreason*. New York, NY: Harper & Row.

Lipset, Seymour Martin & Raab, Earl (1981). "The Election and the Evangelicals." *Commentary* 71(March): 25–32.

Lofland, John & Stark, Rodney (1965). "Becoming a World-Saver: A Theory of Conversion to a Deviant Perspective." *American Sociological Review* 30(Dec): 862–75.

Lofland, John & Stark, Rodney (1977). "'Becoming a World-Saver' Revisited." *American Behavioral Scientist* 20(July/Aug): 805–18.

Lott, John (2010). *More Guns, Less Crime*, 3rd ed. Chicago, IL: University of Chicago Press.

Loy, David (2002). *A Buddhist History of the West: Studies in Lack*. Albany, NY: State University of New York Press.

Luscombe, Richard (2022). "Congressman Echoes Trump's Claim That [Hillary] Clinton Aides Deserve to Die." *The Guardian*, Feb. 15.

Luther, Martin (1974). *Luther: Selected Political Writings*, edited by JM Porter. Philadelphia, PA: Fortress Press.

MacWilliams, M (2016). *The One Weird Trait That Predicts Whether You're a Trump Supporter*. Available (consulted 15 August, 2018) at: https://www.politico.com/magazine/story/2016/01/donald-trump-2016-authoritarian-213533

Marcuse, Herbert (1962). *Eros and Civilization*. New York, NY: Vintage Books.

Marcuse, Herbert (1964). *One Dimensional Man*. Boston, MA: Beacon Press.

Margalit, Ruth (2020). "Built on Sand." *The New Yorker*, June 29, pp. 42–51.

Mathias, Christopher (2022a). *Doug Mastriano's Prophets in Pennsylvania*. Available (consulted 4 Nov. 2022) at: https://www.Huffpost.com

Mathias, Christopher (2022b). *Living with the Far-Right Insurgency in Idaho.* Available (consulted 19 May 2022) at: https://www.Huffpost.com

McAdams, D (2016). *A Psychologist Analyzes Donald Trump's Personality.* Available (consulted 25 August 2018) at: https://www.theatlantic.com/magazine/archive/2016/06/the-mind-of-donald-trump/480771/

McKinley, James Jr. (2010). *Texas Conservatives Win Curriculum Change.* Available (consulted 14 March 2010) at: https://www.nytimes.com/2010/03/13/education/13texas.html

Mehan, Hugh & Wood, Houston (1973). *The Reality of Ethnomethodology.* New York, NY: John Wiley & Sons.

Meloen, JD, Van Der Linden, G & De Witte, H (1996). "A Test of the Approaches of Adorno, et al. Lederer and Altemeyer of Authoritarianism in Belgian Flanders: A Research Note." *Political Psychology* 17: 643–56.

Milgram, Stanley (1974). *Obedience to Authority.* New York, NY: Harper & Row.

Miller, Alice (1984). *For Your Own Good,* trans. by HH Hannum. New York, NY: Farrar, Straus & Giroux.

Miller, Alice (n.d.). *Adolf Hitler: How Could a Monster Succeed in Blinding a Nation?* Available (consulted 29 March 2013) at: https://www.naturalchild.org/articles/alice_miller/adolf_hitler.html

Miller, Paul D. (2021). "What Is Christian Nationalism?" *Christianity Today*, Feb. 3.

Mitzman, Arthur (1969). *The Iron Cage: An Historical Interpretation of Max Weber.* New York, NY: Alfred Knopf.

Monk, Maria (1836). *Awful Disclosures of the Hotel Dieu Nunnery.* Manchester: Milner & Co.

Newport, Frank (2020). *Religious Group Voting and the 2020 Election.* Available (consulted November 25, 2020) at: Https://news.gallup.com/polling-matters/324410/religious-group-voting-2020-election.aspx

Niewert, D (2017). *Alt-America.* London & Brooklyn, NY: Verso.

Nisbet, Robert (1953). *The Quest for Community.* New York, NY: Harper & Bros.

Office of Press Secretary (2009). *Statement by U.S. Department of Homeland Security Secretary Janet Napolitano on the Threat of Right-Wing Extremism.* Available at: www.DHS.gov/news/2009/04/15/Secretary-Napolitanos-Statement-right-wing-extremism-threat

Orwell, George (1944). *What Is Fascism?* Available (consulted 21 January 2014) at: http://orwell.ru/library/articles

Pace, James (1985). *Amendment to the Constitution.* Los Angeles, CA: Johnson, Pace, Simmons & Fennell.

Pagels, E (1995). *The Origin of Satan.* New York, NY: Random House.

Parsons, Talcott (1951). *The Social System.* New York, NY: Free Press.

Parsons, Talcott (1971). *Evolution of Societies.* Englewood Cliffs, NJ: Prentice-Hall.

Perera, Sylvia (1986). *The Scapegoat Complex.* Toronto, Canada: Inner City Books.

Peters, Pete (1992). *Death Penalty for Homosexuals Is Prescribed in the Bible.* LaPorte, CO: Scriptures for America.

Pierce, William (1978). *The Turner Diaries.* Arlington, VA: Vanguard Books.

Piper, Michael C & Hoop, Ken (1999). *A Mockery of Justice: The Great Sedition Trial of 1944.* Available at: html" Https://barnesreview.org/product/the-barnes-review-novemberdecember-1999-a-mockery-of-justice-the-great-sedition-trial-of-1944

Popper, Karl (1965). "Science: Conjectures and Refutations," in *Conjectures and Refutations*, pp. 33–65. New York, NY: Basic Books.

Pronger, Bryan (2002). *Body Fascism.* Toronto, Canada: University of Toronto Press.

Rand, Ayn (1961). *The Virtue of Selfishness.* New York, NY: New American Library.

Rausch, David & Chismar, Douglas (1983). "The New Puritans and Their Theonomic Paradise." *Christian Century*: 712–5.

Reavis, Dick (1995). *The Ashes of Waco.* New York, NY: Simon & Schuster.

Reich, Wilhelm (1980 [1933]). *The Mass Psychology of Fascism.* New York, NY: Farrar, Straus & Giroux.

Reid, Francis (director) (2000). *Long Night's Journey into Day* (video). Burlington, VT: California Newsreel.

Richardson, James & Davis, Rex (1983). "Experimental Fundamentalism: Revisions of Orthodoxy in the Jesus Movement." *Journal of the American Academy of Religion* 51: 397–425.

Ridgeway, James (1996). *Blood in the Face.* New York, NY: Basic Books.

Robison, J (1967 [1798]). *Proofs of a Conspiracy.* Boston, MA: Western Islands.

Ross, A (2016). *The Frankfurt School Knew Trump Was Coming.* Available (consulted 3 December 2018) at: https://newyorker.com/culture/cultural-comment/the-frankfurt-school-knew-trump-was-coming

Ross, Alexander Reid (2017). *Against the Fascist Creep*. Oakland, CA: AK Press.
Ruether, Rosemary (1979). *Faith and Fratricide: The Theological Roots of Anti-Semitism*. New York, NY: Seabury.
Rushdoony, Rousas (1973). *The Institutes of Biblical Law*. Nutley, NJ: Craig.
Sanford, Nevitt & Comstock, Craig (eds.) (1971). *Sanctions for Evil*. Boston, MA: Beacon Press.
Sanneh, Kelefa (2023). "Under God: How Christian Is Christian Nationalism?" *The New Yorker*: 22–5.
Schaeffer, Francis (1982). *A Christian Manifesto*. Wheaton, IL: Crossway Books.
Schatzman, M (1973). *Soul Murder: Persecution in the Family*. New York, NY: Random House.
Schlatter, Evelyn (2009). *Aryan Cowboys: White Supremacists and the Search for a New Frontier*. Austin, TX: University of Texas Press.
Schlesinger, Arthur Sr. (1965). "Extremism in American Politics." *Saturday Review*: 21–5.
Schlesinger, Arthur Jr. (1986). *Cycles in American History*. Boston, MA: Houghton Mifflin.
SCOTUS (Supreme Court of the United States) (2008). *District of Columbia v. Heller 554 U.S. 570*.
Shils, Edward (1954). "Authoritarianism: Right and Left." In R. Christie & M Jahoda (eds.) *Studies in the Scope and Method of the "Authoritarian Personality*. Glencoe, IL: Free Press.
Simmel, Georg (1977). *The Problems of the Philosophy of History: An Epistemological Essay*, trans. by Guy Oakes. New York, NY: Free Press.
Small, Albion (1925). *The Origins of Sociology*. Chicago, IL: University of Chicago Press.
Snyder, Timothy (2018). *The Road to Unfreedom*. London: Bodley Head.
Sokol, Chad (2019). "Working toward the 51st State." *Idaho State Journal*: A-7 & A-8.
Solomon, Sheldon & Greenberg, Jeff, et al. (2015). *Worm at the Core*. New York, NY: Random House.
Stark, Rodney & Bainbridge, William (1985). *The Future of Religion: Secularization, Revival and Cult Formation*. Berkeley, CA: University of California Press.
Stock, Catherine (1996). *Rural Radicals*. Ithaca, NY: Cornell University Press.
Sunstein, C (ed.) (2018). *Can It Happen Here?* New York, NY: Dey Street Books.
Tavuchis, Nicholas (1991). *Mea Culpa: A Sociology of Apology and Reconciliation*. Stanford, CA: Stanford University Press.
Templeton, Amelia, Wilson, Conrad & Haas, Ryan (2016, Oct. 27). *All 7 Defendants Found Not Guilty in Refuge Occupation Trial*. Portland, OR: Oregon Public Broadcasting.
Theweleit, Klaus (1987, 1989). *Male Fantasies*, 2 vols., edited by S. Conway et al. Minneapolis, MN: University of Minnesota Press.
Thompson, Benny (2022). *The January 6 Final Report* (Chairman of the House Select Committee to Investigate the January 6 Insurrection).
Throckmorton, Warren (2011). *Freedom of Religion Only for Christians*. Available at: https://wthrockmorton.com/2011/03/23/bryan-fischer-freedom-of-religion-only-for-christians/
Tolnay, S & Beck, EM (1990). "The Killing Fields of the Deep South." *American Sociological Review* 55: 529–39.
Trangerud, Hanna Amanda (2021). *The American Cyrus: How an Ancient King Became a Political Tool for Voter Mobilization*. Available at: https://doi.org/10.3390/rel 12050354
Trevor, W (1976). *Children of Dynmouth*. London: The Bodley Head.
UMKC (n.d.). *Lynchings by Year and Race*. Available (consulted 14 September 2020) at: https://www.famous-trials.com/sheriffshipp/1084-lynchingsyear
Underhill-Cady, J (2001). *Death and the Statesman*. New York, NY: Palgrave.
Villa-Vincencio, Charles & Doxtadter, Erik (eds.) (2003). *The Provocations of Amnesty*. Trenton, NJ: Africa World Press.
Virilio, P (1983). *Pure War*. New York, NY: Foreign Agent Series.
Wallis, Roy (1982). "Network and Clockwork." *Sociology* 15: 102–7.
Weber, Max (1958a). "Politics as A Vocation." In Hans Gerth & C Wright Mills (eds.). *From Max Weber* (pp. 77–128). New York, NY: Oxford University Press.
Weber, Max (1958b). *The Protestant Ethic and the Spirit of Capitalism*, trans. by Talcott Parsons. New York, NY: Scribner.

Weber, Max (1964 [1947]). *The Theory of Social and Economic Organization*, trans. by Talcott Parsons. New York, NY: Free Press.

Westover, Tara (2017). *Educated: A Memoir*. New York, NY: Random House.

White, John Wesley (1983). *Arming for Armageddon*. Milford, MI: Nott Media.

Wilder, Forest (2011). *Rick Perry's Army of God*. Available (consulted 23 Oct. 2011) at: http://www.texasobserver.org/rick-perrys-army-of-god/

Wilson, Jason (2019a). *Republican Lawmaker and Ally Urged Crowd to Prepare for Civil Unrest*. Available at:https://www.theguardian.com/us-news/2019/may/01/republican-matt-shea-rightwing-rally-guns#:~:text=Washington%20state%20Republican%20representative%20Matt,of%20the%20state%20last%20year.

Wilson, Jason (2019b). *Revealed: Republican Lawmaker Aided Group Training Young Men for 'Biblical Warfare.'* Available at: https://www.theguardian.com/world/2019/aug/13/matt-shea-biblical-war-washington-team-rugged

Wilson, Conrad & Rosman, John (2016). *Malheur National Wildlife Refuge Occupation Ends*. Available at: https://www.opb.org/tag/news/

Winkler, Adam (2013). *Gunfight: The Battle over the Right to Bear Arms in America*. New York, NY: W.W. Norton.

Wolf, N (2007). *The End of America*. White River Junction, VT: Chelsea Green Pub. Co.

Worrell, Mark (2008). *Dialectic of Solidarity: Labor, Anti-Semitism, and the Frankfurt School*. Leiden & Boston, MA: Brill.

Wyschogrod, Edith (1985). *Spirit in Ashes: Hegel, Heidegger, and Man-Made Mass Death*. New Haven, CT: Yale University Press.

Ziemer, G (1941). *Education for Death*. New York, NY & London: Oxford University Press.

Index

Note: Page references with "n" denote endnotes.

Abolitionists 14–15, 33
Adorno, Theodor 27, 30, 37, 79–80, 84
Against the Fascist Creep (Ross) 6
Agenda 21 49
Albright, Madeleine 49
ALEC (the American Legislative Exchange Council) 95
Alien Registration Act (Smith Act) 90
Alien-Sedition Acts 13
al-Qaeda 1
Altemeyer, Robert "Bob" 78, 80, 82–84
Amendment to the Constitution (Pace) 10
American Civil War 14
American Deep South 54
American evangelicalism 37
American far-right 12–21, 68n1, 77, 91, 93, 96; Christian evangelicalism 17; overview 12; peculiarities of 89; right to work campaigns 17; right-wing extremism 12–16; and social psychology 78; status displacement 16–18
American fascism 92; *see also* fascism
Americanization 1
American Legion 89
American Protection Association (APA) 14
American Protestant evangelicalism 22
American right-wing extremism 6, 88
Anglo-American 82–84
anti-conservative bias 80
Anti-Defamation League (ADL) 90
anti-fascism 17
Anti-Masonic Party 14
Anti-Saloon Party 14
anti-Semitism (AS) 79, 84; scale 79
anti-White mainstream 94
apocalyptic millenarian movements 1, 3
Apologia 33–34
Apostle Paul 37
Appelrouth, Scott 53
archaeological digs 48
Arendt, Hannah 16, 47–48, 50, 89

Aryan Nations Calling 9
Aryan Nations Church 3, 5, 7–8, 36, 64, 72, 74, 76; American flag 9; *Aryan Nations Calling* 9; on British 9
Aryan revolutionaries 3
Aryan World Congress 9
Aryan Youth Movement 93
attitudinal clusters 83
Augustine, St. 29, 32n3, 35, 53
Aum Shinriko 1
authoritarianism 6, 77–86; and Anglo-American 82–84; de-eroticization of 84; dimensions of 79; Frankfurt School account of 80–82; and F-scale 78–80; FS school responds 83–86; learning theory of 83; left-wing 80, 86n2; phenomenology of 84; Republican Party 78; social-cultural context 82; variations of 77
authoritarian personality (AP) 6, 77–78, 82–83, 85; concept of 6, 78, 83; de-eroticization of 83; types of 79
The Authoritarian Personality (Adorno) 79
Azazel-Satan 55

Bakker, Jimmy 24
Bannon, Steve 95
Baptist assemblies 81
Barkun, Michael 89
Barrès, Maurice 16
Barton, David 40–41
BATF (the Bureau of Alcohol Tobacco and Firearms) 61, 66
Beach, Harry 91–92
Beam, Louis 91
Beck, Glenn 38, 39, 95
Becker, Ernest 42, 54
Bharatiya Janata Party (BJP) 3, 77
Bible 18, 23, 25–31, 44, 59, 61, 64–65, 73; -based political economics 31; sciences 29–31
"Biblical Basis for War" 45
Biden, Joe 4, 18

Big Lie 48–50; chief cabalist 50–51; infallibility 50; maddening perplexity 48; making of the cabalist 51–54; model of 48–50; motive of 54–56; mystery 48–49; phrase 4–5, 18; prophecy 50; simplicity 49
bin Salman, Mohammad 77
biodiversity 17
"Birth of A Nation" 15
Black Africans 40
Black Legion 15, 89
black-robed Mormans 51
blue-collar workers 77
Bolshevik Revolution 14, 22–23
Boogaloo warriors 12
Book of Revelation 62
Britain 9, 11n2, 47, 77
British 37, 68n9, 73; language 9
British Israelism (BI) 89
Brüders Schweigen (Secret Brotherhood) 42, 64, 65
Brzezinski, Zbigniew 49
Buchanan, Pat 95
Buddhist Myanmar 77
Buddhists 38
Bund Deutscher Mädel 85
bureaucratic manipulator 79
Bureau of Land Management 43, 62
Busch, Wilhelm 81
Butler, Richard 8, 36, 41, 91–92

cabalist: embedment 53–54; labeling 52; making of 51–54; myth-making 52–53; sacrifice 54
Calvinists 53
Camus, Renaud 16
Catholicism 14, 38, 62
CATO Institute 92
Caucasian 17, 72–73, 95
centrifugal pressures of globalization 1–2
centripetal pressures of globalization 1–2
chakra analysis 75
chief cabalist: Big Lie 50–51
child abandonment 35
child-care philosophy 81
Children of Dynsmouth 84
Christian Anti-Communism Crusade 17, 74
Christian demography 30
Christian Dominionism (CD) 3–4, 6–7, 18, 31–32, 33, 36–45, 72, 90, 91; comprehension of Jew 11; ideologically driven 10–11; and modern science 28–29; pre-millennial 37; roots of 22–26; and violence on the inside 36–41; and violence on the outside 41–45; *see also* Aryan Nations Church
Christian Dominionists 21, 33, 35–36, 95
Christian evangelicalism 17
Christian Front 17
Christian historiography 30–31
Christian Identity (CI) 72–73, 89
Christianity 55, 68n7; orthodox 34
A Christian Manifesto (Schaeffer) 25
Christian Nationalism (CN) 3, 6n3
Christian patriot militias 15
Church of Jesus Christ-Christian *see* Aryan Nations Church
Church of Jesus Christ of Latter-day Saints (Mormon) 13
Civil War 72
Clinton, Hillary 50, 77
Colby, Gerard 22
Coleridge, Samuel Taylor 32
collective violence 4–5
COMINTERN 14, 15
Communism 14, 24–25, 79, 90
community-shattering consequences 89
conditions: Dominionist-related violence 44
consciousness raising 17
conservatism 16, 89, 95
Conservative Action Project 12
Conspiracy against All the Religions and Governments of Europe (Robison) 13
Coulter, Ann 95
Covenant Sword and Arm of the Lord (CSA) 91
COVID-19 pandemic 43, 49
COVID fascism 17; *see also* fascism
Crawford, Jarah 42
creation science 30

danse macabre (dance of death) 58–68; embedment 60; grand and terrible ball 61–66; mutual diabolization 58–60; myth-making 59–60; naming or labeling 58–59; riddance 60; Truth and Reconciliation 66–68
Davidians 61–65
Dean, John 78
Deep State 4–5, 11, 15
de-eroticization: of AP 83; of authoritarianism 84
defamatory labels 52
Democratic Party 76
Dennett, Charlotte 22
Dennis, Lawrence 90
Department of Homeland Security (DHS) 44
DePugh, Robert 91–92
Der Struwwelpeter (Hoffmann) 81
Devi, Savitri 88
The Diagnostic and Statistical Manual of the American Psychological Association 59
Diamond, Sara 24
Dilling, Elizabeth 90
Dilthey, Wilhelm 84
Diltheyan methodology 86
disenfranchisement 88
distant aggressive 71
Dobbs v. Jackson Women's Health 33, 69
domestic terrorism 4, 16
domestic violence 69

Dominionism 3
Dominionist-like bigotry 38
Dominionist-motivated violence 42
Dominionist-related violence 4, 42; conditions 44; means 43–44; motivational orientation 42–43; norms 45
Dominionist right 43
Dostoevsky, Fyodor 48
Douglas, Mary 4, 52
Dugan, Alexander 88
Duke, David 39, 85, 92, 93
DuPont family business 89
Durkheim, Emile 60
Duterte, Rodrigo 77

eco-fascism 17; *see also* fascism
Eichner, Edward 90
Eli Oboler Library (Idaho State University) 3, 7
Ellison, James 91
embedment: cabalist 53–54; *danse macabre* 60; defined 60
"endo-psychic demons" 53
engineering 73
epistemological self-consciousness 28
E (ethnocentrism) scale 79
Escape from Freedom (Fromm) 78–79
ethnomethodology 68n3, 68n5
Europeanization 1
Evans, Dale 24
Evola, Julius 88
excremental assault 57n2

Fairness Doctrine 24
Faith2Action.org 37
fake news 29
Falwell, Jerry, Jr. 17, 43
Falwell, Jerry, Sr. 17, 24, 26
fascism 16, 88–96; American 92; COVID 17; eco-fascism 17; fascist creep in America 89–94; homo-fascism 17; Islamo-fascism 17; liberal 17; overview 88–89; and satanism 94–95; technofascism 17
fascist creep in America 89–94
fascist groups 72
Father Coughlin 17, 89
Federal Emergency Management Agency 49
Federal Reserve System 62
femi-nazism 17
Feuerbach, Ludwig 94
Firearms Control Regulation Act, 1975 43
First Amendment 38
First Gulf War 65
First Liberty 12
First World War 14
Ford, Henry 90
foreigners and guest peoples 38–40
14th Amendment 34

"45 Cyrus" 45n5; *see also* Trump, Donald
FOX News 95
Foxx, James Vincent 36, 45n2
France 6, 36, 77, 89
Frankfurt School (FS): and authoritarianism 80–82; school responds 83–86; survey conducted by 78–79, 80
Frankfurt University Institute for Social Research 77
Frazer, James 55, 56
Freemasonry 13
French Revolution 89
Freud, Sigmund 79, 82
Freudianism 79
Fromm, Erich 78–80, 84–85
F-scale 78–80, 82, 84
functional differentiation 2
The Fundamentals: A Testimony to the Truth 23

Gale, William Potter 91–92
Gardell, Mattias 1–2
Garfinkel, Harold 52
German-American Bund 15
German historicism 84
Germany 6, 23, 47, 77
Gerson, Jeanne 34
Gladden, Washington 27, 32n2
globalization 1, 47; centrifugal pressures 1–2; centripetal pressures 1–2; non-isomorphic paths of 2
Goebbels, Josef 47
Goering, Hermann 82
Goldberg, Michelle 32n1
Goldstein, Baruch 1
Goldwater, Barry 93
Graham, Franklin 17
grand and terrible ball 61–66
"The Grand Inquisitor" (Dostoevsky) 48
Grant, George 22
Great Depression 15
"Great Sedition Trial" 89–91
Griffin, Robert 89
Griffin, Susan 82
Grimstead, Jay 25
Groundswell 12
Guns and Ammo 65

Hagee, James 17
Hagee, John 38, 85
Hamm, Mark 65
Hargis, Billy James 24–25, 90
hate groups 5–6; getting into 71–73; getting out of 74–76
Hebrew 73
Hedges, Chris 78
Heidegger, Martin 84
Hidden Hand 11
Himmler, Heinrich 82

Hindus 38
Hispanic-Americans 39
Hitler, Adolf 41, 47, 82, 85, 90
Hochul, Kathy 69
Hoffmann, Heinrich 81
Hofstadter, Richard 27
"Hollywood's Answer to Communism" 24
homo-fascism 17; *see also* fascism
Höss, Rudolf 82
Hussein, Saddam 51
hybridization 88, 92–93
hyper-originalism 69

Iberia 73
Idaho State University 74
Identity Christianity 36–37, 45n2
Identity Christians 64
Illuminati conspiracy 13
Immigration and Customs Enforcement (ICE) 39
implant instruments 75
India 3, 77
individual freedom 34
infallibility 50
infantilized psyche 85
Ingersoll, Julie 25–27, 30
inner-worldly asceticism 81
The Institutes of Biblical Law (Rushdoony) 25–26
internal psychodynamics 6
Internal Revenue Service 62
International Jew (Ford) 90
Islam 34, 53
Islamo-fascism 17, 77; *see also* fascism
Israel 72–73
Italian Catholics 23

Jackson, Jesse 76
Jacobs, Cindy 38
Jefferson, Thomas 13
Jeffress, Robert 17
Jeffries, Stuart 86n2
Jehovah's Witnesses 23
Jewish nationalism 3
Jew York City 64
Jew York Times 39
Jim Crow segregation laws 14
John Birch Society 15, 49
Johnson, F. Woodruff 90
Jones, Alex 49, 50
Judah 73
Judaism 34, 37
Juergensmeyer, Mark 1
Jung, Carl 53

Kaplan, Jeffrey 1
Kennedy, James 37
Kierkegaard, Søren 84
Kim Jong-un 77
King James Bible 14, 28, 41

Kissinger, Henry 49
Klassen, Ben 94
Koch, Charles 92
Koch, David 92
Koresh, David 59, 61–63
Koyré, Alexander 48
Ku Klux Klan (KKK) 14–15, 72, 74, 76, 92

labels/labeling: cabalist 52; *danse macabre* 58–59; defined 52; pejorative 58–59
Late Great Planet Earth (Lindsey) 44, 63
LaVey, Anton 94
LDS Church 14
left-wing authoritarianism (RWA) 80, 86n2; questionnaire 84; scale 82–83; scorers 83
left-wing extremists 5
left-wing servility 80
Lewis, Clyde 49
liberal democracies 77
liberal Enlightenment philosophy 57n1
liberal fascism 17; *see also* fascism
libertarianism 26, 88, 92
"Liberty State" 45
Liberty University, Lynchburg, Virginia 43
Likert-like questionnaire 79
Likert scale 86n1
Limbaugh, Rush 50
Lincoln, Abraham: Emancipation Proclamation 41
Lindbergh, Charles 90
Lindsey, Hal 44, 63
Lipset, Seymour Martin 27
Lofland, John 76n2
Long, Huey 89
Loy, David 42
loyalty oaths 15
Luegenfabrik ("lie factory") 47
lunatic fringe 79
Lyman, Stewart 22–23
lynchings *see* public lynchings

MacWilliams, Matthew 78
Maddow, Rachelle 91
maelstrom 3, 6n2
Making America Great 12
Malheur National Wildlife Refuge (Oregon) 43, 66, 91
Manson, Charles 94
Marcuse, Herbert 83–84, 86n2, 87n5
marginalization 88
Marx, Karl 47, 50, 90
Marxist-Leninist phraseology 89
The Mass Psychology of Fascism (Reich) 79
Mather, Cotton 49
Mauch, Loy 41
Max und Moritz (Busch) 81
McBirnie, William S. 17
McCarthy, "Tail Gunner Joe" 15
McDowell, Stephen 40
McIntire, Carl 17, 23–25, 90

McIntire consortium 23–25
McVeigh, Timothy 15, 65–66, 68n9
means, and Dominionist-related violence 43–44
medieval monasticism 81
Mein Kampf (Hitler) 41, 47
Methodism 81
Metzger, Tom 91, 93–94
Middle Ages 54
Mifepristone (RU-486) 35
Miller, Alice 81, 82, 84, 85–86
Miller, Stephen 85
Mitzman, Arthur 86n3
modernization 1, 47, 89
Moms for America 12
Monroe, Timothy 13
Moral Majority, Inc. 15, 24
Morgan, William 13
Mormonism 23, 38
motivational orientation 42–43
multiculturalism 17, 95
Murphy, Bryan 44
Muslims 38–39, 43, 94
mutual diabolization 58–60
mystery, and Big Lie 48–49
myth-making 52–53, 59–60

NAACP 92, 95
naming, and *danse macabre* 58–59
National Alliance 9
National Association for the Advancement of *White* People (NAAWP) 92, 95–96
National Public Radio 31
National Rifle Association (NRA) 43, 46n6
National Vanguard 9
Nazi Germany 52, 77
Nazism 33, 41, 47, 57n1, 77, 86, 88; in Austria 6; in Germany 6, 81
neo-Calvinist sects 81
neo-logism 84
Niewert, D. 78
nihilistic rebel 79
9/11 terrorist attacks 1, 50; *see also* World Trade Center
Nisbet, Robert 89
Nixon, Richard 78
None Dare Call It Conspiracy (Allen) 49
non-human hominids 36
non-isomorphic paths of globalization 2
Nordic Odinism 94
normal neurotic 78
norms 45
North, Gary 26, 31
Northwest Imperative (NI) 91

Oath-Keepers 12
Obama, Barack 4, 7, 15, 29, 44, 50
objective criteria 69
Occidentalism 1

The Octopus (Dilling) 90
Oklahoma City bombing 5, 15, 44, 50, 58, 61, 66
Old Testament 37, 40
open-carry weapons 69
Operation Midnight Ride 25
Operation Northern Exposure 68n9
O'Reilly, Bill 95
organized diversity 2
oriental despotism 38
The Origins of Totalitarianism (Arendt) 89
Orthodox Christians/Christianity 34, 62
Orthodox Jews/Judaism 39, 53
Orwell, George 16

Pace, James 39
Parsons, Talcott 41
Pascal, Blaise 6
Paul, Ron 92
pedagogy: poisonous 81; of secular humanism 73; of the whip 82
pejorative labels 58–59
Pelley, William Dudley 89
"People's Rights" network 43
personal autonomy 34
Pierce, William 41
Pietism 81
Plot Against Christianity (Dilling) 90
The Plot Against Christianity 49
"pointy-headed elitists" 48
poisonous pedagogy 81
political socialization 60
Pontifex Maximus 94
pop-biology 52
Popper, Karl 29
Porter, Janet 37
Posse Comitatus (PC) 91–92
pre-fascist potential 83
pre-millennial CD 37
Presbyterianism 81
prideful resistance 73
primal emotions 88
private property rights 93
private psychodynamics 5–6
Project Veritas 12
Promised Land 56
Proofs of a Conspiracy against All the Religions and Governments of Europe (Robison) 50
prophecy 50
The Protocols of the Learned Elders of Zion 49
Proud Boys 12
Public Broadcasting System 31
public degradation ceremony 52
public lynchings 14
public schools 73
"pure war" 56
Putin, Vladimir 77
pyramidology 9

QAnon 49, 50, 53

Raab, Earl 27
race science 88, 93
Rand, Ayn 31
Ready, J. T. 95
Reagan, Ronald 15
Reagan Revolution 15
Red Elephants 45n2
red scare 14
reduction 83–84
Reich, Wilhelm 79, 89
Religion and the Racist Right (Barkun) 89
religious conversions 5, 76n2
religious extremism 4; *see also* right-wing extremism
Religious Othering: Global Dimensions (Juergensmeyer) 4
religious violence 1
Republican Party authoritarianism 78
retrogressive sociopaths 79
right-wing extremism 5, 6, 7–11, 88; in America 12–16; Stupid, socially Isolated, and/or Crazy (SIC) 5, 7
right-wing violence 5, 44
Robertson, Jack 45
Robertson, Pat 24, 26
Robison, John 13, 50
Rockefeller, John D. 23
Roe v. Wade 33
Rogers, Roy 24
Roman Catholicism 62
Romney, Mitt 38, 78
Ross, Alexander Reid 17, 88–95
Royce, Josiah 26–27, 32n2
R-scale 80
Rushdoony, Rousas John 25–26, 40, 90
Rutschsky, Katharina 81

"The Sabbat of Orifices" (Aho) 53
sacrifice, and cabalist 54
sadism 32, 82, 85
sado-masochism 79, 86
Sandy Hook elementary school massacre 50
sarin gas 1
satanism 94–95
savage mind 55–56
Schaeffer, Francis 25, 90
Schatzman, Morton 81–82
Schlesinger, Arthur, Jr. 13
Schlesinger, Arthur, Sr. 13
Schreber, Moritz 81
Schwarz, Fred 24–25, 90
Schwarze Pädagogik (Rutschsky) 81
Scriptures for America 9
Second Amendment 16
Second Coming of Christ 39, 44
Second Iraq war 51
Secret Brotherhood *(Brüders Schweigen)* 7–9, 15

secular humanism 73
semi-erudite 79
"Seven Mountains" 37
Seventh-Day Adventist Church 62, 63, 68n7
sexual pathology 79
Shea, Matt 45, 46n8
Shils, Edward 80
Shotgun News 65
SIC-ness theory of conversion 76
Silver Shirt Legion 15, 72, 74
Simmel, Georg 86
simplicity, and Big Lie 49
slavery 40–41
Smith, G. L. K. 17, 89
Snell, Richard 68n9
Social Gospel movement 23, 27, 32n2
socialist revolution 77
Sociological Spectrum 5
sociology 5, 41, 48, 77
sodomy 17
Soldier of Fortune 65
Sons of Darkness 60
Sons of Light 59–60
Sons of Perdition 59
sorority 71
Soros, George 49
Southern Baptists 68n7
Southgate, Troy 88
Sovereign Citizens 12, 17, 91
Soviet Communism 79
speculation 72
Spencer, Richard 95
Spinozism 57n1
Spiritualism 23
"spiritual warfare" 37
Srinivasan, Balaji 95
Stark, Rodney 76n2
Stewart, Jimmy 24
stupid, socially isolated, and/or crazy (SIC) 5, 7, 21, 73, 78
Sun Myung Moon 76n2
superfluous capital 47
superfluous men 16, 88
Supreme Court of the United States (SCOTUS) 33, 69–70
Swain, Joseph Ward 60
Sweden 77
Swift, Wesley 17, 72
symbiotic fusion 79
syncretic absorption 17

Tablet Magazine 3
Taft, Robert 90
Taylor, Jared 95
Team Rugged LLC 45
TEA (Taxed Enough Already) Party 7, 13, 25
technofascism 17; *see also* fascism
terrorism, domestic 4, 16

theophany 31
Theweleit, Klaus 82, 87n6
Thiel, Peter 95
13th Amendment 40
Thomas, Clarence 34
Thoreau, Henry David 53
Thy Will Be Done (Colby and Dennett) 22
Tokyo subway attacks 1
Tomb of the Patriarchs 1
Trevor, William 84
tribe of Dan 73
tribe of Gad 73
Trump, Donald 4, 16, 18–21, 33, 39, 44, 51, 52, 77–78, 85, 95
Trumpism 16, 18–21
"The Trump Prophecy" 45n5
Truth and Reconciliation Commission (TRC) 58, 66–68
The Turner Diaries (Pierce) 41, 65, 68n9
Tutu, Desmond 67

Übermensch 47
"unenumerated rights" 34
US Marshals Service 64
US Rangers 72

Van Til, Cornelius 26
Verein für Sozialpolitik (Union for Social Politics) 32n2
Viereck, George 90
Viguerie, Richard 25
violence 36–45; collective 4–5; criminal 41; domestic 69; Dominionist-related 4, 42; occasion 2; passionate celebration of 87n6; political 4; religious 1; right-wing 5, 44
violent Men's Rights movement 95
Vishnu (Hinduism's God of the world) 2
von Krafft-Ebing, Richard 79

Waco Tribune-Herald 61
Wagner, C. Peter 37

Walker, Edwin 25
Wallace, George 93
WallBuilders.org 40
WAR (White Aryan Resistance) movement 93
war of extermination 47
war on drugs 14
war on modernism 22
Washington Post 90
Weaver, Randall 44, 64–65
Weavers 63–64, 65
Weber, Alfred 84
Weber, Max 12, 32, 33, 80–82, 86n3
Wertrationalität 32–33
Wesley-ism 81
Westernization 1
Westover, Tara 74
Weyrich, Paul 92
Wheeler, Burton 90
White Christian Dominionists (CDs) 7
White ethnic studies programs 17
White nationalism 93
White nationalists 93
White Student Union 93
White supremacist groups 44
White TEA Party 12
Winrod, Gerald 17, 90
Wise Use (WU) movement 92–93
Witness the Know Nothing Party 14
Wolf, N. 78
women of both sexes 79
World Trade Center bombing 1
World War II 51
World War One 47
Worrell, Mark 79

Yom Kippur 55

Zionist fanaticism 77
Zoroastrianism 55
Zweckrationalität 33